Endorsements

The financial system in 10–15 years will only be vaguely recognizable from today's perspective. The system of the future will have five key features: efficiency (including absence of monopoly power), inclusion, security, transparency, and interoperability. Our current infrastructure fails on each of these dimensions. However, to grasp the potential of the future, it is crucial to fully understand our complex current system. Lehalle and Raboun provide a comprehensive analysis of today's landscape. Highly recommended.

Campbell R. Harvey, Professor, Duke University and
Co-author, *DeFi and the Future of Finance*

Charles-Albert Lehalle has been for many years an invaluable member of our Scientific Advisory Committee at the French AMF. For a regulator/supervisor it was a privilege to rely on such an expert of the micro-structure of financial markets, combining an exceptional background both academic and operational and a perfect and updated understanding of the financial regulations. I commend him and Raboun for sharing their deep knowledge of the financial markets and the appropriate tools for analyzing them in this sharp but luminous book; an undisputed reference in this field.

Robert Ophèle, Chairman,
Autorité des marchés financiers (AMF)

This is a unique, masterful, and insightful new interpretation of the global financial system as an ecosystem of asset management firms, financial products, and intermediaries, working together as the components of a giant risk-processing network. The ambition, scope, and authoritativeness of this academic-practitioner blend of scholarship immediately make it the go-to source for graduate students, practitioners, and policymakers who need a way to make sense of modern finance.

Darrell Duffie, Adams Distinguished Professor of Management and
Professor of Finance,
Graduate School of Business,
Stanford University

This book is offering a unique approach to the financial world by reviewing the objectives and constraints of the main financial agents. Without a deep understanding of the interactions between those market participants it is almost impossible to fully comprehend how financial markets function.

Jean-Paul Villain, Director, Strategy and Planning Department,
Abu Dhabi Investment Authority (ADIA)

Financial
Markets
in Practice

From Post-Crisis Intermediation to FinTechs

Other World Scientific Title by the Author

Market Microstructure in Practice
Second Edition
ISBN: 978-981-3231-12-2

Financial
Markets
in Practice

From Post-Crisis Intermediation to FinTechs

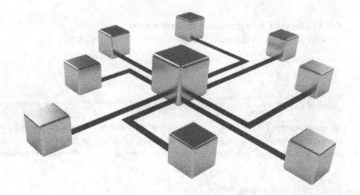

Charles-Albert Lehalle
Abu Dhabi Investment Authority, ADIA, United Arab Emirates
Imperial College London, UK

Amine Raboun
Euronext, France

World Scientific

NEW JERSEY · LONDON · SINGAPORE · BEIJING · SHANGHAI · HONG KONG · TAIPEI · CHENNAI · TOKYO

Published by

World Scientific Publishing Co. Pte. Ltd.

5 Toh Tuck Link, Singapore 596224

USA office: 27 Warren Street, Suite 401-402, Hackensack, NJ 07601

UK office: 57 Shelton Street, Covent Garden, London WC2H 9HE

Library of Congress Cataloging-in-Publication Data
Names: Lehalle, Charles-Albert, author. | Raboun, Amine, author.
Title: Financial markets in practice : from post-crisis intermediation to fintechs /
    Charles-Albert Lehalle, Abu Dhabi Investment Authority, ADIA, United Arab Emirates &
    Imperial College London, UK, Amine Raboun, Euronext, France.
Description: New Jersey : World Scientific, [2022] | Includes bibliographical references and index.
Identifiers: LCCN 2022000994 | ISBN 9789811252570 (hardcover) |
    ISBN 9789811252587 (ebook) | ISBN 9789811252594 (ebook other)
Subjects: LCSH: Finance. | Capital market.
Classification: LCC HG173 .L385 2022 | DDC 332--dc23/eng/20220324
LC record available at https://lccn.loc.gov/2022000994

British Library Cataloguing-in-Publication Data
A catalogue record for this book is available from the British Library.

For any available supplementary material, please visit
https://www.worldscientific.com/worldscibooks/10.1142/12731#t=suppl

Desk Editors: Aanand Jayaraman/Yulin Jiang

Typeset by Stallion Press
Email: enquiries@stallionpress.com

Preface

This book owns a lot to the course "Strategies and Actors on Financial Markets" that I created under the auspices of University Paris Dauphine (part of Paris Sciences et Lettres) in 2010. During the Global Financial Crisis of 2008–2009, some voices raised concerns on the responsibilities of financial mathematics to the crisis. As a mathematician, teaching applied mathematics for finance since 2005, I had to think about the share of responsibility that I had to take in the crisis as a teacher, and as belonging to the communities of financial mathematicians and of practitioners, since I was managing a team of a dozen of "quants" working on trading and liquidity topics in the brokerage arm of an investment bank at this time.

I had a lot of elements to think about: before working in the financial industry, I had a career in the aerospace and automotive industry, and hence had elements of comparison with other practices. Moreover, I had a seat in the front row of the financial turmoil: because liquidity became of primary importance during the GFC, I was involved in a lot of internal meeting, including a top management driven workgroup to "rethink" the business of the investment bank. As a consequence, I was involved into the reorganization of the investment bank towards more standardized products, with a focus on what I would call the "supply chain of financial risk": optimizing the trading flows at a large scale (Equity and Equity Derivative business lines). In the scope of the management of this transition, I had discussions and meetings with diverse market makers, traders, quants, risk managers and regulators.

My first conclusion has been that it is unfair to blame a tool, just because some operators use it badly. But it would have been too easy to stop the reasoning there: most of these operators have been trained as mathematicians or physicists, and have grown internally to reach some managing, operation, or sales positions. Hence they were meant to know the limitations of the models quants used either in their teams, either in other teams serving their business line. How could they have forgotten to make the balance between, on the one hand their management and business-oriented role, and on the other hand the technicalities of the tools they have been taught as Master's students years ago?

Compared to other fields like engineering of construction, or engineering of energy production, I realized that if financial quants are trained far more technically than most other engineers (especially in the practical use of abstract mathematics), the business models of the industry they will work into were almost absent from their courses. Students in engineering in other (and most often older) fields, are taught the organization of the industry they will work into, and especially its stakes, its past failures, etc.

In brief: I convinced myself that if you take young promising scientists and you push them to technicalities and abstractions they will probably have brilliant careers, but once they will have reached a different, probably management-oriented, role, it will be difficult for them to make the link between their technical skills and the stakes at the scale of the firm they have now to serve in a more qualitative way.

With this conclusion, I went to Pr. Bruno Bouchard, who was at this time in charge of the Financial Engineering Master at University Paris Dauphine (MASEF): I was teaching the course "Statistics and Optimal Trading" and wanted to convert it to a far more qualitative course, involving the business models and the stakes on financial markets. Bruno reacted very positively: he immediately accepted. This did not surprised me since he is not only a brilliant mathematician but he has an interest in understanding applications.

Then I had to create the course. I clearly had not the full skillset to teach this. I went to practitioners I knew and I trusted to convey the message I wanted to transmit to the students: "*What you are learning is a small part of a large ecosystem; it is a crucial component of it, because without engineering, there is no rational business process, nor risk management, but you need to understand the purpose of the mechanisms you learn to put in place.*" Luckily enough, I could gather a team of experts who could cover with me most of the aspects of the financial ecosystem: Pascal Gibart, Julien Leprun, Christophe Lesieur, Mark Sinsheimer, and Jérôme Simon made me the honor to accept to be part of this adventure. I followed their sessions myself, year after year, to be able to deliver to the students a coherent message despite the interdisciplinarity of this teaching team. After few years, the course followed a structure that was already very close to the table of content of this book.[1] Other Masters at Paris Dauphine proposed to their students to follow this same course: some years we had more than 90 students attending and questioning the meaning of their future job. From my viewpoint it meant that this course was fulfilling its promises.

When I met Amine Raboun he was following the technical course I am giving since 2005 at another master.[2] I have been impressed by his questions during the breaks: he was not only asking questions on the theorems and financial tools, but also on the meaning of the techniques I was teaching. Following his Master, Amine pursued a PhD thesis under the supervision of Marie Brière and myself, hence I naturally proposed him to write a book inspired by this successful course. The contributors of this book are some of the experts who initially contributed to the course, with the exception of three: Jérôme Simon and René Aïd, who are incharge of the part of the course on energy markets; and Mark Sinsheimer. Amine and myself decided to restrict the book to a subset of the topics addressed in the course to make it more consistent.

Do not misunderstood me: this book is not the transcription of the course. It goes through the same topics, but a far more compact and consistent way, with a very strong punchline: *the financial system is a network of intermediaries who are buying and selling mixed risks; this ecosystem has an overall purpose: to allow actors in the real economy to transform uncertainty on future outcomes into deterministic premia.*

---

[1]The only missing chapter is the green finance and the markets of energies, that would deserves a book by its own.

[2]The "El Karoui" Master in Finance and Probabilities.

On the top of the course, a lot of discussions with important researchers of the field, like Nicole El Karoui, Michel Crouhy, René Carmona, Jean-Michel Lasry, Bruno Bouchard, Mathieu Rosenbaum, Nizar Touzi, Stéphane Crepey, Thierry Roncalli, Marie Brière, Jean-Pierre Zigrand, and Robert Almgren, among others, influenced the way we structured the book and its content.

Charles-Albert Lehalle
Abu Dhabi, the 3rd of December 2021

The financial markets have always been a great mystery to me. From a young age, exposed to Hollywood movies about the euphoria of Wall Street, fascinated by charismatic people taking bold bets on the market, and seeing documentaries about the various financial crises that have completely changed the economic landscape of certain countries, I developed a growing curiosity about this global system that, at first glance, seems extremely complex and difficult to penetrate, but once the dots are connected, seems very intuitive and easy to grasp.

My journey in the financial sector started with my applied mathematics courses at the Telecom ParisTech Engineering school. With a mathematical approach, these courses develop the technical background, skills, and knowledge necessary for quantitative jobs in financial institutions. This was my first opportunity to learn the application of some of the abstract mathematical concepts of stochastic calculus, such as random walks or martingales, to the design of risk-neutral strategies for option pricing and hedging. Although the notions of risk packaging and risk intermediation were largely present in these lectures, focusing on the technical aspects hasn't given me the whole picture I was hoping for. Aware that what I had learned so far was only the tip of the iceberg, I wanted to deepen my knowledge of financial markets. I decided to enroll in the prestigious master's degree in probability and finance (El Karoui) at the Ecole Polytechnique and UPMC. Things became clearer for me thanks to the variety of subjects discussed in the courses covering the different financial assets (Stocks, Bonds, Rates, Derivatives, etc.) and the different financial applications ranging from structured products pricing, asset management, and asset allocation to high-frequency trading and statistical arbitrage. It was then where I met Charles-Albert Lehalle, who was in charge of the course on market microstructure. The interaction we had together made me realize how vast the world of finance is and how much I wanted to learn about it. It made me want to become an "expert" in financial markets and I decided to enroll in a Ph.D. program with Charles-Albert and Marie Brière, head of the investor research center at Amundi, as co-advisors. The beauty of this experience was its format, an industrial partnership between a company and an academic laboratory (Those who know the french system, we refer to the program by CIFRE Ph.D. thesis). In my case, the company was Euronext, the largest pan-European stock exchange, and the laboratory was Paris Sciences et Lettres (PSL) Dauphine University, the French leading University in finance.

Euronext is the epicenter of finance in Europe. Working there, for 4 years now, I have there the opportunity to interact with all kinds of market participants: operators of the real economy looking to finance their projects or future acquisitions either through bond issuance or capital increase via listing or new shares; banks and brokers looking to access the trading platform to create new derivative contracts (futures or options, etc.) to meet the growing needs of the economy; regulators raising interesting points about liquidity, risk concentration, and fair information dissemination; and FinTech companies trying to sell us their innovations to improve our infrastructure. Not to mention that Euronext is present in several countries in Europe: France, the Netherlands, Italy, Belgium, Ireland, Portugal, and Norway; it allows me to observe the commonalities as the divergences of the different market operators across Europe. Without exaggerating, Euronext is the place to be to develop a 360 degrees view on the market and to scrutinize the complex interactions between market participants. Moreover, as an index structurer in the Euronext Index Department, I am responsible for designing equity portfolios for three types of players: QIS desks of investment banks, that are issuing structured products and certificates using Euronext's indices as an underlying, ETF issuers and passive managers that replicate liquid and capacitive open indices, and pension funds who seek to invest in rules-based quantitative strategies optimized for their needs. Each player is looking for a proper combination of sources of rewarded risks to achieve a particular risk-return profile.

In a complementary way, PSL-Dauphine University put me in contact with researchers thanks to the multitude of seminars and conferences I had the chance to participate in and to animate. I would like to thank in particular Tamara Nefedova for our discussions on corporate finance, Serge Daroles and Gaëlle Le Fol for our discussions on liquidity and the role of flows in asset management, René Aid on the particularities of the electricity market, Thierry Roncalli for his insight on risk parity and ESG investing, and the many other researchers who helped me mature my thinking on these topics. I especially appreciated the scientific viewpoint that academics adopt on the financial problems I simultaneously had to address with industrials: the formers ask "Why?", whereas the laters ask "How?". Overall, setting me in the middle of these two approaches, the CIFRE thesis pushed me to confront academic theories to the daily challenges of the company, and to gather the points of view of practitioners and academics on my topics of interest.

After my thesis, and in order to keep in touch with the academic world, I now succeed Charles-Albert in teaching courses and organizing seminars for students on topics related to "the organization of the financial system" at the PSL-Dauphine University.

After several years, I am probably still not an expert, but I have had the privilege of deepening my knowledge on various aspects related to finance. Having had that feeling of sometimes being lost with all these concepts during my PhD, I wanted to co-author this book to convey the message and logical reasoning that I would have hoped someone would have given me when I first started learning finance. If I had understood the logic of intermediation and "risk packaging" from the beginning, all the concepts that seemed independent at first, which I initially tried to understand separately, would have seemed like lego bricks adding up to form the big picture of the financial ecosystem. The goal of this book is not to be overly technical in its content, but to convey the kind of insights and knowledge that can only be gained through experience and interaction with professionals and academics. Readers interested in a more in-depth quantitative approach will find more details and guidance in the "*for more details*" sections closing each chapter.

Amine Raboun

Paris, the 6th of December 2021

About the Authors

Charles-Albert Lehalle is currently Global Head of Quantitative R&D at Abu Dhabi Investment Authority (ADIA). Charles-Albert Lehalle holds a PhD in Machine Learning and "habilitation à diriger les recherches" on modelling and controlling the price formation process; he is a leading expert in market microstructure and optimal trading.

Prior to joining ADIA, Charles-Albert Lehalle held positions as Senior Research Advisor at Capital Fund Management (CFM, Paris), the Global Head of Quantitative Research at Crédit Agricole Cheuvreux, and the Head of Quantitative Research on Market Microstructure in the Equity Brokerage and Derivative Department of Crédit Agricole Corporate Investment Bank. He studied intensively the market microstructure evolution since the financial crisis and regulatory changes in Europe and in the US. Pr. Lehalle is often heard by regulators and policy-makers like the European Commission, the French Senate, the UK Foresight Committee, etc. He has been a visiting researcher at the Collège de France (2013) and is a visiting professor at Imperial College London.

Charles-Albert Lehalle chaired the Index Advisory Group of Euronext, has been a member of the Scientific Committee of the French regulator (AMF), and of the Consultative Workgroup on Financial Innovation of the European Authority (ESMA). Moreover, Charles-Albert Lehalle received the 2016 Best Paper Award in Finance from Europlace Institute for Finance (EIF) and published more than 50 academic papers and book chapters. Amongst his contributions, he is the co-author with Sophie Laruelle of the book

Market Microstructure in Practice (2nd edition 2018, WSP) and the Co-Editor with Agostino Capponi of the book *Machine Learning and Data Sciences for Financial Markets: A Guide to Contemporary Practices* (2022, Cambridge University Press).

Amine Raboun is currently an index structurer in the index department of Euronext Paris. After graduating from Télécom ParisTech engineering school and obtaining a master's degree in applied mathematics at Ecole Polytechnique, Amine Raboun completed a PhD in finance at Paris Dauphine University — PSL Research University. His research focuses on market frictions, market microstructure, and asset allocation. In his research, he studies the effect of institutional investors' trades on overall market liquidity, the market impact of popular institutional trading strategies, stock price reactions to news, and market makers' trading regimes.

About the Contributors

Charles-Albert Lehalle is the main contributor of chapters 1, 2 and 6 and Amine Raboun is the main contributor of Chapters 3 and 4. The following distinguished practitioners contributed greatly to this book:

Pascal Gibart is the main contributor of Chapter 5

Pascal Gibart started his career in 1987 with Credit Commercial de France (CCF) in the Brussels Branch as a Money Market Trader. He then joined Forex Finance, a joint venture between CCF, COFACE and Coopers & Lybrand which offered dedicated advice to corporate customers for the management of their FX and Interest Rate exposures.

In 1994, Pascal Gibart moved to Credit Agricole Lazard Financial Products, a joint venture between Lazard and Crédit Agricole that offered tailor made solutions to Lazard's corporate and institutional clients. He started as a member of a group of early joiner that designed and developed an in-house Front-to- Back system that was then used successfully to risk manage the bank and produce all accounting and regulatory reporting. He then spent 2 years in Singapore as a structurer covering the Asian region and managed to land reference transactions with prime Lazard clients. Finally, from 1998 to 2003, he came back to London to head the Trading team.

Pascal Gibart joined CAcib's market risk department in 2003 and was in charge of the pricing model validation team. In 2012, he became deputy head of the Market Risk Department. In 2019, he took over the direction of the MASAI FRTB program, an ambitious project to transform the market risk ecosystem in order to enhance the operational efficiency and prepare the bank for the ever renewed challenges of regulatory reporting.

Julien Leprun is the main contributor of Section 1.7

Julien Leprun is deputy head of the surveillance and data department of the French market regulator AMF, which he joined in 2009. Prior to the AMF, Julien worked with BNP Paribas Investment Partners as credit structurer after positions in Axa Investment Managers also in structured credit and Societe Generale in equity derivatives. He graduated in finance from Ecole des Mines de Saint-Etienne. Julien was awarded the CFA charter in 2013.

Christophe Lesieur contributed to Chapter 3

Christophe Lesieur is currently Chief Risk Officer and Head of Financial Engineering at LFIS Capital. In this position, he oversees the pricing capacity and risks of several cross-asset hedge funds. He joined the LFIS group in July 2013 first as the Head of Financial Engineering and Chief Operating Officer of La Française Global Investments.

Prior to LFIS, Christophe spent 17 years at Crédit Agricole Corporate & Investment Banking (CAcib) where his last position was co-head of the Global Equity Derivatives department. Christophe was Head of the Corporate Equity Derivatives trading and supervised different trading activities as well as the sale of structured products throughout his career. Christophe has used during all his career a various number of pricing models to create structured products and financial solutions to match client needs. He also has extensive experience of banking and asset management organizations and systems. Christophe graduated from IMT Atlantique.

Acknowledgments

Editors would like to thank Mark Sinsheimer, whose lecture on asset managers shaped Chapter 4; and Louis Lacasse, who reviewed the full manuscript of this book. Besides, editors would like to thank Nicolas Kornman for valuable discussions about the role of brokers in financial intermediation; Chapter 2 owns a lot to these discussions.

Contents

From a Quantitative Perspective

Chapter 1

Financial System as a Network of Intermediaries

1.1 Motivation and Objectives

The aim of this book is to provide a compass for quantitative analysts (i.e., *quant*, or *strat*) working in financial institutions. It describes the most common business models surrounding a quant in her or his day to day professional life, in a way to help the reader develop a deep understanding of the business models in finance. It draws the global picture of the financial system focusing on the major business lines, and presents the role of each participant in the system. By highlighting the interactions between agents and principals operating in financial markets, it aims at following a very simple viewpoint: In most cases, *business units of a financial institution operate risk transformations*. Once the reader will have understood that the complex financial system is no more than a "simple" supply-demand chain of risks, where participants buy, transform, sell and net different kinds of risks inside the financial system, it will be very easy for her or him to deeply understand the stakes of a quantitative occupation in financial companies: trader, portfolio manager, risk officer, structurer, etc. Such an *intermediary-driven* viewpoint helps in choosing promising projects and in proposing fruitful ideas.

This book is structured as follows: First, we define the financial system, introduce market participants, their role, the interconnection between their activities and their impact on the well functioning of the real economy. This includes an in-depth analysis of the role of regulations. Second, we describe the price formation process and the

1

importance of information dissemination in the system. Next, we present the structuring business, which is the typical way of packaging different kind of risks together. This book's focus is not modeling and technical aspects of pricing, but how structured products are built and for what purpose. Then, we turn to asset management, with an emphasis on the process followed by asset owners to select a manager and some details about factor investing. The latter started to shape the industry of asset management in the years 2010, defining a simple vocabulary to describe risky exposure to economic factors. The following chapter describes the risk management process from an investment bank viewpoint. It presents the basics of risk management models and gives examples where inappropriate or wrong model outputs resulted in unexpected consequences. Finally, the last chapter deals with FinTechs and recent innovations led by Machine Learning and Artificial Intelligence.

1.2   A Tale to Understand the Basic Functioning of the Financial System

To understand the position of each market participant and the interactions between them, a first step is to understand the role of the financial system itself. With the following story, we would like to illustrate the nature of the financial industry while highlighting the interactions between market agents The story begins like this:

Start with the story of micro-credit. *Once upon a time, a traveler was sightseeing in New Delhi, India and came across a shoe-shiner. He decided to get his shoes cleaned since it costs only \$1. While speaking, the traveler realized that the shoe-shiner had usually 30 customers per day, which made him an average of \$30 a day. Speaking with this hard-working guy, the traveler suddenly understood that unfortunately, the shoeshiner did not own the brush and had to pay borrowing costs of \$29 per day to use it. With only 1 remaining dollar, the shoe-shiner could hardly buy food for him and his family. The traveler made a deal with him: he offered to lend him \$40, the price of the brush, for a period of 5 days, in exchange for a \$10 yield. Hence, the shoe-shiner could buy the brush, make an average of \$150 revenue in 5 days, pay the traveler back, earning \$100*

(=150−40−10) in those 5 days while keeping the brush forever. In exchange, the traveler will get a 25% return in his lending for 5 days. The shoe-shiner accepted the offer, and both made a profit and lived happily for the rest of their lives.

Up to that point, the story is a very simple example of micro-credit: the traveler performed the most basic risk transformation: a liquidity transformation. He accepted not having access to his money for 5 days, transforming a fraction of his bank account into a loan; that he is then rewarded for. This reward is made of a mix of pure liquidity transformation and of course a counter-party risk: the chance that the shoe-shiner may not pay the money back, either because of a lack of skill or a lack of luck.

Creating an agency with a global balance sheet. *But this tale does not end so soon. The traveler came back to his city, let's say Paris, and shared the experience with his friends. By word of mouth, this investment opportunity spread out in the city to where each time someone was going from Paris to New Delhi, she looked for a shoe-shiner around town to offer him the deal. Besides, other French investors were ready to invest in this tempting opportunity, if only they could avoid the* fixed *costs related to the plane ticket to potentially meet a shoe-shiner. A smart entrepreneur identified the growing need of an intermediary agent who will answer both appetites: On one hand, the New Delhi shoe-shiners looking for capital, and on the other hand, Paris based investors ready to take a counter-party risk in exchange for a yield. This entrepreneur created an agency named NDP Investments (that is, New Delhi–Paris Investments) with two subsidiaries, one in each city. After the launch of the company, French investors could henceforth put their deposits in the French subsidiary. NDP Investments immediately transfers the money to its second subsidiary in India, where shoes-shiners can visit to borrow this same money. Of course, the agency does not provide this service for free. It takes a 5% cut from each transaction, leaving the final investor with a 20% return.*

At this stage of the tale, we have seen the creation of a pure agency broker: *It does not commit its own capital in the intermediation. It simply seeks liquidity for Indian shoe-shiners and provides standardized contracts to both sides of a trade. Its added value is to replace the* fixed *costs of plane tickets per investor with the cost of maintaining a balance sheet in France and another one in India. It allows the broker to make wires at low costs once the administrative and regulatory expenses have been paid.*

Basic role of intermediaries: Unconflicted advices and contribution to the stabilization of the system. *Now that the business of NDP Investments runs at a large scale, the issue of shoe-shiners not being able to pay back the $40 occurred often enough to push the company to take new measures. The agency decided to add some clauses to the contract with shoe-shiners, stating that when a loan is provided the borrower must buy a brush, and in case of default on the payment, the agency gets back the brush. By reselling it or re-lending it to other potential shoe-shiners, the agency is able to recover part of the invested capital; that is called the* recovery rate *of the broken deal. With the addition of a limited liability clause in the contract, the broker introduced* collateralization: *this is one of the common ways to improve the resiliency of the financial system because it limits the risk borne by participants who committed capital in exchange of promises of future, and thus uncertain, returns.*

Moreover, to give more transparency to investors, enabling a best match between different investors' risk-appetites and borrowers' profiles, the agency broker puts in place new contracts with a large range of yields corresponding to different levels of risk (investors willing to finance riskier projects get higher return on investment). In parallel, the agency published a weekly newsletter, the "NDP Blueprint", with information of the pending offers and transparent rankings of the contracts in terms of risk and yield with a system of "stars": the higher the number of stars, the lesser the risk and the yield for the investor. The edition of such a "blueprint" is very close to what brokers are doing with their business of financial analysis *or* strategists' publications. *It is commonly accepted that brokers agencies, because of their position of intermediaries with no skin in the game, are in a good position to provide recommendations on financial products and give neutral advice to natural risk-takers. By adding these two features to their business model, unconflicted intermediaries play a pivotal role in the financial system.*

Making the markets. *As a pure agency broker, NDP Investments structurally maintained a balance sheet with two legs: one in*

Paris and the other in New Delhi. As soon as a French investor makes a deposit in Paris, a wire goes to New Delhi where a loan is structured correspondingly. This set-up worked because an agreement between a shoe-shiner and an investor took place few minutes before each deposit. After some months as a pure agency business, NDP Investments estimated that on average 5 new French investors make deposits per day and 5 shoe-shiners come to New Delhi's desk to borrow it. At the same time, it noted that some investors coming to Paris' desk lose patience and leave before the company could provide them a contract. The waiting time between two consecutive arrivals is on average over 2 hours: the market is not liquid enough. The founder of NDP Investments decides to create another company: NDP Bank, to make this market: It will play the role of the counterparty of buyers and sellers in both agencies. NDP Investments will be able to create contracts on the fly to temporarily borrow money from French investors if no shoe-shiner is at New Delhi's desk, and then sell back the contract, with a markup, to the next shoe-shiner coming at NDP Investments' desk in India. This markup occurs also when the shoe-shiners come before the investor. NDP Bank creates two different prices for the same contracts: a bid-ask spread is born, that is the difference between the best buy and the best ask offer waiting for a counterparty. Now NDP Bank, sharing part of its capital with NDP Investments, has some skin into this game, but the market is far more liquid. On average, 10 contracts are signed per day, whereas there were only 5 before the involvement of a the market maker. Of course, the inventory of NDP Bank is usually to be flat at the end of the day and its business remains profitable.

The addition of market makers had big consequences on the market: on one hand, the market becomes more liquid: More clients (on both sides) are signing contracts, even those who were not patient enough to wait can now make a deal. On the other hand, the prime broker is now making money thanks to the bid-ask spread he sets and as far as he has a good management of his inventory of pending contracts. The agency also raised its incomes because more transactions are made every day. The drawback of this new set-up is that the company is exposed to a new risk and in case of bankruptcy of NDP Bank, all clients who were dealing via the NDP holding will not be able to see the term of their contracts. This adds systemic risk:

if the holding falls, this financial system will stop functioning, and the real economy will take a heavy blow.

A remark on blockchain. *It is the perfect moment to make a comment about one of the potential nice feature that blockchain can bring to financial markets. It has been underlined that to conclude a deal, the investor and the shoe-shiner have to first agree; then the investor has to make a deposit on his NDP account, NDP has to make the wire to New Delhi to fill another NDP account, and from this account, the contracted shoe-shiner can borrow the money. If there is any issue or delay in one of these steps, the deal cannot occur. With a blockchain, all these steps are resolved simultaneously: a smart contract can be created on a blockchain specifying the term of the agreement. Following its creation, the contract will be valid as soon as the money will be taken by the shoe-shiner, and all the intermediate steps can be written in the blockchain, to guarantee their veracity, or can be concluded outside of the ecosystem, by relying on what is called an* oracle *that will check that the steps really occurred. The more steps are written in the blockchain, the more automated and the less "flaws" in the system.*

Inventory risk, one-sided risk, and systemic crisis. *After several years of flourishing business, almost all shoes-shiners in New Delhi bought their brush and stood on their own feet. NDP Investments suddenly faced a sharp decline in Indian desk affluence. But following their habits based on historical analysis, the traders of NDP Bank continued to guarantee returns to depositors before actually lending the money to shoe-shiners. If this lasts for too long before the management of the company decides to shut down the market making activity, its inventory will become largely imbalanced, with very large exposure to interest rates.*

The important part of this tale is that once NDP Holding goes bankrupt, all its clients are let without any way of unwinding their contracts, because NDP traders are part of all the deals: In practice, the trader first signs a contract with one side, then concludes the offsetting trade with the other side. Instead of having a direct link between one French investor and one shoe-shiner in each trade, we have two links: one between the investor and NDP traders, and the other one between NDP traders and the shoe-shiner. The whole system gets frozen if NDP traders suddenly vanish. It is very similar to what happened during the financial crisis when Lehman Brothers went bankrupt.

To prevent this intrication of contracts, the post-2009 regulation insists on the clearing *of contracts: if A bought an exposure to B and B sold the exact same exposure to C, then when feasible B should be thrown out of the deal, seeing only A being exposed to a risk sold by C. This is done via* Clearing Houses.

Lessons learned from this tale. This story of a shoe-shiner and a traveler making a deal in New Delhi allowed us to cover important components of the financial system:

1. First of all, we need to have natural buyers and sellers of the same risk outside the financial system.
2. In such a configuration, a pure agency business can be introduced between buyers and sellers. It concentrates the liquidity, provides unconflicted expertise and pays fixed costs that are now split between all participants.
3. Market makers can improve the liquidity of the market by putting themselves between buyers and sellers who would not be synchronized enough otherwise. They are rewarded by a markup, or by the bid-ask spread. As far as the market is not *one sided*, the balance between buyers and sellers is enough to maintain a smooth and orderly functioning market.
4. Collateralization is a good way to guarantee, at least partly, promises of future returns.
5. If intermediaries' inventories grow too much in one direction, the risk of bankruptcy increases and when it happens the whole system freezes.
6. Clearing and careful monitoring of intermediaries' inventory are key measures allowing to anticipate these issues.

Of course, in reality, it is very rare to see buyers and sellers of the same exact opposite risks (except in very specific cases like Credit Default Swaps (CDSs) and Credit Linked Notes, see Chapter 3). As a consequence, intermediaries have to internally decompose the exposure of their balance sheet to different "unitary" moves of economic variables (like GDP, interest rates, prices, uncertainty, i.e., volatility, etc.). Once it is done, they can "net" these exposures to each kind of move, to measure the exact remaining exposures.

1.3   Why Do We Need the Financial System?

In 1995, Robert Merton listed six features of the financial system:

(1) a payment system for the exchange of goods and services;
(2) a mechanism for the pooling of funds to undertake large-scale indivisible enterprise;
(3) a way to transfer economic resources through time and across geographic regions and industries;
(4) a way to manage uncertainty and control risk;
(5) price information that helps coordinate decentralized decision-making in various sectors of the economy;
(6) provides a way to deal with the asymmetric-information and incentive problems when one party holds privileged information that the other parties ignore.

We will not focus on the first feature, which is more related to the retail banking business. The second and third points are kind of obvious and out of the scope of quants. Whereas, managing uncertainty is clearly at the center of the role of quantitative analysis. The two last features (price information and asymmetric-information related problems) are very important to understand. Because of that, we dedicated a large part of Chapter 2 to detail both of them.

1.3.1   Intermediation everywhere

The simple tale of a traveler and a shoe-shiner can be generalized to any natural risk buyers and sellers. For instance, a farmer and the owner of a hydro-electric plant being concerned by exact opposite weather risks, or a plastic manufacturing company and an oil refinery, etc. As soon as there are people or firms inside the real economy that would like to exchange risk, it is preferable and more efficient to put intermediaries between them, because the exchange of risk is not always feasible in a one-to-one scheme. Take for example, a CDS (insuring against the default of a company A), a corporate bond of company A, the stock price of company A, a government bond of the country where the activity of company A seats, and interest rate swaps. The risks of buying or selling those products are linked together, in such a way that there is a portfolio (i.e., a linear combination of them) such that its value is constant and no more exposed to all these atomic risks. When such portfolios exist, an intermediary is able to contract with actors of the real economy who would like to be protected from each atomic risk, and at the end of the day, replace exposures to uncertainty of real businesses by deterministic premia and margins. This kind of N to M combination of risk exposure is only feasible if (unconflicted) intermediaries are taking care of writing, selling and buying contracts, in a collateralized and cleared environment, under the scrutiny of regulators.

Such a financial system is a large network of intermediaries, where leaves are made of buyers and sellers from the real economy. Thanks to this system, a large part of the uncertainty real actors are exposed to is replaced by deterministic money flows. They exchange a future uncertainty, i.e., risk, against a present deterministic premium. For instance, a plastic manufacturing company buying a contract guaranteeing a fixed price of crude oil is far less exposed to the future variations of the price of its raw material but pays a monthly premium for that. Note that thanks to this, its balance sheet is far more deterministic, and can go for instance to a bank and borrow some money to expand its business. However, the company is no longer "exposed" to any "good luck" as well: the premium it pays is the discounted cost of future uncertainty. If the financial institution providing the contract has a natural buyer of the same risk amongst its clients (for instance an oil refinery), the cost can be extremely low, otherwise, it is the exact value of contrarian moves multiplied by their probability of occurrence. This process is based on netting and risk replication.[1]

The very subtle nature of the financial system is that: On the one hand, the more intermediaries are making the market, the more agents in the real economy can take profit from the system. On the other hand, multiplying the number of intermediaries increases the risk of unbalanced inventories, hence the probability

---

[1]Risk replication has been invented by Louis Bachelier in 1900 and refined by Black, Scholes, and Merton. In essence, it says that if an intermediary is exposed to a pending risk, there is a way to progressively buy and sell related tradable instruments to counterbalance this exposure. This is a theoretical result that deeply relies on the existence of correlated tradable instruments; the technical term is *being in presence of a complete market*, and the capability to replicate this pending risk in continuous time.

of the occurrence of a financial crisis. Such a crisis could have negative consequences on any agent of the real economy involved within
the financial system. Stated differently, the best way to allow the
financial system to serve more real business exposes the system to a
larger risk of failure. This risk can be mitigated if a proper regulation
monitors the levels of inventory imbalances. In fact, it is not that a
big problem if an intermediary A is highly exposed to a source of
risk in one direction if there is another intermediary exposed to the
opposite direction with the exact amount. To take care of such a configuration, it is enough to make A and B net their inventories against
each other. If they cannot do it directly, the process of *risk replication*
should achieve the same result without anyone being aware of it. For
example, in the case of exposure to interest rate, Intermediary A will
sell Interest Rate Swaps (IRS) on public markets to cancel its exposure while intermediary B will buy IRS at the same pace. They will
then *net their respective exposures on exchanges*. As a consequence,
they will not have this exposure anymore.

1.3.2   Contribution of the financial system to the economic growth

The financial system does not only provide a way to structure contracts embedding different sources of risks. It takes place in a very
large life cycle of flows of capital: Once they had fruitful activities,
people and firms start to save some capital. Instead of keeping them
on a bank account, they prefer to invest them to protect their savings
against inflation. It is also tempting to try to obtain some yield on
top of inflation.

   To protect a given amount against inflation, it would be enough,
on paper, to invest this amount in "productive goods". In short,
to protect $100 in an idealized world where the value of productive
goods (factories, raw material, etc.) is $10,000; it should be "enough"
to "buy" 1% of each good as an investment. Thanks to this investment, 20 years later, this $100 will have evolved according to the
productive goods' price evolution, and as a consequence, in a closed
economy, to "inflation" (because the value of productive goods is in
theory perfectly linked to *any source of inflation*: a factory producing chairs will follow the prices of chairs whereas equities of high
tech companies will follow any "tech bubble"). Note that this way to

Table 1.1:   Active vs. passive investing: Breakdown of investment vehicles.

	Index funds/ETFs	Mutual funds	Hedge funds	Endowment fund
Passive	x			x
Active		x	x	

invest is *purely passive*: it would be a "buy and hold strategy" (even if, to free some cash as to buy new sources of production when they appear, asset managers would have to sell some of their assets).

In practice, it is of course not as simple as that: Even in a simple and closed economy, identifying *up-and-coming businesses* constitutes a challenge. For instance, how could we identify that Google or Facebook will be soon part of the "producing companies" at their early age? In fact, there is a cost associated to missing some sources of value in the economy; either because it is difficult to identify their existence (refer to the Grossman–Stiglitz paradox, explained in a few paragraphs), or their existence is known but it is impossible to invest in (think about forests in Romania or real estate in a small region of China). To compensate for these "blind spots", asset owners have to "take risk" by investing in active investment vehicles: Human discretionary asset managers cherry-picking promising companies, experts in medical industry studying the files of the Federal Drug Administration (FDA) to invest in new drugs, systematic "technical" hedge funds to take profit from temporary inefficiencies in liquidity, etc. Table 1.1 show the breakdown of assets by very generic classes of investment vehicles. Chapter 4 deals with the ways asset owners choose between a very wide offer of funds and strategies.

Capital allocation. Another way to see the role of the financial system on capital flows is the way it allows asset owners to allocate capital to *rewarded risky investments*. Capital allocation is linked to price formation since when asset managers buy or sell exposures to economic factors,[2] a real-time balance between offer and demand

---

[2]At this stage the term "economic factor" has to be understood in its very generic meaning: investing in the equity of a company means being exposed to its direct success or failure, investing in an interest rate swap means being exposed to the relative health of the economy of two countries.

takes place and modifies the prices in a natural way. More buyers
than seller pushes the price higher, and vice-versa. We will focus in
Chapter 2 on the way exchanges set prices according to a *matching process*. In theory, as stated by the welfare theorem, a Walrasian
equilibrium on prices where agents have fair access to unbiased fundamental and technical information, and make rational choices leads
to an efficient allocation of resources.

Thanks to the shoe-shiner tale, we have seen that the dissemination of unconflicted information is part of the role of brokers. But we
know since the identification of the Grossman–Stiglitz paradox that a
world where information is available for free will never exist: in such
a world the cost of information processing will never be rewarded.
Hence, the information will never be processed. Of course, some technological progress can lower the processing costs, like the current
trend in *now-casting with alternative data sources and data science*.
But, even if more and more data on the current state of the world is
available (these alternative data cover satellite images, traffic on web
sites, consumption coming from credit cards, etc.), and data science
techniques allow to make sense of them using now standardized software packages given almost for free by GAFAM,[3] there is still a cost
in putting all this in industrial projects, allowing to build dashboards
monitoring the economy almost in real-time.

Not only information will never be perfect, but the rationality of
market participants is far from obvious. All the progress in *behavioral finance* shows that a lot of biases are dictating the way we make
decisions. These biases could stem from a bad appreciation of risks
associated with given investments, or more simply by the ignorance of
some costs (typically *transaction costs*).[4] Implicit biases are not the
only cause of irrationality of market participants: *moral hazard* is also
at the root of a lot of "bad decisions". It is widely documented that
the interests of companies and the interests of decision-makers are
often not aligned. A simple example is the bias of financial analysts
working for brokers: since brokers are making money with fees associated with their clients' trading flows, and because most of the assets

---

[3]GAFAM: Google, Amazon, Facebook, Apple, and Microsoft; to be completed
by Asian BATX: Baidu, Alibaba, Tencent, and Xiaomi.
[4]transaction costs are often badly estimated since they are not only made of
"explicit transaction costs", i.e., fees, but also of the bid-ask spread costs and
ultimately of *market impact*.

under management are invested in long-only strategies, there is a "buy" bias in their recommendations. They are implicitly trained to issue more "buy" recommendations than "sell" ones.

All these biases show that capital allocation is not that rational and does not take into account perfect information. Nevertheless, regulators are working on documenting all these flaws as much as possible to help market participants in curing them.

Flows inside the financial system. The reader has understood that the definition of the "financial system" in this book is: *the network of financial intermediaries*. We simply take a constructive and structural view on the financial system: let's have a look at its components, let's understand the operations it allows. It is made of institutions that are mainly operating as intermediaries on "financial products"; that can be products providing insurance, or exposure on properly defined "risk factors". As intermediaries, they buy and sell a lot of these products made of given mixes of risks. They pay some fixed costs that are now split across all their clients, who would otherwise have to pay 100% of these fixed costs. The "leaves" of this network are outside of the financial system: they are made of *natural risk takers*, part of the real economy. If the system is well balanced, the sum of the internal flows goes to zero (in terms of remaining exposure), hence intermediaries are acting as pure channels between natural actors of the real world. We have seen that it is expected from some participants to "make the markets", i.e., to risk their own capital to provide temporary liquidity on the buy and sell sides, waiting for the next "natural buyers" and "natural sellers". The subtle task of the regulator is to define, product by product, the "risk budget" that is needed to make a market. Beyond this limit, the intermediaries are no longer providing a service to the system or to actors of the "real world", but are storing a supplement of risk, probably because this risk is rewarded by large fees or markups. Very often, attractive margins beyond the natural demand are more due to a leak in the valuation of some product (most often a misvaluation of some liquidity costs), rather than a "free lunch" for intermediaries, which results in crisis when it degenerates.

Figures 1.1 and 1.2 show shows some basic flows operated by the financial system:

- After a few years of successful activity, individuals and companies accumulate some savings.

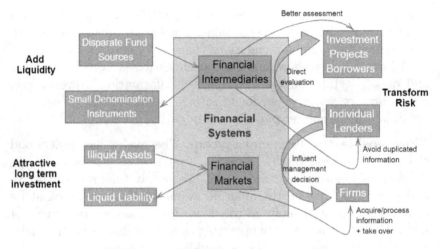

Figure 1.1: Flows in the financial system.

Figure 1.2: Comparative roles of financial intermediaries and markets.

- This cash can be "reused" thanks to financial products: it is typically liquidity transformation (convert cash into loans and be rewarded for that), or more risky investment used to finance "projects" (companies or start-ups) via equity shares or bonds.
- A chain of intermediaries is needed to issue equity shares and bonds: they structure the contracts, guarantee a price for these tradable instruments, and rely on exchanges (or similar intermediaries) for a secondary market.

- Asset managers, and especially hedge funds that can structure long-short vehicles, allow asset owners (the same individuals or companies) to assign a pocket of their capital to the riskiest products.
  As a result, the financial system allows "cash-rich" agents and "risk-taking" agents to share different parts of risky vehicles packaging different types of risks.
- Moreover, investment banks offer "insurance-like products", essentially to provide hedging means to corporate.[5]
- Besides, intermediaries are *making the market*, committing their own capital in providing liquidity to other participants and actors of the real economy. They are naturally rewarded for that; this aspect is detailed in Chapter 2.

Another way to look at the role of intermediaries is to split their features into two categories: risk packaging and liquidity transformation. Of course, liquidity transformation should be seen as a subcategory of risk packaging (since liquidity risk is a type of risk), but putting liquidity on the side provides an interesting viewpoint on the financial system. It is the purpose of Figure 1.1 and is the occasion to list the transformations in both directions: risk and liquidity.

- Provision of liquidity:
  - Financial systems mobilize savings by aggregating and pooling funds from disparate sources and creating small denomination instruments. These instruments provide opportunities for individuals to hold diversified portfolios.
  - Financial markets can also transform illiquid assets (long-term capital investments in illiquid production processes) into liquid liabilities (financial instruments).
  - Financial intermediaries and markets make longer-term investments more attractive and facilitate investment in higher return, longer gestation investments and technologies.

- Transformation of risk characteristics of assets. Enhance risk diversification by reducing information and transaction costs. Resolve

---

[5]Keep in mind the example of a company manufacturing goods in plastic that would like to be protected against price variations of oil.

an information asymmetry problem that may otherwise prevent the exchange of goods and services. Financial markets:

– Avoid duplication of the production of information faced by multiple individual lenders.
– Develop special skills in evaluating prospective borrowers and investment projects.
– Create their own incentives to acquire and process information for listed firms.
– Improve the ability of investors to directly evaluate the returns to projects
– Monitor and increase the ability of investors to influence management decisions
– Facilitate the takeover of poorly managed firms.

1.4   Focus on Two Main Features of Intermediaries

This section focuses on two important roles of intermediaries: ensuring fair access to fundamental information, and managing financial flows. On the one hand, it is good to focus on the first one since it is changing because of the emergence of *alternative data* and *machine learning*. On the other hand, intermediation of flows is a way to list most of the market participants because almost all of them are involved in this activity.

1.4.1   Fair dissemination of public information

Remember that only 40 years ago, the information delivered quarterly by central banks were very difficult to obtain. Central banks used to give official speeches regarding changes in monetary policy; and without being physically in the press room, it was impossible to get the correct information. As usual, when there is a high fixed cost in the financial system, intermediaries invest. In this case brokers took in charge the cost of sending people in the conference room to convey information to investors. They were somehow competing with journalists but added a "market color" to the disclosure of central banks' decisions by explaining how it should influence the price of financial instruments they offered to buyers and sellers. After a while, this information was made available by central banks themselves;

and if you go today on the web site of a central bank, you will find detailed information such as transcripts of the Directors' speeches, time series reports commenting *ex-ante* and *ex-post* the impact of banks' decisions. The fixed cost associated with the digestion of this kind of information decreased so much that brokers had to find enough added value elsewhere to be packaged in the services to their clients.

The next natural information having a large fixed cost to acquire has been the earning announcements of companies. Brokers position themselves as intermediaries between companies and investors. Surprisingly enough, exchanges, offering the listing to companies, have too little relationships with investors to be able to put them in contact with companies, while brokers, who are very often associated with investment banks, have a natural access to investors on one hand, and to issuers on the other hand. Investment banks and prime brokers advise companies when they issue new shares and bonds, and then act as *book runners* during the first days (or weeks) of issuance. It has been natural for them to propose to investors shares and bonds and to provide fundamental analysis on companies, i.e., "blue book", so that asset managers can take decisions on allocating capital. Investment banks took in charge the costs associated with understanding the components of balance sheets and proposing actionable decisions, and to comment on earning announcements of CEO and CFO of companies which gave birth to "financial analysis", i.e., reports commenting on the performances and expected return on equity of companies.

This research is one of the components of the links between investors, intermediaries, and corporations; concentrating the market of financial information in the hands of brokers. Their activity in this area is regulated to *ensure fair and synchronous dissemination of information among all market participants*. Brokers' business models have long been focused on this position around a "pay once trading fees and take profit of a wide spectrum of services" and is now jeopardized by MiFID 2, a European directive that demands for brokers' clients to explicitly pay for what they consume. This demand for unbundling is simultaneous to the commoditization of financial analysis: companies' web sites, papers of academics, internet forums and Wikipedia are seriously challenging the business of brokers' research (see Section 6.1.3 for details on this transformation).

With the emergence of factor investing, brokers started to produce sectorial analysis first, then recommendations by analysts from their equity derivative departments, and quantitative reports on sophisticated strategies. AI and alternative data offer another playing field to brokers: the slow move out of fundamental to more data-oriented research, in their never-ending evolution towards areas with high fixed costs. Investment banks owning computer farms and hosting a lot of quantitative analysts will soon produce this next generation of information at a cheaper price.

1.4.2 Intermediation of flows

Intermediation of flows can be seen from different perspectives: on one hand, investors' flows are intermediated, this perspective follows capital starting at issuance; and on the other hand, each intermediary is running a *flow business* of its own, this other perspective investigates flows generated inside the financial system.

1.4.2.1 Intermediation of investors' flows

The capital injected in the financial system comes from different sources: individuals and institutions. Individuals earn money from working or through inheritance, while legal entities (companies or governments) make profits operating their businesses. A very important source of capital for companies comes from the issuance of their shares and the issuance of corporate bonds. These *Issuances* are two simple ways to generate flows inside the financial system.

A simple definition of bonds. When an external agent buys a bond from the institution, she gives a fixed amount of money for a fixed period of time to this institution. The money will be given back after *maturity* of the bond. In between, the institution pays *coupons* as yield rewarding the "deposit".

The exchange is simple: the issuance of a bond is an adequate instrument when the institution needs temporarily (usually 3–5 years) liquidity to finance a project. The risk associated with a bond is the risk of bankruptcy of the issuer.

The coupon can be seen as a "rent" paid by the issuer to the buyer of the bond. Financial institutions (typically banks) issue bonds.

It is also one of the primary sources of financing for governments. Since the main source of risk for the buyer is the bankruptcy of the issuer, stable and developed countries can easily obtain financing via bonds.

Structure and issuance of bonds. The *structure* of a bond can be fine-tuned; generally, an investment bank takes care of this: what is the good duration, not only from a financing perspective but from potential investors' perspective. Similarly for the coupon: the amount should balance between investors interest and potential investors concerns about the high yield? Moreover, bonds are the basic financial instrument to build *structured products*; Chapter 3 gives a detailed view of this kind of financial product: the coupon can be indexed on complex formulae depending on market conditions, this is typically a way to package sophisticated mixes of risk in a financial product.

Not only its coupons but the bond itself can be shaped to include risk in it: *convertible bonds* are a typical example of that, under specified conditions they can be converted in equity shares. This transformation is clearly a subtle way to package risk coming from the real economy. Let us look at the associated sequence of risk exposures:

- The owner of the bond is exposed to the risk of bankruptcy of the underlying company, it is clearly an exposure to the business success of this company in the real world.
- Under specific economic conditions, the bond can be converted into equity shares. This event itself provides exposure to the real world.
- The buyer of the bond is now owning equity shares, corresponding to another kind of exposure to the success of the company.

In terms of the *smoothness of the exposure to the business of the issuing company*, the owner of a convertible bond goes from an exposure to the crossing of a threshold (that is triggering the bankruptcy) to a jump (the occurrence of the conversion) towards a continuous exposure (since the owner of equity shares is progressively exposed to the successes or failures of the company).

A simple definition of equity shares. Another way to obtain financing is the issuance of equity shares. Equity shares are the

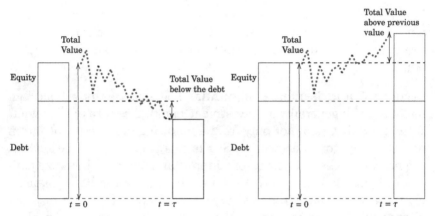

Figure 1.3: Stylized diagram of a balance sheet and of its evolution through time (on the left the corporate face a credit event, on the right it creates value).

simplest way to invest in a company: while bonds embed a *liquidity risk*,[6] it is usually very easy to sell an equity share (at the cost of a liquidity premium that is at least the *bid-ask spread* of the stock). The buyer of the shares is exposed to the bankruptcy of the underlying company (like the buyer of a bond), but in a different way: if the company goes bankrupt the shares' owner gets nothing while the owner of a bond has chances to get some money back (see the next paragraph).

Figure 1.3 stylizes two possible futures once the capital structure of a Corporate is fixed (here simply between the equity and the debt, both financing the business of the company): either (on the right hand side of the picture) the business value of the company increases (because it made profits) and in such a case the equity value increases (proportionally with its structure) and hence the value of each share increases, either (on the left hand side of the picture) its business value decreases so much that it goes below its debt, and in such a case it faces a credit event: the value of one share of equity is zero and the value of the debt is reduced to its recovery rate.

The exposure provided by equity shares is straightforward: in a simplified world, a company would deliver each year dividends

---

[6]Once the buyer of a bond converts some cash into a bond, it is not very easy to get the cashback: the secondary market of bonds is less liquid than the secondary market of equity shares.

corresponding to its profits. The fact that a company decides to make investments in different projects to enhance its future activity will decrease its profits but increase its potential future value. This increase in value should be reflected in the value of its shares of equity.[7] The change in the value of a listed company during a given period of time is the sum of the dividends received by the owner of one share plus the difference between the selling price and the buying price. A discount rate should be applied, and if someone is interested in the yield beyond the risk-free rate, such rate should be subtracted. To be very accurate, the "liquidity cost" is taken into account given that when one share is bought, the price is the Ask price (which can be written as the *mid price* plus half of the bid-ask spread), and after a while, it is sold at the bid price (which can be written as the mid-price minus half of the bid-ask spread). All in all, one could say the share is bought and sold at the mid-price and a bid-ask spread of "liquidity costs" is then paid. This cost is an infinitesimal one since it is paid for one share; but when an investor buys or sells far more than a single share, he influences the offer and demand equilibrium, creating a *market impact*, which increases the transaction cost.

Bonds, equity, and balance sheets. Since the two main sources of financing for a company are equity shares and bonds, it should be reflected in their balance sheet. In short: on the liability side, there is the equity and debts (essentially loans and bonds); and on the asset side, there is the production means of the company, plus the cash. Figure 1.3 shows a simple diagram and illustrates different scenarios at the end of a quarter: the company makes a profit or losses. When the company makes a profit, the debt does not change, hence the equity value adapts so that assets match liabilities: the value of one share increases. Inversely, when the company faces losses, the value of its equity decreases. Should the decrease in equity reach the debt level, the company will then not be able to face its own debt. This raises a credit event.[8] In a simple world, it

---

[7]The value of one share is the total value of the company divided by the number of shares: when the value of the company increases, the price of one share increases.

[8]In the US, the "Chapter 11 of the Bankruptcy Code" addresses the different cases and consequences of the credit event.

would mean that the company has to face bankruptcy. In such a case, owners of equity shares lose all of their investments, whereas owners of corporate bonds share between themselves the remaining value of the company, once its assets have been liquidated. The fraction of the value of the bond they obtain this way is called the *recovery rate* of a bankruptcy.

It is important to understand how the real economy interacts with the financial system. In this case, it is clear that the life-cycle of companies' activity (the "asset" side of their balance sheets) is part of the flows intermediated by the financial system via the "liability" side of their balance sheet: equity shares and bonds are traded by and via financial intermediaries. They are one of the basic components of "risky exposure" that can be traded on financial markets.

These basic "bricks" can be combined: the simplest combination being indexes (like the local indexes: the S&P 500 or the Russel 1000 for the US and the CAC40 or the DAX for France and Germany), and the most sophisticated ones being exotic options[9] written on stocks. If indexes seem simple in appearance, the linear combinations of stocks they provide exhibit very different properties than stocks themselves. As an example, capital-weighted indexes (the "standard" equity indexes) have more (negative) skewness than stocks. Chapter 4 presents other combinations shaping specific risk profiles, like the Fama–French portfolios; these family of portfolios became the basis of the "factor investing" industry that started in the years 2010. Intermediaries offer trading on indexes via baskets replicating their components with the correct weights (usually packaged in Exchange Traded Funds, ETF), typically structured by large asset managers, or via swaps that are themselves structured by investment banks, and via Futures that are designed by exchanges. Three types of intermediaries (asset managers, investment banks, and exchanges) offer the same kind of exposure to agents of the real economy or other market participants. As usual, the way the exposure to these indexes is packaged adds some different kinds of risks: ETFs[10] include some "liquidity risk and cost", while swaps include certain counterparty

---

[9]We do not elaborate here on options, see Chapter 3 for details.

[10]We make here as if all ETFs were physically replicated, and ignore the "synthetic ETFs", that are embedding other types of risks, like counterparty risk.

risk and financing costs (and hence an exposure to interest rates), and futures face "delivery and liquidity costs".

Another investment vehicles providing a different type of exposure are (CDSs): they provide insurance against the credit risk of a corporate bond. In short, you pay a monthly premium to obtain a gain when a given company will face a credit event (in practice, if some clauses of "Chapter 11 of the US Bankruptcy Code" is activated by the company). The fixed income market provides a lot of basic bricks to build financial products too, like Interest Rate Swaps (IRSs), enabling investors to obtain exposure to variations of interest rates of a given kind. Investment banks typically structure these kinds of products, as with a lot of others; they have the expertise in writing the contracts, being regulated in a lot of jurisdictions, and in the process of netting a lot of risks, having few of them in their balance sheets and *replicating the remaining risks*.

Primary and secondary markets. Since intermediaries are offering investment vehicles to agents of the real economy or to other market participants, there is a need for "market places" to buy and sell these products. Participants usually make the difference between the *primary* and the *secondary market*. The former is encompassing the first issuance of products: there is one seller (usually the structurer of the product) and a lot of buyers, while the latter allows the exchange of the products during their life.

For example, the primary market for equity shares takes place during the Initial Public Offering (IPO) of the shares of a company. A prime broker that has been elected by the company board to be the "book-runner" of the IPO helped to choose the initial price at which the shares will be initially sold. The book runner has contacted potentially interested investors, in a *liquidity seeking*[11] process. Usually, the book runner guarantees to commit its own capital by buying for itself a large number of shares. It will use it to package instruments or will provide liquidity on this stock by selling part of these shares in the future. Immediately after this IPO, the secondary market opens and offers the shares to trading. To be authorized to have its shares

---

[11]They look for "buying liquidity" because their expertise is also to know the appetite of different investors.

traded on the secondary market, the company has to be "listed" on an *Exchange*.[12] Only some market places are authorized to list companies, they are called "regulated exchanges" under the MiFID European Directive. Once a stock is listed, other market places are authorized to offer them for trading, they are named "multilateral trading facilities" (MTFs) under MiFID. Chapter 2 elaborates on trading practices.

Emission of corporate or government bonds follows the same process (under two different regulations): they can be bought at issuance on the primary market, or after a while on the secondary market. Since the corporate bond market is less liquid[13] than the equity markets, investors have a preference to buy them on the primary market. This gives a powerful position to investment banks that are structuring the issuance of corporate bonds, acting as "book-runners" and helping companies raise capital.

1.4.2.2   From flows to capital

Equilibrium considerations and leverage. Understanding the way companies raise capital helps to have an investor-driven viewpoint to complement the usual flow-driven viewpoint on the financial system and on financial intermediation. In a simple and closed economic environment: if companies raise capital using equity and bonds via an average repartition key of 60% vs. 40%, then final investors (typically large asset managers and investment banks) cannot own a different repartition than 60% of equity shares and 40% of bonds (in market value). There is usually no creation of new sources of risk in the financial system. Nevertheless, some financial products provide *leverage*. Leverage can be created when it is not mandatory to put the exact value of a provided exposure in collateral. The practice is often that when you structure a product embedding some exposure, an intermediary is not asked to put as collateral 100% of the "value"

---

[12]Examples of exchanges are the New-York Stock Exchange, Euronext, or the London Stock Exchange.
[13]Simply say at this stage that "less liquid" means a lesser number of transactions. In 2019, a liquid stock trades around 50,000 times a day, while a liquid corporate bond trades less than 20 times a day.

of this exposure, but rather 20%[14] of it. This means that on the paper, the available risk traded on financial market places can be 5 times the real value of the corresponding risks in the real economy.

The rationale of leverage is to give an incentive to intermediaries to make the markets. Providing liquidity with a very low inventory in good condition and using a quantitative approach (see Section 1.5.6) is meant to generate a profit that is on average positive but can be very small. With leverage, small but positive profits can be multiplied by the leverage, hence greater than any fixed costs if the leverage is large enough. Of course, a simple multiplication of a strategy not only linearly increases its average profit, but also increases its standard deviation (i.e., volatility: the square root of its risk). Fortunately, enough financial mathematics provide methodological tools to decrease the risk of a strategy, but at a cost in terms of average profits. If the loss in profit to linearly decreases the risk is sublinear, it is feasible to use leverage to simultaneously increase the profits and maintain the risk below a (regularly, or safety) threshold.

Following asset owners' capital. On the one hand, agents of the real economy (retail, companies, and governments) raise capital or borrow money. On the other hand, other agents of the real economy ("risk takers") are looking for returns at the cost of some risks. Financial intermediaries will fill the gap between them: they will structure regulated instruments to mix different nature of risks so that the resulting risk profile corresponds to the exact appetite of risk-takers: maybe no one wants to take simultaneously risk on the business success of a given company and on future moves of yield curves while a corporate bond on this company is mixing the two kinds of risks. In such a case an intermediary (i.e., in this case an investment bank) could "strip" the yield curve to remove its exposure from an investment vehicle designing a product to provide pure exposure to the business success of the company. For this specific example, the investment bank will have some pure exposure to moves of the yield curve in its balance sheet: to cope with regulation and to reduce its exposure to economic variables (the yield curve being

---

[14]20% is not an exact number but is indicative of what could be asked to a reliable counterparty in 2019.

one of them), the bank has two choices: find external clients having appetite to opposite exposure to moves of the curve, or to *replicate its exposure* in the markets using a Black–Scholes–Merton approach.

This example is typical of the role of intermediaries: they engineer investment vehicles decomposing and recomposing risks so that risk-takers and risk providers can match. The overall goal is that the sum of risks bought and sold are exactly the same, hence each agent of the real economy will face exactly the kind of risk it wants to buy or sell.

The expression *asset owner* has to be clarified: individuals (i.e., retail), companies and governments have savings. As soon as they plan on when they will need to spend them, they know how long they can accept to "lock" them on an account. Rather than letting this cash stay on an account, and to be protected against inflation (see Section 1.3.2), they will seek for a yield. At this point they can be called "asset owners": they seek investment vehicles to reach a given goal that is a combination of *risk, returns, and duration*. This combination can be named the *risk profile* of the investment vehicle. Asset owners can buy financial products directly, or can select an *asset manager* who will do it on their behalf, and who will have a *fiduciary duty* (see Chapter 4). Such fiduciaries have expertise in investment vehicles; they will themselves invest directly or via other asset managers. In this way, money, alongside a given appetite for risk will propagate into the financial system, to reach an adequate financial product.

1.5   Market Participants

Each participant has a different viewpoint, depending on his time scale, and his utility function. For the purpose of modeling and understanding market dynamics, it is useful to split participants across:

- *The Buy Side*: Investors and Asset Managers. They make buying and selling decisions. They consume (i.e., "buy") financial services, that is why they are called "the buy-side".
- *The Sell Side — Agency*: Intermediaries who provide (i.e., "sell") financial services, that is why they are called "the sell-side". For a better description of the roles, we will restrict this category of agencies only to intermediaries. Activities involving capital

commitments and leverage will thus be in other categories, respectively "market-making" and "structuring".

- *Structurers*: Intermediaries that build (i.e., "structure") financial products. We prefer to isolate this feature from the "sell-side" for two reasons: first of all, this is a very specific activity with a specific skillset, especially from the viewpoint of quantitative analysts (i.e., "quants" or "strats"). Second because with the modularization of financial activities, it is now possible to have intermediaries that are only taking care of structuration.
- *Investment Banks* are making operations to provide leverage. They also net risk inside their balance sheets (that are often global balance sheets, allowing capital to cross boundaries at a cheap cost), and they replicate residual risks on markets using Black–Scholes–Merton like procedures. Note that structuring teams of Investment Banks are not in the "Investment Bank" category for us, but in the "Structurer" one.
- *Market Operators and Vendors*: Exchanges, trading facilities, providers of trading software and hardware, etc. These intermediaries sell technology and services around trading, from trading facilities (i.e., "matching engines") to high-frequency data acquisition, storage, recovery, and processing.
- *Market Makers and Proprietary Shops* (including high-frequency trading, HFT, firms): Their core business is trading, they involve their own capital in making the market or trading at a frequency that is on average faster than one week. A market-making desk inside an Investment Bank will fall into this category.
- *Regulators*: They aim at monitoring market operations to ensure a smooth and orderly functioning market.

Let's elaborate on each type of market participant. We will see that these categories allow to have a clear view of operations: the Buy Side is where inflows of capital reach the financial system, they can directly access Market Operators to buy or sell by themselves, but usually, they do it via the Sell Side. The latter sells and buys simple exposure to equity and bonds or asks Structurers to build products answering to their clients' needs. In between, Investment Banks net risks and replicate any undesirable risk-on markets. Market Operators are needed for risk replication, and Market Makers and Prop Shops provide liquidity to markets at different time scales:

very fast for HFT on equities and slower for some others. Regulating
Authorities supervise all these entities to ensure that rules are followed. They are in charge of identifying new sources of undesirable
risk to issue new adapted regulations.

1.5.1   The buy side

The Buy Side is made of asset owners or of fiduciaries acting on behalf
of asset owners. Typically Asset Managers (including pension funds)
and insurance companies make up the *Buy Side*. Their business is
mainly to combine investment vehicles (offered by Structurers via the
Sell Side) to reach a given risk profile. The risk-reward analysis is at
the root of their skill set. They have a focus on fees and transaction
costs to make sure that they pay the right price for each product.
Since the 2010s, they have been challenging active portfolio managers
with low fees ETFs and swaps provided by the Sell Side.

From a quantitative perspective (1)

Portfolio construction (especially Modern Portfolio Theory)
and market impact analysis is the basic knowledge needed for
the Buy Side. Of course, generic knowledge of structuring is
good since it allows to better understand what to invest in.

1.5.2   The (agency) sell side

The Sell Side is firstly made of "pure agency brokers": they do not
commit any capital in making the market or in proprietary trading. On the paper, it guarantees that there is no conflict of interest
between them and their clients: it is impossible to *front run* their
clients' orders.

Other brokers are traditionally named "prime brokers": they commit capital in their business. Thanks to this, they can make markets, provide leverage and build structured products or derivatives.
To develop a clear and simple view on market participants, we will
split the description of this kind of companies operating different
businesses under the same umbrella. Each "business line" will be

described independently: the market making and liquidity provision activity will fall under the "Market Makers and Prop. Shops" category, while leverage will fall under the "Investment Bank" category, and structuring will be developed under the "Structuring" subsection.

It is nevertheless important to underline that very often pure agency brokers are named "executing brokers" and that most agency brokers offer a "facilitation" service. This service allows them to "provide liquidity" to their clients; thus allows them to provide exactly the opposite feature to front running. For instance, they accept to sell to a client the requested shares at a price close to the current market price but do not immediately buy them on exchanges, they keep a short/negative inventory for the time needed to buy them back on exchanges at a preferable price. It is considered as a "lazy market making activity", and without market-making expertise and active business, it is difficult for the broker to make money out of it. Around 2015, investment banks started to put in place a *central risk book* to stabilize this kind of activity around a team close to the brokerage business. See the "Market Maker" category for details.

From a quantitative perspective (2)

The expertise needed on the Sell Side is one of market microstructure and optimal trading. It allows us to develop and tune algorithms splitting large orders (i.e., metaorders) of the Sell Side in "child orders" to achieve "best execution". Such trading algorithms can be used by the Sell Side to execute their large orders, the optimal split of a large order has to take into consideration two dimensions: time and space. "Time splitting" is also named "trade scheduling", and "space splitting" is a way to face *fragmentation of market places*.

Front running. Front running is the typical example of the bad behavior of brokers: a client calls him to buy a large number of shares; the broker could then buy these shares before the client, thus impacting the price and then sell them back to his client. An "isolated way" to understand this is that the broker is "gaming" its client's order, which is clearly bad because the broker is not providing a *best* *execution* but the *worst possible execution*. Another more holistic and deeper way to understand front running is that the broker is riding on his client's information. More generally, rather than using a single client's information, a broker could aggregate all of his clients' orders before deciding whether to front-run or not, which would be far more reliable: One-half of the clients calling to buy while other clients are selling is not the same as a configuration where all clients are buying. This is of paramount importance because it allows for understanding that *flows are moving the price*. They are not only moving the price because of mechanical pressure that one could name *market impact*, but also because the Buy Side is buying or selling according to information it has on future price movements. Front running is not simply "stealing some pennies in front of one client", it is free-riding on clients' information. In a simply separated world with only a Sell Side and a Buy Side: the Buy Side invests in means (data, technology, and knowledge) to extract information on future price moves, while the Sell Side spends money in developing expertise in executing large orders (usually named *metaorders*). It is not so simple, because brokers (i.e., part of the Sell Side) also sell reports on the "fair value" of tradable instruments: they have developed expertise in assets valuation. Therefore, they can invest according to their information in a similar fashion as their clients should they have capital. This raises concerns about conflict of interest, which is why they are regulated to avoid price manipulation, either while they are disseminating information, or trading.

1.5.3   Structurers

Structurers "build" financial products, which are engineered to answer to risk appetites of the Buy Side. The essential difference between structuring and portfolio construction (i.e., the main activity of asset managers) is that structuring involves leverage and nonlinear payoff. The payoff is a generic term used in financial mathematics to name a formula that will be computed in the future (the time between the issuance of the product and the computation of its payoff is called the *duration*). The result of the formula is the amount of money the seller of the product must give to the buyer at maturity. The simplest payoff is the one of a Contract For Difference (CFD): the payoff of a CFD is written on a stock, its duration is one day, and the payoff is equal to the daily return of the stock. A more sophisticated payoff is the one of a vanilla Option: a Put or a Call. The payoff of a Call written on a stock corresponds to the right to "call" one share of the stock in the future (at maturity, i.e., after the duration of the Option) at a price decided in advance (i.e., the "strike" of the Option). Since the buyer of a Call will not exercise this right if the strike price is greater than the market price of the stock at maturity, the payoff of a call is the maximum between zero (because the Call will not be exercised) and the market price minus the strike of the Option.

In terms of financial engineering, structurers can embed returns linked to equities in fixed income-like products. Autocalls are of this kind: they are corporate bonds issued by a bank with a coupon that is a formula on returns of equity products (typically indexes). They allow the Buy Side to allocate in their "fixed income pocket" returns indexed on equities. Structuring is developed in detail in Chapter 3.

From a quantitative perspective (3)

Structurers need to know option pricing and risk replication. As such they at least need bases in stochastic calculus and dynamic programming.

1.5.4 Investment banks

Investment banks are the backbone of modern financial markets; they commit capital to provide leverage and maintain a balance sheet with an exposure to the different financial products they bought and sold. They have teams of traders and quants knowing how to replicate the risk in their books to reduce their exposure to changes in economic variables such as prices, interest rates, yield curves, uncertainty (i.e., volatility), etc.

They usually have teams of structurers and of market makers because once a product is designed, it is useful to make the market on it since the Buy Side prefers to buy liquid products (i.e., products having a reasonably active secondary market). They often have a brokerage business too, which can be a pure agency, or prime broker business. Before the financial crisis, they usually had *proprietary trading desks* as well as implementing short-term investment strategies on behalf of the bank for its own account with its own money. But since the bankruptcy of Lehman Brothers, which simultaneously had a prop trading business and a brokerage business, regulators realized that the capital of a prime broker could be used to take risks which could lead to bankruptcy, and that for a large broker (Lehman Brothers was one of the largest brokers in the world at this time) this kind of event could be a systemic risk. A systemic risk refers to the risk that the financial system stops operating as expected, hence stops providing the features expected to the real economy. The 2008–2009 financial crisis has been of this kind. Learning from the lessons of this crisis, the Dodd–Frank Act (DFA, 2010) brought on many different regulations, one of them demanding that the business of serving clients and proprietary trading be separated.

Since providing leverage and making the markets is a way to serve clients, Investment Banks are allowed to maintain a balance sheet that is embedding the financial risk corresponding to bought or sold financial products. Because of this, the boundary between stopping any prop trading activity and having proprietary traders is not that clear (somehow market makers are prop traders: traders buying and selling on behalf of the Investment Bank). Moreover, the DFA is part of the US regulation and European countries do not all have a similar regulation.

From proprietary trading to central risk book. Nevertheless, a large movement of displacing proprietary trading outside of Investment Banks started globally in the years 2010. Different strategies have been taken: from externalizing prop trading desks in the asset management arm of banks (becoming as such asset managers, in which Investment Banks can then invest), to converting their prop trading activity in "market-making" (or an equivalent). A simple way to understand how to convert prop trading strategies into market-making strategies is the following: take short-term strategies, especially ones based on mean reversion. The strategies are giving a "paper price", that is the expected price (according to prop trading predictors) a few hours, minutes, or seconds later. Once they are in place, they can accept to provide liquidity to a client who wants to buy if such paper price is lower than the current price (or respectively to accept a sell order if the paper price is greater than the current price). If the predicted prices are accurate enough, this market making strategy will earn money. And if they are very good, it is even possible to provide price improvements to clients.

These predictors are only good "on average"; which implies that the more they are used in one day, the closer they are to the average profits at the end of the day. There are two ways to have the opportunity to use predictors in a day: either having a lot of clients resulting in more opportunities within the day (but there is no guarantee that the predictors will predict the price direction corresponding to the demand of the client, i.e., price up for a sell and price down for a buy), either by offering liquidity provision for as much tradable products as possible. This is why large Investment Banks have put in place a *Central Risk Book*: a service or a desk offering liquidity thanks to this kind of price predictors on as many products as possible. Moreover, the more products offered to trade, the easier it is to balance its exposure to directional market moves. It gives, for instance, the opportunity to be "long"[15] in one stock and "short"[16] on another, positively correlated one. Additionally, if a liquidity provider bought 10 shares of a stock and sold 20 shares of another stock, and if the later has a correlation of 0.5 with the former, the liquidity provider has, on average,[17] no exposure to price moves.

In practice, it is difficult to put in place a Central Risk Book: it is a large industrial project as it needs to convey the needed information and to compute predictors and risk management analytics on time. It is a wide change of habits too: the mindset of proprietary traders have to evolve from a selfish one to a more "client-oriented" one.

Risk management in an investment bank. Investment Banks invest a lot in risk management: they have to cope with regulation by computing many analytics regarding their exposure to potential changes in economic variables, to perform stress tests, and to assess the global level of exposure of the balance sheet (or of the balance sheets, because most Investment Banks have a lot of different balance

---

[15]Have a positive inventory.

[16]Have a negative inventory.

[17]Of course, it is only an average, since the correlation is indicative, under stationarity assumption, of the usual joint moves of the two stocks.

sheets) of the bank to different risk factors. Chapter 5 details risk management practices for Investment Banks.

From a quantitative perspective (4)

Quantitive analysts working in an investment bank have to know how to compute the costs and revenues of each business line, and to perform breakdowns by clients, by market conditions, etc. They need to have skills in risk management. For an Investment bank, risk management is focused on exposure to non-linear payoffs, with a bias on interest rates (that are very useful for Asset and Liability Management, ALM). This is different from risk management operated by asset managers who allocate capital on risk factors.

1.5.5 Market operators and vendors

The "Exchanges" are a crucial component of the financial system as transactions (i.e., trades) take place there. Very early in history, market participants understood that having a central place to buy and sell goods was a great idea. That is obvious for physical goods since there is a cost to carry them to different places, but it is also true for "paper goods", like equity shares, or bonds, because when all buyers and sellers meet at the same place, price formation will be more efficient.[18]

An exchange has different features: creating and monitoring listed instruments, concentrating flows, and regulating its members (usually brokers and market makers). An instrument is listed by a company (typically a company has to list its equity shares and its corporate bonds), by a government or by the exchange itself. For instance, Future contracts are created and managed by exchanges. Traditionally, exchanges have been associated with countries (or states), and have created indexes of the most liquid companies

---

[18]Simply because if you have 99 buyers and one seller in one place and 99 sellers and one buyer at another place, you will have two different prices, and only two participants will have an attractive price (the lonely buyer and seller) whereas 198 participants could have a better price if they would have met at the same place.

they listed. Such an index reflects the wealth of the economy of a given country, like the CAC 40 for France or the Nikkei for Japan. The corresponding Future contracts are thus financial instruments providing exposure to the economy of these countries. Other firms provide indexes, like MSCI, S&P or MorningStar, that are often specialized by country and by sector, providing another type of exposure.

Once regulation allowed competition between exchanges, other trading venues (such as Alternative Trading Venues, ATS, or MTFs) were born and *fragmentation appeared* (for more details about this, see Chapter 2). While information technologies are used to communicate with exchanges or any kind of market place, technology vendors appeared on the playing field, competing to offer (often in association with trading facilities) the means to submit orders and receive transaction reports. Thanks to fragmentation, most market participants should they have or want to, can check whether they traded at the best place, in the best condition, and at the best price. Software companies started to sell tools, connected to large databases, to perform such Transaction Cost Analyses (TCA).

Moreover, once a transaction occurred, it has to be settled and if it is a contract with a payoff in the future, a clearinghouse is needed to ask for initial margins and potentially subsequent margin calls.

This long list of activities around trading venues shows that it is difficult today to isolate "exchanges" as the unique kind of market participants needed to trade, there is a constellation of companies that have business models around transactions, which can be called "Market Operators and Vendors".

1.5.5.1 Exchanges

Basic features of an exchange. To make it simple and to help understanding the most important features of a market place, it is useful to focus on these four simple properties:

1. An exchange is *a place to finance the economy*. This is clearly the viewpoint of companies or governments listing instruments on the market to raise capital.
2. An exchange is *a place where sellers and buyers meet*. This underlines the way market places centralize trading flows in one place: traders know that they should find a counter-party when they come to a recognized trading facility.

3. An exchange is at *the origin of the price formation process*, simply because the trading process is a mechanism matching buyers and sellers, where the price is the adjusting variable reflecting the directional views of market participants. Trading venues implement matching engines that are operating this *double auction game* in real-time.

4. An exchange is a *place where risk decreases* since trading is the way used by structurers and investment banks to continuously hedge their exposure to variations of economic variables, thanks to the Black–Scholes–Merton risk replication methodology.

Different ways to trade. The main feature of trading venues to offer a place to match buyers and sellers. They are two main ways to ensure a buyer and a seller agree to transact:

• A *bilateral* way:
  This is an asymetric setup: the *liquidity consumer*, buyer or seller, come to a specific counterparty, typically a bank, that makes the market (they are usually named "market dealers"). The process is the following:

  1. The consumer tries to announce as vaguely as possible its intention, for instance: "I would like to trade (never disclosing the direction, buy or sell) this kind of instrument for a "big" size (never disclosing the exact size)".

  2. The dealer answers with *quotes*: a quote is made of two prices (one for a buy and one for a sell) and associated quantities (usually the same quantity for both sides), like: "For a size around 1,000 lots, I can buy at \$9.9 and sell at \$10.1". This quote has a bid price and an ask price, the former being lower than the later, and associated bid and ask quantities.

  3. The liquidity consumer then decides to *activate* or not this quote, i.e., he can simply not trade with this counterparty (perhaps because he was offered a better quote).

This process is typically named a *Request For Quotation* (RFQ). In this configuration, the roles of the "client" and of the "maker-dealer" are very different, for many various reasons:

  – The dealers are the sole liquidity providers, whereas the clients are the sole liquidity consumers.

– Each dealer knows her clients "by their names", she can conduct "liquidity analyses" (that are also called "information analyses" or "toxicity analyses"). The goal of such analysis is to understand (or model[19]) the usual cost of providing liquidity to a client. One expects that the usual level of information of the client on future price changes is of paramount importance, but the market context and the type of traded instruments are influencing the cost of liquidity provision too. Thanks to these analyses, a dealer can customize the cost of liquidity for each client which may also depend on market conditions. The state of the dealer's balance sheet is often taken into account too: if the dealer has too much of an instrument, she will probably unwind it for cheap. Inversely, a client will have to pay an additional cost for the dealer to accept accumulating an inventory of this instrument.

– Because of these very different roles, bilateral trading structurally exhibits *information asymmetry* between clients and dealers. On one hand, clients are meant to have more information on long-term price changes. On the other hand, dealers have more information on the short-term flows of institutional investors. Since the pressure exerted by the net order flows influences price moves, larger dealers have more accurate information on future prices (hence on the cost of providing liquidity).

– In such a bilateral market, there is usually an *inter-dealer brokers market* (IDB), where dealers can unwind their positions between themselves. Such a market can use a multilateral mechanism; in any case, the IDB market is less asymmetric than the bilateral one.

- A *multilateral* way:
  The other way to organize the trading process is via multilateral platforms. Buyers and sellers, liquidity providers and liquidity consumers have exactly the same status, and cannot be distinguished. Any participant to the double auction can send orders (i.e., buy 1,000 shares up to price $10.5, or sell 500 shares at a price better or equal to $9.5).

---

[19] With the emergence of Artificial Intelligence and Machine Learning, dealers are improving their "toxicity analysis" using modern tools.

All these instructions are usually collected by an automated mechanism called a *matching engine*: At the start of the trading session, orders are simply stored in memory, up to the point where a buy and a sell order can be matched. For instance, if a buy order for 100 shares at $10 is already stored, and a sell order for 250 shares at $9.5 reaches the matching engine, a trade of 100 shares is generated (and three messages are sent by the matching engine). As a consequence, the order of the buyer (of the 100 shares) is "fully filled" at $10 (first message), the order of the seller (owner of the 250 shares) is "partially filled" for 100 shares at $10, the seller is satisfied since he sells at a better price (second message), and the observers of the auction are seeing a "trade" of 100 shares at $10. For more details about matching mechanisms, see Lehalle and Laruelle (2018). These orders are stored in a limit order book (LOB).

It is easy to understand that in such a mechanism, the sole asymmetry is between the first comer (in our example the buy order) and the second one (for us the sell orders). The first comer is the liquidity provider while the second one is the liquidity consumer. The important difference with bilateral trading is that each participant can be in turn provider or consumer.

The common belief is that bilateral is better suited for low liquid instruments and multilateral for liquid ones. This is not necessarily true as corporate bonds (which are not liquid) were traded in the US in a multilateral way before 1929.

Another belief is that within a bilateral system the dealers can make different prices for each client whereas it is not possible in a multilateral process. This is in fact not true. The behavior of High-Frequency Traders, monitoring the state of the order book and amending their orders accordingly, makes that in the multilateral process, participants aware of order book liquidity in real-time will not pay the same price (i.e., they will pay less) than those not paying attention to the state of liquidity. But what is important to notice is that:

- In bilateral trading: market participants with more knowledge on (long term) price changes will pay more for liquidity.

- In multilateral trading: market participants with less knowledge on order book dynamics (short-term price changes) will pay more for liquidity.

There is no consensus in the academic sphere on the cost of liquidity in each "quadrant" of this bivariate configuration: It is certain that participants with little knowledge on the long-term price changes and the order book dynamics will pay the most in both trading mechanisms. However, is it really possible to be paying less with high knowledge on long-term price moves or order book dynamics? The answer is not trivial, as market participants, even the sophisticated ones, initiate large orders unrelated to future price changes, typically when they need to unwind part of their positions because of risk constraints or to reduce the exposure of their books to some economic factors.[20] This kind of liquidity quest is endogenous to the participant.

Is one trading system "better" than the other? In practice, there is a trend towards electronification for several reasons. First, traders are satisfied because they can automate some of their trading processes (which became cheaper with the rise of "data science" techniques). Regulators are also satisfied because electronification allows tractability (intentions, orders to transactions, are all recorded). Hence, they can watch trading members' behavior with scrutiny. Besides, since the financial crisis, all market participants would like to lower their information asymmetry, which favored limit orderbooks. Nevertheless, there is a huge legacy of RFQ systems (especially in fixed income markets). Thus, software vendors and some exchanges are making efforts to create RFQ platforms with some of the LOB attributes, moving toward more anonymity in their engines to lower information asymmetry. Moreover, certain market makers try to extend their business on less liquid markets using RFQ-like systems. They have the feeling that it is easier for them to provide liquidity if they can segregate their clients.

---

[20]Except in a "run for exit" situation: when flows are crowded because all participants are selling their inventory (like during the "quant crash" of 2007).

Is it "better" to segregate clients? Looking at liquidity provision via RFQ from a welfare viewpoint can be summarized as follows:

- From a market maker's viewpoint, the ability to set different prices for each type of clients seems interesting.
- But from the client's viewpoint, the answer is not clear. Because if clients cannot be distinguished, each client will pay the same price, one of a "representative client".

To understand the importance of differentiating prices across clients, let's consider the following example: You have two clients A and B, trading on average the same amount each day, but client A has accurate information on the future price whereas client B does not. It means that when the market maker provides liquidity to client A at "market price", it suffers from a loss of ℓ (basis points), and when it provides liquidity to client B at market price, the market maker's PnL[21] is zero. Since the market maker has operating cost c and needs a commercial margin m, the cost of liquidity for client B will be $c+m$, whereas it will be $\ell + c + m$ for client A for a *risk neutral market maker*.[22] Now if the market maker is not able to distinguish A from B, the average loss is $\ell/2$, and a risk-neutral market maker will ask $\ell/2+c+m$ to each client. On average nothing will change, except that client B will pay more and client A will pay less to access liquidity.

The interesting point to look at is when the market maker is *risk averse*, i.e., when its cost is a nonlinear function $U(\ell)$ of the loss ℓ. In such a case, when it is possible to make the difference between A and B the former will pay $U(\ell) + c + m$ and the later will pay $U(0) + c + m$ to access liquidity. It is natural to assume that $U(\cdot)$ is an increasing function (i.e., A will pay more than B). In this risk-averse case: when clients cannot be distinguished, they will both be paying $U(\ell/2) + c + m$. Is it better for A and B to be differentiated or not? It depends on the shape of $U(\cdot)$: when the utility function is *convex*, i.e., such that $U(ax + (1 - a)y) < aU(x) + (1 - a)U(y)$, the overall cost will be cheaper when clients are merged. When U is concave we have the opposite: it is not use for clients to be merged.

---

[21]PnL means: "Profit and Loss".

[22]In this context, "risk-neutral" means that taking a risk does not cost to the market maker.

Imagine now that A and B are two accounts of the same client, for instance, a large asset manager who is able to know that he has informed trades and non-informed ones. In such a case, declaring or not the two accounts to a market-maker makes a difference (if the utility function of the market-maker is not linear).

To sum up, both bilateral and multilateral mechanisms have their pros and cons. The resulting cost of liquidity depends on the composition of the landscape: are market makers highly risk-averse or not? What is the shape of their utility function? Are clients large and mature enough to be able to label and segregate their flows themselves? Answers to these questions lead to knowing if bilateral trading is more expensive or not, and which participants will take profit of a potentially lower cost.

From a quantitative perspective (5)

Exchanges and Vendors need quantitative analysts with expertise in market microstructure, good skills in statistics, a good knowledge of market participants, and some bases in optimization.

1.5.5.2 Central countreparties

The role of Central CounterParties (CCPs) and Clearing Houses is to ensure the settlement, the physical transfer of money and the change of assets ownership. CCPs are becoming more and more important with post-crisis regulations. Since the G20 Pittsburgh Summit in 2009, the trend is to secure most of the transactions in cash or collateral deposits and regularly call margins and net positions.

A Central Counterparty Clearing House is a pure intermediation agency. Following a transaction, the clearinghouse acts as a "middleman" between the buyer and the seller to ensure that both counterparties will be able to respect the terms of the contract. To this end, the seller of potential future financial flows (typically the seller of a swap), will have to post margins to the CCP proportional to the amount it will have to deliver at expiry. The value of the margin evolves according to market conditions. These margin calls will demand to post collateral with a value close to the future flows.

The buyer and the seller have to be members of the CCP. Moreover, the members of the CCP have to contribute to a "Default Fund"[23] that will be used to face potential losses when a clearing member defaults and there is not enough collateral (accumulated thanks to margin calls) to face its obligations. The "Waterfall Process" of the CCP describes the process of resolution of such events.

Margin calls. Clearinghouses collect initial margins from members to cover potential losses in the event of a default. The initial margin aims to cover standard market conditions. For EMIR-regulated CCPs, that would be a 99% confidence interval for listed markets and a 2 days holding period. The Initial Margin has two components:

(1) *The Negotiation Risk or Contingency Variation Margin*: Covers the evolution of the valuation by comparing the transaction value and the mark-to-market at the last known settlement price. It aims at covering the past market risks.
(2) *The Liquidation Risk*: Covers the potential price variations between the potential event of member default and the effective liquidation of the positions by the clearinghouse. This component aims at covering future market risks.

Once the initial margin has been collateralized, additional margins can be added during the life of the exposure. They have three origins:

1. **Market Risk:**
   - *Liquidation and Concentration Risk Margin*: Aims at covering the cost that the CCP should support in case it has to liquidate a portfolio with concentrated positions or illiquid assets.
   - *Wrong Way Risk*: Used to cover the risk that arises when a Clearing Member has positions on products that are issued by its own group companies. In this case, the clearinghouse knows that if the member defaults these assets will have their value fall to zero
   - *Volatility Exposure Monitoring*: to take into account the second-moment sensitivities, in order to better capture the volatility surface and the volatility risk at different maturities.

---

[23] A fund created from the contributions of its members in order to face losses greater than the collateral.

- *Single Stock Dividend Future*: A dividend investment can be seen as corresponding to an equity investment, while often being more resilient and less volatile than stocks.

2. **Settlement**:
   - *Delivery Margin*: Post maturity date, the settlement for physical delivery on commodities can occur in a one month delay. In order to cover the price move related to the CCP exposure until the actual settlement of the goods, the CCP calls the delivery margin.
   - *De-netting Risk*: Better risk coverage due to de-offsetting of accounts structures, different settlement dates.

3. **Counterparty Credit Risk**: Credit risk margin linked to the financial profile, operational capabilities, T-ratios and ratios on capital.

Default fund and stress testing. Clearinghouses collect mutualized default funds from members to cover losses incurred in the event of a default. For EMIR-regulated CCPs, this implies to withstand at least—under extreme but plausible market conditions—the default of the member having the largest exposure or the second and third largest members combined. There is a waterfall process that is enabled only in case the losses are higher than the defaulting clearing member's resources plus the allocated part of clearinghouse capital.

Risks of CCPS and open questions. By becoming the only physical counterparty in all the transactions, clearing the multilateral exposures and mutualizing potential losses between members, clearinghouses help reduce counterparty risk (the risk of default). However, it positions itself as a systemic player that needs to be closely monitored by supervisory and macro-prudential authorities. Before the Brexit, the clearing of certain financial products in euros such as interest rate swaps, forward rate agreements or certain credit derivatives such as the CDS were carried out in London. The perspective of the Brexit raised interesting questions about the relocation of compensation inside the Union's territory for the most vital systems to its financial stability: What are the optimal characteristics of a European-wide compensation architecture, encompassing aspects of financial stability, resilience, and cost of implementation? Taking into consideration the characteristics of the products (swaps, interest rate futures, Repos, CDS, equities derivatives, etc.) is there a natural equilibrium to which the market will converge? Would it be a monopoly (single CCP), oligopoly or free market? While the existence of multiple clearinghouses ensures fair competition, more efficiency, and limited margins, the concentration of liquidity in a single house ensures economies of scale. Besides, in terms of financial stability, the coexistence of several clearinghouses increases the resilience of the financial system in the case of service interruption (cyberattack, bankruptcy, etc.).

> ### From a quantitative perspective (6)
>
> CCPs need quantitative analysts with expertise in the computation of margins. Hence they need to understand derivative products, and to be able to compute the value at risk (VaR) or extreme quantiles of returns at given time horizons. A good understanding of estimation of correlations (with a dynamic component) is also needed because the way returns of financial instruments correlate when some participants start to default is of paramount importance to calibrate Default Funds.

1.5.6 Market makers and proprietary shops

This category "market makers and proprietary shops" covers not only independent market-making firms or "boutiques" using their own capital to provide liquidity to the market, but also market-making desks of banks or of broker-dealers. In short: all activities committing capital to provide liquidity to market participants fall into this category.

Most often these firms are "recognized marker makers" in some trading venues. This status allows them to have specific agreements with the exchange: sometimes they pay fewer fees (or even benefit from a "rebate" on trading fees or get paid to trade), sometimes they have access to specific mechanisms (like "order types": intentions to trade that benefit, for instance, from a *last look*), and may also shortcut the waiting queues of matching engines, etc. Such agreements come in exchange for continuously providing liquidity to the market, fulfilling certain constraints during their presence in the market, as well as how aggressive they are in providing liquidity. The rationale behind this is that trading venues need liquidity providers to be present in the market as to encourage other market participants to trade, making the instruments more liquid. Otherwise, a lower amount of transactions will be made, which at the end of the day results in less money for the trading venue (trading venues' incomes are essentially made of trading fees).

The mechanisms allowing market makers to trade have been detailed in Section 1.5.5.1. In short, they have two ways to provide liquidity to other market participants: a bilateral way and a multilateral way. In the former, they have detailed information on each participant they provide liquidity to, in the latter, they have to compete with other market participants (including other market makers but not only) to provide liquidity to counterparties they do not really know. In such case, they use advanced statistics (one could call them " machine learning" or "artificial intelligence" algorithms) to cluster the orders they are answered to in different categories; somehow they do not know by name with whom they trade, but they choose under which conditions to trade and that is sometimes very close (and largely enough).

In any case, market makers have a very specific role in financial markets: they increase the probability of transactions to occur. Without them, buyers and sellers must be synchronous; thanks to market makers, the buyer can come first, buy from the market maker, and when the seller comes a few hours or days later it will find the market maker as a buyer. Of course, the market maker will ask for a "markup" on both prices: the buyer will buy at a (slightly) higher price (the *best ask* price), and the seller will sell at a (slightly) lower price (the *best bid* price). These two prices are called the "quotes" provided by the market maker, and if the price did not change while the market maker was waiting for the seller, the market maker's profit will be the bid-ask spread (i.e., the best ask minus the best bid). This simple feature is very useful, but not completely straightforward to implement:

- Without a "middleman" between the buyer and the seller, the buyer will bear the risk of not buying the financial product at the moment he really needs to. Market makers allow other market participants to decide to reduce their exposure (i.e., their risk) whenever they want at a markup price. This is a risk transfer from the liquidity consumer to the liquidity provider (i.e., the market maker).

- Once it is almost sure that buyers and sellers will find a counterparty to unwind their positions, it is easier for them to accept to buy or sell. In other terms: when there is a "liquid enough" secondary market, investors hesitate less to buy instruments, and hence provide capital more easily to companies in the real economy (typically via equity shares and corporate bonds).

- Nevertheless the risk borne by market makers does not disappear: it remains very important they keep good practices in risk management. Typically, once their inventory reaches a threshold (for instance long 10 Average Trade Size), they stop providing liquidity to sellers. Before reaching this threshold, the market maker will have to progressively modify its bid-ask spread, gradually providing liquidity to the seller at a higher cost (i.e., at a lower price) and to the buyer at a cheaper cost (i.e., at a lower price too). This is a very natural way to link the probability matching buyers and sellers to the current state of its inventory: when it is properly done, it provides mean-reversion to zero of the inventory.

- To help market makers to provide liquidity, they are often exempted from certain constraining rules. One of them being the "*short selling*[24] bans". Market makers need to be able to sell contracts they do not own, waiting for a seller to come back to a flat inventory; otherwise, it would be more difficult for them to provide liquidity to buyers.

- It is difficult to provide liquidity while being restricted to strict thresholds in terms of inventory, especially for a market maker working on one contract only. But the more contracts in the universe of the market maker, the easier it is to control the "net risk of its overall inventory". For instance, having bought \$150,000 of company A shares and having sold \$150,000 of company B shares, a market maker is less exposed to market moves if the correlation between A and B's returns is close to one rather than close to zero. One important quantity is the expected variations of the global inventory with respect to risk factors.

---

[24] A market participant "Short Sells" when he sells contracts he does not own. During specific market conditions, like crises, short selling may be banned.

It is specifically effective to combine market making activity on both packaged products (like an ETF or a Future) and their underlying components: having bought 10 Future contracts of a bucket and having sold the equivalent basket of underlying securities results in an exactly flat position (with no statistics involved). It is even possible to really flatten this kind of position by doing an Exchange For Physical (EFP) at the end of the day: the Future against its exact composition, at the cost of the "basis" of this EFP (that is often few basis points).

Reasoning in terms of net inventory and making the market on a wide universe allows providing more liquidity to market participants. Nevertheless, it is important to keep in mind that "expected variations" are estimated via statistical models, that are themselves exposed to some risks (the most common risk is the non-stationarity of economic conditions; see Chapter 5 for details about Model Risk).

Looking for Market Makers. Having market makers to provide liquidity is so important for exchanges that some of them provide capital to "prop. shops" or retail-like organizations so that they make the market on their contracts (especially on markets of Options). It is an interesting case of intermediation: an exchange hasn't got the infrastructure or the know-how to make the markets, but it can provide capital to small organizations to do so, much like when a big company seeds a start-up that will help in stabilizing its business.

From a quantitative perspective (7)

Market makers need quantitative analysts that are skilled in statistics and stochastic control. On top of these highly technical skills, they will need to have good knowledge of market microstructure.

1.5.7 Regulators

Regulators are a specific category of "market participants". They enforce the rules of "the game that is played" by other participants.

Moreover, they conduct studies and analyses to allow policymakers to adjust existing rules or to create new ones. Chapter 5 is detailing the role and the scope of Regulators.

An important point to note at this stage is that in financial markets, all participants are in charge of being careful that rules are being respected. For instance, a broker, an exchange or an investment bank have to monitor the flows of their clients and take certain actions if "some strange" scheme is noticed. The role of *compliance departments* of market participants encompasses this "local implementation" of "market rules".

An exchange typically has "alarms" in place, to identify abnormal behavior of flows in real-time, on a member by member basis. A real-time team processes these automated alarms, and if it detects something suspicious, a case is opened and the member is usually called to provide explanations. As a consequence, this member can be immediately banned from trading for the day (or for the time needed to have its operations go back to normal). The cases that are not closed within the day are sent to another team, in charge of "offline investigations". If it happens that a member needs to be reported to the regulatory authorities, it is done by the aforementioned team.

To prevent abnormal behaviors "by mistake", brokers and exchanges provide certain "risk controls", that is a client by client setup of thresholds on flow characteristics: messages per second, involved capital within the day, etc. Each client can ask for a specific setup of the risk control layer, to protect itself against a potential unexpected behaviour within the software and its code. Exchanges themselves can have "bugs" in their matching engine (see Section 2.3 for examples), in such a case a resolution procedure can help to curb its consequences: trading can be halted and some trades can be canceled. Since market participants buy and sell risk to agents of the real economy, such agents may employ this framework to launder money coming from illegal activities. Banks, asset managers, and brokers have to put in place good practices to detect suspicious activities of this kind too.

Protection from asymmetry. One of the missions of regulators is to protect customers from bad practices. On the one hand, the information delivered to customers has to be fair, not biased or misleading. On the other hand, the customers of a given product need to have the necessary level of education to understand the risk profile of the products. These two aspects can be simply deduced from the assumptions of the welfare theorem: to take the "correct" decisions, agents have to be rational and well informed. The European PRIIPS Directive on investment products is largely inspired by these principles too.

Nevertheless, studies in anthropology and sociology have shown that humans have behavioral biases that impede on their capability to make rational decisions. A typical cognitive bias is the "lottery effect": having the choice between two games with the same expected returns (having a one in 10,000 chance to win $100,000 vs. having 50-50 chance to win $20), people will generally choose the one with the potential maximum gain (in our example the game with the potential to win $100,000), regardless of the associated risk.

Regulators have to find ways to protect customers from this kind of biases. Another guideline of regulation is to consider that small participants have to be more protected than large ones. It is generally true that when an investor has billions to invest, he can afford to pay experts to help him collect a good level of information, and thus make adequate choices.

Leveling the playing field. Regulators have to ensure that all market participants are "playing the same game". This is a very subtle concept since each participant has the freedom to invest money on the business model he believes in, to make mistakes and to incur expenses with a low return on investment. It is the principle of competition to allow some companies to be better than others. Nevertheless, they need to be able to see the whole menu of possible choices. For instance, an exchange cannot create a feature and offer it to one company only, this is clearly unfair; of course, the price and the conditions to benefit from this feature can be very selective, but any company deciding to invest in this feature should be able to do so. This guideline clearly drives the way in which regulators try to ensure an "equal access to data" and to financial information.

Negative externalities. Moreover, authorities have to protect the ecosystem as a whole against practices that could have "bad side effects" (i.e., *negative externalities*). This argument has been used during the rise of high-frequency trading: when a High Frequency

Trader (HFT), who only commits its own capital, trade on a market, the number of orders and transactions increases substantially (sometimes it multiplies by 10); market participants having to comply with the Best Execution regulatory principle in Europe, have to face (simply because of this increase in messages) higher costs in recording, storing and processing market data. This creation of a cost to a majority of participants, due to the legal activity of a few actors, can be questioned. Only policymakers and regulators are in a position to prevent "side effects" of this kind.

From a quantitative perspective (8)

Analyst working for regulators (or compliance departments of other market participants) often have more background in law and economics than in quantitative skills. However, with the rise of technology and big data, regulators are now hiring statisticians and data scientists, with a good knowledge of products and market practices.

1.6 Intermediation Everywhere

The real economy is composed of corporations and households. They are not part of the financial system but interact frequently with it. For instance, households have savings and need to invest them in order to protect them from inflation. They then buy assets on the market and simple products like loans from banks. Both corporations and households constitute the natural buyers and sellers of risk in the market. They use structured/derivatives products to hedge their exposure to risk factors. In addition, corporations need financing for their future development. Thus, they issue shares on the market or sell bonds to investment banks. For this purpose, they need first to interact with the exchange to list their product and have the right to be traded. They also need to increase liquidity on their instruments. They hence use the service of market makers. Shares issuing is similar to selling a huge block of the same security. If there is no market maker in front to provide liquidity and absorb the shocks, price movement resulting from the selling pressure could be very detrimental to the company. In the case of a public offering, "Book runners" get all the shares at first and disseminate them gradually to market participants. We note that Investment banks are in the center of the system. They provide funding, custody as well as investment tools, they make the market, and help in the trading process.

1.6.1 Flows of information

Figure 1.4 allows to understand the way information propagates in the financial system. Two kinds of information affect the financial system:

Information about the real economy. Any generic news about the health of the economy have influence on market participants' behavior, and hence on prices. Macroeconomic news, regarding GDP, inflation, unemployment rates, etc., condition the actions of the governments and central banks, which will simultaneously influence the

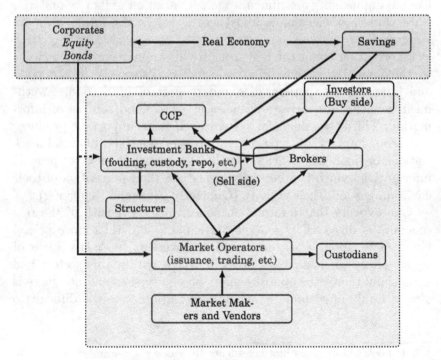

Figure 1.4: The financial system.

health of private companies and of households.[25] Their actions may also have an impact on the financing of Investment Banks (via the interest rates, the availability and costs of government bonds, etc.).

Moreover, business news on economic sectors, such as Energy, Materials, Industrials, Health Care, Finance, Real Estate, Information Technology, Communication Services, Utilities, Consumer Discretionary and Consumer Staples (based on the Global Industry Classification Standard for instance), affect companies producing and consuming within these industrial groups. However, on top of such type of information about macroeconomic conditions and specific economic sectors are a series of *idiosyncratic news*, which are specific to individual companies. For instance, the profitability of a company producing plastic flatwares is subject to price variations of plastic, to variations of the demand in the country it operates, to the weather if we assume that people use more plastic flatwares during sunny days (which suggest a yearly seasonality in this business); but such profitability is obviously impacted by its own governance decisions like buying hedging instruments against variation of its raw material price. This last element is idiosyncratic, while the former is more *systematic*.

Information about the real economy disseminates in various ways to the financial system: First, journalists, especially in economic and financial newspapers, disseminate part of it. Second, government agencies and private agencies are also good sources of information. Third, the financial system itself is an important producer and propagator of information: via brokers' analysts, financial associations or financial agencies. Finally, companies themselves provide information, which is necessarily biased, on their perception of their environment and their activity (Quarterly Financial Reporting).

One expects that information concerning the health of the real economy is digested by market participants and thus move prices. Good news about a sector should, on average, move up prices of equity shares of companies doing business within this sector; bad news should have the opposite effect on equity shares. Since there is always a mix of systematic and idiosyncratic news, it is difficult to

---

[25]This book will of course not investigate the chicken-and-egg debates on consumption and production: which one influences the other the most.

anticipate in which direction prices will go. Moreover, the time scales at which prices are digesting information can vary substantially. To come back to the example of the firm producing and selling plastic flatwares, which let's say is in France: imagine that the French government announces that a new norm (on the structure of flatwares to prevent kids from getting intoxicated if they ingest by accident a small piece of plastic fork) will come into force in 3 years. This will probably demand to the firm to spend more in R&D to produce safer products. If this firm also has difficulties to access capital, it faces the risk of bankruptcy within 3 years. So, when should the price move? Probably a part of these future costs will impact the cost right now, but some of the market participants could consider that the company has enough time to adapt and reduce the uncertainty regarding its business relative to these future expenses. This reasoning is called a *forward looking valuation* of the company. It consists of valuing the business (profits, cash flows, etc.) of the company in the future and applying a discount rate to this value to estimate the "rational" value of holding one share of the equity of the company today. This future valuation is not solely based on objective elements, but on subjective elements as well. Think about the dot com bubble, in which future values of ICT companies were partly estimated by looking at the number of clicks on their websites.

It is important to underline that even if the previous example focuses on the impact of information on equity share prices, it actually affects the capability of the company to raise capital or at least the cost it will have to pay to raise capital, whatever the way it decides to implement it. One of the best channel to raise money for corporations being bonds, news then affect the characteristics of the contract. Typically bad news should make the company pay higher coupons to reinsure investors for the additional risk, while good news should allow the company to replenish its treasury at a cheaper cost.

Information about the financial activity. Another kind of information is the one generated by the financial system itself. The state of the inventories, the amplitude of the exposures and especially the flows moving from one institution to another, or from one portfolio of financial products to another, are of paramount importance. It is primarily due to the fact that during the process of selling an instrument to buy another, market participants modify the offer-demand balance: more offer on the first instrument and more demand on the second one. The price being the adjusting variable guaranteeing the offer to be equal to the demand at any point in time, the first instrument (the one that is sold) experiences a decrease in price, while the bought one experiences an increase in price. Section 1.5.5.1 exposed the two main mechanisms enabling to achieve such a balance in real-time via limit orderbooks and requests for quotation.

The reasons behind changes in ownership are diverse. Either because of changes in the structure of risk factors in the real economy or a subsequent order to new information available in the market, as detailed just before, or some institutions like banks trying to hedge their exposure to different economic variables (continuously trying to balance their risk). This generates flows either in an isolated way or in crowded directions, which increases the probability of a "Rush toward the exit door" scenario if the market reverses. Regulators try to monitor these flows and to understand them. They often issue "risk dashboards" to share a very generic version of what they understood, so that market participants be aware of these crowded directions, and avoid them.

The way information about the financial activity is disseminated is less transparent since each participant sees a fraction of the activity taking place under its umbrella. Regulators, exchanges, associations, and agencies publish anonymized figures of what their members are witnessing. On their side, some brokers publish, with some delay, the generic directions of their clients' flows.

To sum up, the information influencing the financial system and forming prices is of two kinds. First, the "natural" information from events outside of the system itself, describing what is happening to the real economy. Second, the flows inside the system. Both types influence the price formation process: the first because market participants are anticipating the consequences of such information on the value of goods and businesses, and the second because of the "mechanical pressure" it will have on the balance between offer and demand. These effects can potentially impact all financial instruments simultaneously: all the instruments related to a company (equity shares, corporate bonds, loans, derivatives, etc.) or to a country (rates, yield curve, government bonds, etc.). However, these type of information propagate consistently between instruments sharing common characteristics (the yield curve potentially influencing all fixed income instruments, sectorial news influencing all companies, related sectors, countries, etc.). An analogy with waves on the surface of the sea can be useful: exogenous events (like storms) locally influence the shape and strength of the waves, but very soon they interact with one another, with the sea bed, with beaches and islands. The physics of wave dynamics are usually modeled using partial derivatives, converges towards more stationary phenomena, "diluting" the initial effects of exogenous events over the surface of seas. During this "stationarization" process other exogenous events occur, resulting in dynamics that are never stationary, although endlessly evolving towards stationarity.

1.6.2 Flows of capital

Capital is transferred almost each time there is an arrow in Figure 1.4:

- Companies and households look for efficient ways to invest their savings. The financial system answers this need. The expected good property of such investments is that:
  - Agents follow the risk-reward profile of the economy, or of any subset of the economy.
  - These investments will be *productive*, i.e., they will provide capital to other citizens and other companies.
- Companies, citizens and states can obtain loans.
- States can issue government bonds.
- Companies have additional ways to interact with capital. Issuing equity shares (during an IPO, a secondary offering, or through share buyback). They also have the possibility to issue corporate bonds.

One of the features of the financial system is to allow companies and citizens with savings to buy equity shares, corporate or government bonds so that they will own a portfolio with a risk profile compatible with their expectations and needs.

As soon as someone makes a deposit in a bank, his savings can be used by the bank as collateral to issue some loans to other citizens. His money allows to inject more money in the real economy, the borrower can now buy goods or build a company. This is a *liquidity transformation* (i.e., the deposit becomes less liquid and a loan with a given duration is created), it generates the following flow of capital: the deposit, some collateralization, the wire to the borrower.

Equity shares, corporate and government bonds are not always directly bought by citizens (or companies), most often asset managers are buying them on behalf of their clients. Asset managers are *managing* the money of citizens (or of other asset managers): they take the investment as a deposit on a commercial bank account, then use it to buy financial instruments. When these financial instruments are equity shares or bonds (at the primary market), this money is directly injected in the real economy: a company or a government uses this capital to produce goods and services. When the financial instruments are derivatives, like Futures or Options, one should first notice that leverage is provided to the asset manager. This means that a deposit (via a wire, some margin calls or collateral posting) is made in an Investment Bank. Moreover, the asset manager accesses to a customized risk profile. To go further with this, we can take the example of a Future contract on a commodity,[26] let's say on wheat; the investor does not simply buy the wheat directly, he rather buys it *in advance* (say three months in advance) at a given price. The risk profile of such a transaction in the future is quite different from simply waiting these three months and buying that wheat at the given price, as its price will certainly have changed within this timeframe. If the price increases during the next three months, buying a Future can be considered as a good decision, otherwise it can be seen as a bad decision. But it is still interesting for the buyer: now that the contract is bought, there is zero uncertainty on the cost of wheat in three months, which enables the investor to make more thoughtful decisions. This *reduction of uncertainty* is a *risk transformation* that is often necessary to companies or individuals; it needs collateral and hence several capital transfers:

When a company or a citizen invests in a Fund managed by an Asset Manager (first capital transfer), there are several capital movements that follow:

- If the Asset Manager uses part of this money to buy equity shares during an IPO, it goes through a broker, an exchange, a settlement

---

[26]See Chapter REF:commo:futures for details about the structure of Future contracts.

house, and at least one commercial bank. The money is immediately transferred to the company. It is very similar to buying corporate (or government) bonds on the primary market.

- If the Asset Manager uses part of this money to buy equity shares on the secondary market, it goes through a broker, an exchange, a settlement house at least a commercial bank again, but the money goes to the seller of the shares who previously bought them, and not directly to the company who formerly issued the shares. The seller retrieves his money and can buy goods, services or other financial instruments with it. From the viewpoint of the company who issued the shares, the main effect is that it contributes to pushing the price of this share so that if the company needs more capital in the future (using new shares, bonds or loans), it will have access to such capital at a cheaper cost.

- If the Asset Manager buys derivatives, the money will go through a broker, an exchange, a clearinghouse (that will ask for margins as a guarantee if the price goes down) and an investment bank. The effect of such a transaction is indirect: either the other party of the trade wanted to take the opposite risk. In such a case this is a *risk transfer*[27] and one can assume that it corresponds to specific needs in the risk-reward profile of the two parties of the trade. Either the other party created (i.e., issued) the financial instrument for this customer. It is probably an exchange or an investment bank, and in any case, if the exchange created the Future contract, the other party of the trade is an investment bank. If the investment bank had the exact opposite risk in its inventory, it is equivalent to the previous case: this is a simple *risk transfer*, otherwise, it implies that the inventory of the investment bank is increasing in this direction. At a certain point, the investment bank will have to reduce its exposure to the corresponding economic factor (for a Future on an equity index it is probably a risk exposure to the economy of a country[28]); it will have to *hedge* (i.e., replicate) this exposure. Throughout the hedging process, the investment bank may find a natural counterparty, and again this is a *risk transfer*. If there is no natural counterparty among market participants, the

---

[27]Such a risk transfer is similar to the ones described in Section 1.3.1.

[28]France for a Future contract on the CAC40 and the US for a Future contract on the S&P500.

process of hedging will push the price up to pay the exposition to this factor.[29] The transfer of capital is indirect but on its course it modifies the price of risks in an offer vs. demand logic.[30]

1.6.3   Flows of risks

Most of the arrows of Figure 1.4 can be understood as a transfer of some kind of risk. Keeping in mind that *a risk factor corresponds to an uncertain future payoff*. As a consequence, owning an equity share is a risk factor, the same for owing a government bond, a Future contract on an underlying (index or commodity) or Options. When a market participant accepts to make a cash deposit, he accepts to be exposed to the liquidity risk factor (i.e., will the bank be able to give back this cash in a few months?).

A risk transfer occurs when the ownership of such a risk factor changes from one participant to another. All the examples that have been described starting at page one of this book are risk transfers, and most of them have a specificity: when a market participant "holds a risk" (or "is exposed to a risk factor") and wants to sell it, he may face difficulties to find a counterpart, thus may need to pay a certain premium. That is why

- Exchanges are places centralizing potential buyers and sellers of some standardized risk factors (equity shares, Future contracts, Options, swaps, etc). *Centralization increases the probability to "find a match".*
- Market makers accept to buy or sell risks and to keep the position (i.e., to be exposed to this risk factor) long enough to find a seller or a buyer to unwind their exposure. Their reward is the bid-ask spread or a markup. To avoid taking exposure to too much risk (i.e., important possible losses), they hedge their positions. This hedging process generate trades selling the risk factor to which they are exposed to the most.

---

[29]To continue with the example of the S&P500 the prices of companies being part of this index will go up as well.

[30]One can hope that if too many investors want to buy the same exposure, its cost will rise and as a consequence fewer investors will be interested, preventing too much crowded orders.

This is a risk transformation: Say, for example, a market maker accepts to buy shares of US companies, from different traders who wanted to get rid of the corresponding risk factor. After the transaction, the market maker is the one exposed to the US economy. It decides to hedge this position by selling Future contracts on the S&P 500. The market maker operated a risk transfer: a mix of idiosyncratic and systematic risks versus systematic risk only (the idiosyncratic risks, once put together in the same book, reduce the risk of the resulting portfolio thanks to the Central Limit Theorem. The systematic risk, however, can not be diversified).

- Investment banks continuously design financial products, corresponding to the demands of their clients. Again, their books are made of many exposures to risk factors. Some of them exactly compensate the others (such as Credit Linked Notes compensating CDSs, see Chapter 3); the remaining risk factors, when they reach a threshold, have to be hedged. Hedging of nonlinear risks is done using a "Black and Scholes approach": thanks to the nice properties of the Taylor expansion,[31] the exposures to each term in the expansion of all products owned by the bank can be added up, and only the "net risk"[32] has to be *replicated* in the markets. This replication process consists of selling tradable risk factors to neutralize the remaining risks, component by component of the Taylor expansion.[33]

  This again is a risk transformation: a basket of sophisticated risks is converted in a list of net exposure to a list of risk factors, and then few of these risk factors (provided that they can be traded) are sold to other market participants, in most cases on Exchanges.

- Asset managers transform deposits (that are frozen in their books, their investors being hence exposed to a liquidity risk) in exposure to risk factors that should be clearly defined by their "investment philosophy". For instance, large asset managers provide index trackers or ETFs, corresponding to a mainstream exposure to the

---

[31] The only important point is to keep in mind Ito's lemma to properly write the Taylor expansion along a diffusion.

[32] "Netting the risk" means to add all the terms of the Taylor expansion of a basket of products: only the "net sum" of the exposure remains.

[33] All the success of replication is based on writing a Taylor expansion on the "adequate list of risk components", see Chapter 5 for details.

economy of some countries, or the health of some sectors; and certain hedge funds specialized in medicals and drugs use their investors' money to buy and sell equity shares and corporate bonds of companies in the medical and drug business, following a careful investigation on their patents and research publications.

Asset managers transform liquidity risk into exposure to a well-defined risk factor. Moreover, to provide more risk, certain asset managers need leverage, that they obtain at investment banks in exchange of involving certain assets as collateral. This is once again a risk transformation: collateral immobilization (i.e., liquidity risk) versus risk exposure. Investment banks accept to operate this transformation mainly because they have a client mix that can "net" the different risk exposure they would like to be exposed to, and because regulators agreed that investment banks have more leverage than other institutions.[34]

- Market operators, especially Exchanges and CCP, operate very simple and atomic risk transfer: the former designs *but does not issue* products (like equity shares, bonds, and Futures), it hosts the transactions without bearing any risk; the latter, via the process of clearing products, ensure that the buyer and the seller of a risk factor will both have enough money to face it at expiry. One of the parties will have to pay the other, and the margin calls will ensure that the payer will have the money to pay at the due date.

1.6.4   Flows of fees and markups

The economics of intermediation is not only made of the mechanisms allowing risk transformation, it also relies on sustainable business models of intermediaries. Intermediaries are paid in several ways: the simplest one is *fees*, a more complex way to be paid is a *markup*, and a third way is to make a profit during the process of intermediation.

Market operators and structurers. The simplest configuration is one of the market operators: Index providers, like MSCI,

---

[34]In exchange investment banks are more regulated, and hence have to invest in governance procedures, accountancy, and lawyers, etc.

FTSE-RUSSEL, S&P, or Euronext make money thanks to licensing fees, benchmarking fees and market data. As soon as a market participant uses one of its indexes to structure a financial product or if it explicitly provides exposure to the risk factor corresponding to this index, it should pay the licensing fees. They also sell information about the historical compositions of their indexes To be a member of an Exchange or a CCP, market participants have to pay *membership fees*, and CCP asks for *clearing fees* for each "line" (i.e., type of contract), that they clear. Exchanges are paid by trading fees (when two traders make a transaction on an Exchange, both[35] pay fees), as well as by the companies that are *listed* by them (their equity shares or bonds are issued on this Exchange), and another source of revenue is made of sales of data and technologies associated to accessing data owned by this Exchange. Structurers make a margin when they sell a product that are similar to the management fees.

Brokers. Brokers have different businesses: market access, corporate access, and research. Under the scope of market access, brokers pay memberships and fees to Market Operators, and they offer to their clients to use these memberships, asking for another layer of fees on top of these mutualized fees. It is easier to ask for high fees when they offer services associated with market access, like *execution services*.[36] Corporate access is a very subtle business: it allows brokers to introduce investors to companies, and the opposite: on the one hand, companies are happy to present their business plans to investors so that it will be easier to sell their equity shares and corporate bonds, and hence to raise capital. On the other hand, investors are happy to be able to access corporate executives (especially their CFO or CEO) to ask questions and understand if it is worthwhile to invest in them. It seems to be a very simple and lucrative business to be the middlemen between two categories of participants that would like to discuss at any price; the difficulty comes from the competition between brokers to attract the most promising companies and the wealthiest investors at their meetings and conferences. Regulators

---

[35] In some cases only one of them pay fees, and this other is paid by the exchange, see Section 1.6.4 on *reverse fees* or *rebate*.
[36] See Chapter 2 for details.

are keen to be able to regulate a handful of market participants to avoid too much insider trading. The last service brokers sell is "research": it is made of reports and unconflicted recommendations to investors on the real value of the instruments brokers give access to. They provide research on equity shares, on corporate bonds, on sectors, on factor investing, on derivative-based strategies, etc. The way Brokers are paid for this research is subtle; for long they simply asked for trading fees, which partly covered market access and the right to consume Corporate access and Research. It has been seen as "soft dollars" for some time: depending on how much a client paid in execution fees, she had the equivalent of a virtual account of dollars that she could spend to use Corporate access and obtain reports and interviews with Research. Regulators have long insisted that the decomposition of these soft-dollars has to be clear: what is exactly the price of one report produced by the Research? What is the price to access to a meeting with the CFO of a company? Having clear and transparent accountancy for this is needed to have a sane competition between brokers. One way to level the playing field between brokers and their clients is probably to ask for an "unbundling" of services and expenses: just pay for what you consume, at the same price for all clients. European policymakers made a step in this direction within the second version of the MiFID European directive on the market of financial instruments, in January 2018.

Asset managers. The business model of asset managers is simple to explain: they ask for *management fees*, which are a small percentage of the asset under management they have, and sometimes they ask for *incentive fees* too, that are due only when they over-perform a well-defined benchmark. As an example, hedge funds management fees and incentive fees have been for long respectively 2% and 20%.

Investment banks and market makers. It is very unusual that market makers ask for fees: they earn money by doing their job of selling and buying from other market participants well. In the very simplistic case where the price does not move and a market maker buys to sellers at the "fair price" minus half of a bid-ask spread, and sell to buyers at the same "fair price" plus half of a bid-ask spread, they earn one bid-ask spread as soon as they intermediate liquidity. Of course, it is more complex than that because the "fair price" is unknown and moves. Moreover, liquidity providers compete within themselves to provide liquidity. Investment banks make a commercial margin when they sell a product. Similarly to market makers, they can also make a profit while they are hedging their exposures to different market risks. Both need to have (on average) correct views on the direction of prices of the risk factors they intermediate to make money.

1.7 Regulating the Interactions Between Intermediaries

Without a proper regulatory framework, the financial system has the potential to cause severe damages to the whole economy and undermine its stability for long. Interdependencies of market participants across borders can exacerbate these effects far beyond the only financial sector and country from which the problems may originate. Regulation is therefore essential to avoid the risks of crisis and ensure financial stability. A decade ago, the financial crisis had revealed a large number of vulnerabilities of the financial system. It has shown how, intermediating risks between actors of the real economy could also harm it when the financial system suffers from a systemic crises, i.e., stopped to provide the intermediation functions that it is meant to provide. The magnitude of the crisis has led the international community to undertake a broad overhaul of the regulatory and supervisory framework. A far-reaching reform agenda was set in place to increase the resilience of a global financial system that was severely impacted during the crisis. Over the last 10 years, the financial industry has experienced a range of regulatory reforms on an unprecedented scale. Although some areas still require adjustments, a lot has been achieved, leading to a regulatory framework that is now fairly stabilized. These regulatory reforms have focused on four main objectives:

(1) restoring and enhancing the resiliency of the banking system,
(2) setting up resolution regimes for systemic financial institutions,
(3) making the derivatives market more robust,
(4) strengthening the supervision of shadow banking.

These four topics are developed in the following sections.

1.7.1 Restoring and enhancing the resiliency of the banking system

The prudential framework applicable to the banking industry has been deeply reformed and revised over the past decade. This important transformation was driven by the Basel Committee.[37] Largely in response to the crisis, this group of banking authorities has developed a set of reforms known as Basel III designed to improve regulation, supervision and risk management within the banking industry.

It is first important to understand the concept of systemic banks: they are institutions that are involved in so many risk intermediation activities, and with so many counterparts, that the difficulties they could encounter have high probability to propagate to other market participants, freezing the circulation of liquidity and risks among the financial system, and hence affect the functioning of the real economy. There is a paradox of being a systemic participant in the sense that it is positive for its operations: we will see that the more clients, the higher probability to be able to net the different risks in its balance sheet (because there is a high probability that the investment banks sold to a client the risk it is already buying from another client, reducing its global exposure to zero), this is the virtue of being a big institution (coined by the expression "big is beautiful"); but on the other hand if the demand or offer of risk is only one way, then the balance sheet of the systemic bank is very quickly largely imbalance, expositing it to huge losses and preventing it to take any new client. Chapter 5 is dedicated to risk management of intermediaries and exposes this kind of mechanism. The following paragraphs are detailing how the Basel Committee worked in two main directions targeting to improve the balance sheet of market participants via an increase of the capital they own and limiting their leverage. The leverage reflects the amplitude of the balance sheet before any netting: if a participant sold 1 dollar of risk and bought one dollar of risk to another client, its net position on this risk factor is zero (i.e., $1-1$) and its gross exposure is 2 (i.e., $1+|-1|$); its leverage is hence 2 divided by its own capital, i.e., its assets.

---

[37] The Basel Committee on Banking Supervision (BCBS) is a committee of banking supervisory authorities that was established by the central bank governors of members of the former Group of 10 countries, successively extended to 20.

1.7.1.1   Increasing the level and quality of equity

Solvency ratios, which require banks to retain capital to absorb unexpected losses, are the cornerstone of the prudential regulation. Although they had already been revised with Basel II, the crisis showed their inadequacies with the actual risks that banks accumulated. On the one hand, the prevailing ratios were circumvented by banks in the context of securitization. On the other hand, they proved insufficient to limit the leverage of banks and excessive risk-taking compared to their capital reserves. Indeed, many states had to recapitalize their banks or nationalize them at the height of the crisis. The reform of the capital of banks was therefore one of the highest priorities among regulators. The Basel Committee issued in December 2010 new rules on bank capital.

The minimum capital that banks must hold has been significantly raised: the minimum regulatory capital requirement (Tier 1 and Tier 2) for risk-weighted assets has remained unchanged at 8%. However, the minimum hard capital ratio (Core Tier 1) has been increased from 2% to 4.5% of total risk-weighted assets. In addition, a "safety cushion" equal to 2.5% has been introduced that banks can draw on in the event of difficulties so that they can maintain a minimum level of capital.

As a result, the minimum Core Tier 1 ratio has been set at 7% (compared to only 2% under Basel II) and the minimum solvency ratio has been raised from 8% to 10.5%.

To take into account the fact that the financial system is a network of intermediaries, Basel III has also introduced a number of measures to extend the risk coverage, especially to counterparty risk which had been often overlooked before the crisis. For instance, capital requirements must be determined using stressed market conditions when calculating counterparty credit risk. Counterparty risk is made of the impact of a failure of a counterparty on the balance sheet of the considered institution. Since the risk that intermediaries are buying and selling is essentially made of future promises (i.e., the result of a formula in the future), current estimation of risk in the inventory of an investment bank take into account these future engagements of other intermediaries, hence the netting is conditioned to the capability of the other market participants to comply with these commitments. If they go bankrupt in between, large parts of the balance sheet reveal to be far more imbalanced than expected. Banks also have to implement a new capital charge to cover mark-to-market losses on the counterparty risk to OTC derivatives.

1.7.1.2 Limiting the leverage

Shareholders of a company may have an interest in this increasing debt to finance profitable assets rather than increasing capital, as debt is cheaper than equity. In this way, they increase the earnings per share. But the banking system, which had accumulated significant leverage both on and off the balance sheet, saw the profitability of its assets decline sharply at the time of the 2008 financial crisis. In order to be able to meet their repayment obligations, banks were forced to sell their unprofitable assets, which accentuated downward pressure on asset prices, thus amplifying the spiral of losses, the erosion of their equity capital and the contraction of the credit supply.

The Basel Committee therefore decided to limit the leverage, or the accumulation of debt aimed at financing the investments and activities of banks, in order to mitigate the risk of deleveraging spirals during such an economic downturn. It introduced a leverage ratio, corresponding to the amount of core (Tier 1) capital to the bank's total risk-weighted assets. The minimum requirement has been set at 3%.

The largest institutions qualified as global systemically important banks by the FSB (i.e., the Financial Stability Board, made of 30 institutions as of November 2020) are subject to higher leverage ratios.

1.7.1.3 Improving the liquidity of banks

To address this risk of liquidity which was not covered under the prevailing prudential regulation, Basel III has introduced new requirements in the form of two ratios: a short-term liquidity ratio, the Liquidity Coverage Ratio, requiring banks to hold sufficient liquid assets to cover their needs for 30 days in times of stress. The regulation requires the banks to perform a stress test simulating events that are likely to cause severe liquidity stress, such as withdrawals of a significant share of customer deposits or a rating downgrade that weakens the institution's reputation.

A long-term liquidity ratio, the Net Stable Funding Ratio encourages banks to maintain a stable funding profile in line with the composition of their assets and off balance sheet activities. It aims at limiting excessive maturity transformation risk, and complements the former ratio (LCR) over a longer time horizon.

Focus on the net stable funding ratio (NSFR). The NSFR is defined as the amount of available stable funding relative to the amount of required stable funding. This ratio should be greater than or equal to 100% on an ongoing basis. At the numerator, the liability items making up the available stable resources are weighted degressively according to their stability over a 1-year horizon, with the weighting depending on the type of resource but also on the counterparty. For instance, the equity capital of the institution, its preferred shares and all other liabilities with a term of more than 1 year are weighted at 100% while deposits without maturity or with a term of less than 1 year from individuals or SMEs are weighted at 85% (50% from large companies). At the denominator, the required stable financing consists of assets to which variable weightings are assigned according to their degree of liquidity: for example, cash and short-term securities that are actively traded are not included (weighting of 0), while loans to individuals with a maturity of less than 1 year are only included at 85%. Bonds issued by companies are accounted for 20% if they are rated AA or higher, but the weighting rises to 50% for those of lower quality (A-rating) and for corporate loans with a maturity of less than 1 year. All other assets (including long-term loans) are weighted at 100%.

1.7.1.4 Limiting the pro-cyclicality

One of the lessons of the Global Financial Crisis is that when a risk factor is not yet identified (the leverage of US individuals on the real estate market), there is a high probability that most market participant take an exposure to this factor: since they to not monitor the projection of their balance sheet in this direction, there exposure to this factor is "invisible". It becomes hence rewarding to buy products increasing the risk in this same direction (like the subprimes): the system faces the worst case of a one way market, because the financial system is on-boarding risk without any capital, and accepts to buy more of this risk, allowing actors in the real economy to increase there exposure to it. In practice it was very easy for an individual to obtain leverage on real estate because market participants were eager to buy this risk.

To prevent this risk, Basel III has introduced a counter-cyclical buffer, which banks are required to build up in times of strong economic growth to serve as extra protection for periods of economic stress. This capital cushion, ranging from 0% to 2.5%, is added to the regulatory capital and imposed on banks when, according to the assessment of their national prudential regulator, a credit bubble is growing and is deemed to carry a systemic risk. Conversely, this steering wheel can be removed in the lower periods of the financial cycle. This additional constraint remains at the discretion of national regulatory authorities.

1.7.2   Setting up resolution regimes for systemic financial institutions

In addition to strengthening the resilience of banks, important regulatory steps have been taken to deal with institutions that are failing or likely to fail and put an end to the "too big to fail" paradigm. This concept is the natural continuation of the "big is beautiful" aphorism: since the largest intermediaries are easier to run (less influence of fixed costs, higher probability to net risks in the direction of identified factors), the financial system ends up with few very large, systemic, actors. Once it is the case, regulators and governments cannot afford to let them fail and will help them at almost any cost, this is the "too big to fail" paradigm.

Systemic risk is inherent to the banking and financial system, due to the interconnections in this sector between different institutions and markets. Systemic risk in the financial sector is all the more dangerous because the negative effects are likely to spread to the real economy. This explains why states had to commit so much resources as a last resort during the financial crisis to save a number of key institutions using taxpayers' money.

In the aftermath of the crisis, new regulations have come into force to prevent insolvency or, when insolvency occurs, to minimize the consequences for the overall economy and the public finances. The supervision role is handed over to the Resolution Authorities. These regulations addressed four main issues:

(1) *Preparation*: Regulation requires institutions to prepare a recovery plan containing the measures they would take if their situation were to deteriorate seriously. If the resolution authority identifies legal or operational impediments to the rapid dismantling of the institution in the event of a crisis, it is able /has the power to impose structural changes in particular with the group organization. National authorities have also to prepare resolutions plans for each institution they supervise.

(2) *Prevention*: *Ex-ante* resolution funds have been set up to assist in the rescue of failing institutions. These funds, which are financed by the banking sector, may provide temporary support to banks in the form of loans, asset purchases, guarantees, etc. They can be used ultimately to absorb the losses or recapitalize the bank only after its shareholders and creditors.

(3) *Early intervention*: Resolution authorities are now able to step in at an early stage when the capital ratios fall below certain thresholds, for example by appointing a temporary director or call a shareholders' general meeting to pass the necessary reforms.

(4) *Resolution*: More importantly, new regulations have granted more power to resolution authorities to restructure the ailing institution. The new resolution tools allow authorities to:

- sell a subsidiary or a part of the business;
- temporarily transfer performing assets to a bridge institution such as a government-managed entity in order to continue the most important functions of the institution;
- separate good assets from non-performing ones, the latter being transferred into an asset management entity (bad bank);
- apply bail-in measures: impose losses — discounts — or a conversion of debt into shares. In this way, losses are imposed on the institution's shareholders and creditors, not on taxpayers. Similar powers have been provided to the regulator in the US by the DFA.

1.7.3   Making the derivatives market more robust

Prior to the 2007 crisis, most derivatives were traded in the US by mutual agreement OTC, i.e., out of regulated exchanges. While trading OTC enables to tailor contracts to each counterparty's specific needs, it exposes them to a risk that the crisis revealed in many cases neglected or underestimated, the counterparty risk. This risk refers to the likelihood that the counterparty of the transaction might default on its contractual obligations. The risk is of particular importance for derivatives given their leverage effect, especially when their long maturity exposes counterparties to the risk of substantial change in price over a distant time horizon.

Managing the counterparty risk is all the more challenging when transparency is scarce and limited. During the crisis, few if any had a global vision of everyone's exposure to risk. This lack of information contributed to freeze the markets: the risk of loss in the event of counterparty default had become far too high to take the risk of lending to a bank you don't know about. As early as September 2009, the G20 summit in Pittsburgh called for a major overhaul of the derivatives market and resulted in a new regulatory framework set in particular by the DFA in the US and EMIR in Europe among other jurisdictions.

New regulations require the clearing through CCPs of sufficiently standardized contracts, such as some interest rate swaps and CDSs. Among these instruments, most liquid ones are subject to an obligation to be executed on trading platforms. One of the guiding principle is "any instrument that is clearable has to be cleared". This is a virtual rule since is pushes CCPs to provide clearing to new instruments to attract more clients. The more products are cleared, the better, since clearing remove dependences in the chain between the current buyer and the current seller. Without clearing, if the initial buyer A traded again a seller a, and then if A sells back the contract to B, while a buys back to another participant b, the full chain at expiry of the product is $B - A - a - b$, whereas only $B - b$ would be enough. Without clearing, if a goes bankrupt between the initial transaction and the expiry of the contract: the chain is broken and it is difficult for B to obtain the payoff by b. With clearing the chain is really $B - b$, without any counterparty risk from A nor a.

For other derivatives whose clearing is not mandatory, mechanisms of counterparty risk mitigation are required, which include: timely trade confirmation, daily valuation, portfolio reconciliation, dispute resolution process, portfolio compression and exchange of margins. Most regulations also introduced reporting obligations for transactions and positions. This reporting is usually intended for trade repositories in first place, which ensure data quality through regular reconciliations, as well as transparency, through the publication of various aggregates per asset class (e.g., transaction volumes in nominal, open positions, MtM value). Ultimately, the reporting is also made available to the regulators, which can thus conduct their market and prudential oversight. While data is more and more widely used by authorities and participants, its usefulness is however still affected by data quality issues.

As the new regulations enhanced the role of CCPs and put them at the heart of the derivatives market, it was also necessary to increase their resiliency. CCPs are now subject to more stringent requirements, in terms of solvency and supervision. A supervision exercised/ undertaken independently at national levels is not suitable to increasingly interconnected markets. In the EU, their authorization and ongoing supervision are assigned to a college of regulators in order to ensure the strictest and harmonized standards. This is particularly useful as the competition among CCPs may lower their requirement levels towards their members (i.e., clearers).

Regulation has also introduced specific measures to manage the recovery and resolution of CCPs in case of extreme but possible events of serious financial distress. Much like for banks, the key objective is to protect the stability of financial markets and avoid the use of public funds.

In the US, the DFA also imposes enhanced capital requirements to the major participants including the swap dealers.

1.7.4 Strengthening the supervision of shadow banking

Shadow banking, to which the regulators prefer the less connoted term of non-banking financial intermediation (NBFI), refers to the various activities similar to those pursued by banks but that are subject to a different, usually lighter, regulation and supervision. Up to now, all financial intermediaries are not regulated the same way: the closer to the center of the financial network, the more regulation on participants. As a consequence the buy side (i.e., asset managers) are less regulated than the agency sell side (i.e., brokers) that are even less regulated than investment banks. The main drivers of the intensity of the regulation are

- the more leverage needed to operate, the more regulation,
- the more client facing, the more regulation too.

As a natural consequence investment banks (with leverage and a lot of clients) are under more scrutiny than asset managers (using less leverage and having less clients — except if the retail is considered).

The participants operating shadow banking typically encompass insurance corporations, broker-dealers (other than banks), hedge funds, money market funds (MMFs), investment funds (other than hedge-funds and MMFs), captive financial company and money lenders (CFCML).[38]

Many of the unexpected losses during the financial crisis resulted from separate activities parallel to banks regular operations, and thus did not fall directly under the banking regulation. NBFI required enhanced scrutiny from regulators (Figure 1.5).

Since the first G20 leaders' summit in 2010 calling for developing the oversight and the regulation of shadow banking, a range of reforms have emerged. Efforts have focused on two main areas:

Area 1: Identifying and monitoring the risks. Thanks to a better exchange of information and regular data collection exercises from an increasingly larger coverage of economies accounting for 80% of the world GDP, regulators have gained a better knowledge of NBFI. An important step for the oversight of the shadow system was the introduction of the annual global monitoring reports on NBFI, which assess the main trends, the scale of operations and risks of this sector.

Area 2: Strengthening the regulatory framework through targeted regulations. Important steps have been made to reduce the systemic risks associated with NBFI, by targeting directly the entities or activities of the NBFI, but also the banks that may have close interactions with NBFI business/operations/entities.

---

[38] A CFCML is a wholly-owned subsidiary of a corporate company that provides loans and other financial services to the customers of this company. For example, captive finance companies of retailers provide store credit cards and full-scale banking while captive finance companies of automakers provided loans to their clients.

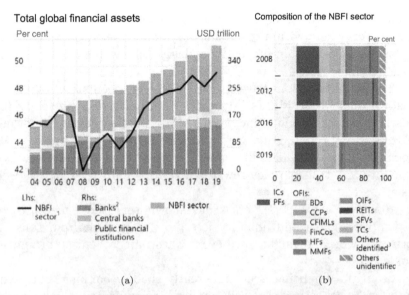

(a)   (b)

Figure 1.5:   Total global financial asset (a), and composition of the NBFI sector (b).
Source: Financial Stability Board, Global Monitoring Report on Non-Bank Financial Intermédiation, 2020.

Securitization, which was at the heart of the financial crisis, could not avoid a serious regulatory overhaul. Following recommendations from OICV in 2012 and Basel Committee in 2015, a number of jurisdictions have implemented incentive alignment obligations, which require issuers to retain a share, typically 5%, of the credit risk of the securitization. Other regulations also aimed at increasing the standardization of securitized instruments. To this end, the EU Securitization regulation entered into application in 2018 introduced a specific framework for simpler, more transparent and standardized securitizations (STS) in order to promote products qualifying as such. This regulation also prohibits re-securitization, i.e., a securitization in which any one of the underlying exposures is a securitization position (e.g., CDO).

Regulators also wanted to reduce the systemic risks of MMFs, which are part of NBFI alongside other investment funds. The financial crisis showed that MMFs can be exposed to serious risks of runs, which played an accelerating role in the turmoil.

The constant net asset value applicable in 2008 to MMFs in the US maintained the illusion of a safe investment but it also casted doubts on the true value of the portfolio assets when losses started to surge everywhere within the financial system. The suspicion towards these funds resulted in preventive redemptions, which in turn amplified the fall in price.

Several jurisdictions have strengthened their regulation, requiring institutional prime MMFs in the US to adopt a floating (mark-to-market) net asset value, increasing MMFs disclosures and allowing MMFs to impose liquidity gate and fees. In the EU, the new MMF regulation imposed eligibility criteria for assets, new requirements of liquidity and transparency towards investors and regulators, as well as stress-tests.

However, the COVID crisis has shown that these measures of redemption gates and liquidity fees did not prevent from runs on prime MMFs and might have even exacerbated them according to some studies.

Securities financing is not inherently shadow banking, but regulators were concerned that collateralized instruments like repo might facilitate excessive leverage, regardless of which type of participants uses them. While banks are already subject to prudential regulations limiting their leverage, measures applicable to a broader range of participants including the NBFI entities was therefore needed. In 2013, the FSB called for measures relating to the supervision of the reuse of collateral and the implementation of processes for collecting data in order to increase transparency and regulatory oversight. These have resulted in the EU regulation on securities financing transactions (SFTR), which requires a reporting obligation on counterparties to a SFTs with central data repositories (pretty similar to derivatives transactions in the EMIR regulation); a requirement for transparency of the fund managers to their investors on the use of SFTs; and a supervision of the reuse of titles used as collateral.

While core activities of banks are subject to regulation and close monitoring by regulators, banks often conducted less-standardized or sophisticated activities before the crisis, usually off-balance sheet, known to be more difficult to monitor for regulators and investors. For instance, banks used to finance mortgages through OBS, ABS, and hedged risk through CDS, as well as OBS. In addition to making more difficult a correct assessment/determination of their risk, this OBS practise resulted in lower capital ratios according to the rules of the Basel Committee prevailing at the time. Following FSB recommendations, accounting rules were amended to limit the use of OBS.

Important steps were taken by regulators to reduce the risks arising from interactions between banks and shadow banking entities. These interactions may take the form of a bank supporting unconsolidated but closely linked entities in difficulty (under stress) for which the bank has no contractual obligation, known as step-in risk. This type of situation was particularly observed during the crisis, when banks brought support to many MMFs, SIVs and conduits.

The Basel Committee has published in 2017 a framework for self-identification by step-in-risk banks (as long as the banks assume a role as sponsor of the entities located outside their accounting and prudential consolidation group) and of notification to the regulator. These guidelines, which should in particular be implemented into European law by 2020, may result in complementary prudential charges. While step-in situations are covered in different regulations, including through the LCR standard covering contractual or non-contractual liquidity risks and capital requirements for banks' exposures to funds, this framework published by the Committee acts more as a safety net for situations where step-in risks may remain and therefore complements existing regulations.

From a quantitative perspective (9)

Regulation is more and more using models and data to monitor and analyse the risk embedded in the financial system. Either as a whole, from a systemic risk perspective, analyzing the true network of relationships between market participants, either focusing on one participant or one class of participants. The regulation can be principle driven or data (i.e., result) driven; it is sure that the more data driven it is, the more need of quantitative analysts.

Moreover, regulators have access to unique data, very often is the identity of the buyer and of the seller of each contract; it allows to foresee liquidity issues or to isolate classes of participants that should be regulated differently.

1.8   For More Details

Paper on financial intermediation are available for long (see, for instance, Pyle, 1971 to start with), but they often focus on balance sheet intermediation, and not on market intermediation; see Adrian and Shin (2010) for a paper about the change in the nature of intermediation. This book focuses on market intermediation since it seems that regulators are pushing in this direction, essentially to increase the transparency and to reduce the information asymmetry that takes place when intermediaries are using their balance sheet as main tool of intermediation. In most cases, information asymmetry increases transaction costs for counterparties (see Edwards *et al.*, 2007 for an illustration on the market of corporate bonds).

To underline the way the financial system operates as a network of intermediaries, it is good to go back to Merton (1995), in which Robert Merton defines the functions of the financial system; this paper is cited in multiple places within this book.

Papers on shadow banking are a good reference to understand money and risk flows on financial markets since they explained how banks may use non bank participants to exfiltrate risk from their highly regulated balance sheets (see Pozsar and Singh, 2011 for a good example).

Details on market microstructure can be found in Lehalle and Laruelle (2018), its second edition summarizes the state of the art knowledge on liquidity from a trading viewpoint, trading algorithms, market fragmentation and high frequency trading.

The best place to find information on regulation are the web site of regulators: the ESMA, the SEC, the AMF (for France) or the FCA (for the UK) have a lot of whitepapers containing quantitative information. The FSB issue interesting reports like Board (2021) too.

References

Adrian, T. and Shin, H. S. (2010). The changing nature of financial intermediation and the financial crisis of 2007–2009. *Annual Review of Economics*, 2(1):603–618.

Board, F. S. (2021). Global monitoring report on non-bank financial intermediation 2020. *Financial Stability Board*.

Edwards, A. K., Harris, L. E., and Piwowar, M. S. (2007). Corporate bond market transaction costs and transparency. *The Journal of Finance*, 62(3):1421–1451.

Lehalle, C.-A. and Laruelle, S. (2018). *Market Microstructure in Practice*. World Scientific.

Merton, R. C. (1995). A functional perspective of financial intermediation. *Financial Management*, 23–41.

Pozsar, M. Z. and Singh, M. M. (2011). *The Nonbank-Bank Nexus and the Shadow Banking System*. International Monetary Fund.

Pyle, D. H. (1971). On the theory of financial intermediation. *The Journal of Finance*, 26(3):737–747.

Chapter 2

Intermediation of Trades, Market Microstructure and Liquidity Provision

2.1 The Specific Position of Brokers

2.1.1 A little bit of history

> [The Buttonwood Agreement] *We the Subscribers, Brokers for the Purchase and Sale of the Public Stock, do hereby solemnly promise and pledge ourselves to each other, that we will not buy or sell from this day for any person whatsoever, any kind of Public Stock, at a less rate than one quarter percent Commission on the Specie value and that we will give preference to each other in our Negotiations. In Testimony whereof we have set our hands this 17th day of May at New York, 1792.*

More than two centuries ago, 24 brokers decided to make an agreement under a buttonwood tree on Wall Street, New York City; thereby constituting the New York Stock & Exchange Board, known today as the NYSE. It illustrates the complexity of the relations between brokers, exchanges and how they shape markets' microstructure. First of all, brokers had a monopoly. Similarly in France, Louis the XVth via an *Arrêté du Roi* made the obligation to trade publicly around the pit in 1774. Everyone could buy and sell but had to do it openly, with full transparency, in order for the transaction price to be known and to limit price manipulation. Without such measure, a broker could quote a price to someone while simultaneously doubling it for some other person. However, if transactions are public, the information about the price is shared between all the clients of the broker; thus, he or she cannot give different prices to different clients without any good reason. In France again, Napoleon the First decided in 1801 to concentrate the flow in the hands of a few brokers, by giving the right of trading stocks to the only 71 existing brokers and preventing new parties to join the market; thereby creating a monopoly.

Two concepts of paramount importance are illustrated here: *transparency*, and *concentration*. When intermediaries are taking part in a business, transparency is a must because it levels the playing field. Concentration and centralization are also required because having fewer places to trade limits the choice of natural risk-takers and increases the probability of a natural buyer meeting a natural seller. In any case, it decreases the time intermediaries have to wait between a sell and a buy.

If transparency and concentration are good for the market, one can question the fact that the creation of NYSE is about creating a *monopoly*: the 24 initial brokers will not buy or sell to any other intermediary, and they will agree on fees. This monopoly of exchanges has not been perceived as a bad thing by regulators, and before MiFID 1 (November 2007) in Europe, shares of companies listed on one exchange could not be traded on another exchange. As such, this monopoly increased the centralization of flows, which is accepted as a good property of market microstructure.

Another important lesson to learn from the Buttonwood agreement is that initially, Exchanges were associations of brokers, and brokers were the *members* of Exchanges. In 1971, NYSE became a listed company with new clients, selling services associated with trading: listing, market data, and technology. They are at the crossing of the real economy (i.e., listed companies seeking capital and financing), and market participants (brokers, asset managers, structurers, investment banks, market makers and regulators). Indeed, a transaction is an atomic risk transfer. The buyer of a risk factor either wants to get exposure to this risk or wants to cancel the opposite risk factor that she already owns.

2.1.2 Brokers: The middlemen

Intermediation of transactions. Brokers are meant to be the perfect middlemen: first and foremost, they allow clients to buy or sell to other investors. If they are both clients of the same broker, and if they come simultaneously, the transaction is a *cross*.

If they are both clients of the same broker, but they did not disclose their intention to buy and sell simultaneously, a market maker may have taken a position between the buyer and the seller. She accepted to be exposed to a risk, but because managing this kind of risk is the business model of a market maker, she probably had a systematic (and cheap) way to hedge most of the risk or to diversify it. The buyer could buy from the market maker an exposure that is made of idiosyncratic and systematic risks; if the market maker has enough activity, she can diversify the idiosyncratic risks she takes, and the remaining risk, that is systematic, can be hedged thanks to cheap contracts like Futures on indexes. The seller can then unload those contracts to the market maker at a later time. Ultimately, it is the broker who puts those parties in contact. Another way for clients of the same broker to trade even if they did not disclose simultaneously their intentions is when the first one mandated the broker to *seek liquidity* on his behalf. In such a case, a buyer comes to the broker saying: "I would like to buy shares of this illiquid company from northern Europe, could you find a counterparty?" Indeed, the buyer hopes that the broker (or to be accurate one of the sales traders of the broker) knows another client who bought such shares a few months ago and would be keen to sell some of them. One of the roles of the broker is to anonymize the interests of his clients: if the buyer randomly calls a few asset managers who, by chance, could own shares he wants to buy, the effect would be very bad. Once potential counterparties know that you have an interest, they will raise their price to accept selling these shares. As a middleman, the broker takes care of this information asymmetric aspect of the double auction mechanisms that fix the price to protect both parties.

A broker can also contribute to a transaction between one of his clients and the client of another broker. In such a case, they trade via an exchange, or to be more generic and use the terminology coined by the MiFID European directive, an MTF, i.e., a *multilateral trading facility*. An MTF is a place that hosts *limit orderbooks*, to which traders send their interests. Another way to trade is to ask to a market maker for *quotes*: she will answer with two prices (one, the ask price, for a buy and the other, the bid price, for a sell), the trader will generally have requested for quotes to several market makers, and will choose the most favorable price.

Intermediation of information. Brokers have been providing advice to their clients far before the regulation of this activity by the *Investment Advisers Act* of 1940 by the Securities and Exchange Commission in the US. Nevertheless, the nature of the area covered by "analysts' research" of brokers evolved, following the availability of information by investors. This phenomenon is driven by the fact that it is worthwhile for a broker to investigate a new source of information if the fixed cost to extract meaningful advice is high enough so that paying it and "selling back" the advice to all of its clients is efficient for the ecosystem. In short: instead of having each investor paying the fixed cost, the broker pays it and asks each client a small fraction of these costs. A consequence is that when the cost to acquire information decreases, it is less efficient for the ecosystem to go through the intermediation of a broker. A typical example is the availability of annual reports of listed companies and of the associated balance sheets: with the convergence of accountancy norms and with the progress of companies' websites, which now include a section for Investor Relations, the value of collecting and commenting these information decreases. Moreover, with FinTech startups providing platforms to independent analysis (see Chapter 6 for examples), the specificity and the value of brokers' traditional research is decreasing. A counter-example is analysts' research about *factor investment*: being able to collect data and process it to identify "rewarded risk factors" is not available to all investors, moreover, being able to comment the nature and composition of these factors demand a specific set of skills that any asset manager cannot afford to have in house.

The position of brokers is perfectly adapted to absorb and dilute fixed costs. It is true for information acquisition as for other services linked to trading. Brokers provide a different kind of analysis:

- *Fundamental Analysis*: This analysis requires a deep knowledge of the analyzed company's business, and to be able to understand

and anticipate the consequences of strategic decisions of its board. It is necessary to understand how microeconomics and macroeconomics influences the perspectives of the company, and to be able to understand its balance sheet. Moreover, analysts performing such research have to be able to convert their understanding in a valuation of one equity share of the company; the usual way to do so is borrowed from the field of *asset pricing*.

• *Credit Analysis*: Surprisingly, credit analysis is often conducted in a separate way from Fundamental Analysis. This is probably due to the fact that stock brokerage and brokerage of fixed income instruments are usually conducted by different departments of the same brokerage firm, or because stock brokers are not always intermediating fixed income products. Nevertheless, it is worthwhile to underline that when a brokerage firm is associated with an Investment bank, the senior bankers of the latter institution advise companies in their debt financing; as such, they are experts in credit analysis. There may be a conflict of interest between the bankers and the analysts: the former have skin in the game, whereas the latter do not.

That being said, Credit Analysis is based on the way the future value of a company changes when the structure of its capital evolves. Typical events changing the capital structure of a company are the issuance of new shares or corporate bonds, loans, spin-offs, mergers and acquisition of companies.

Robert Merton established a generic relationship between the value of a company, the value of its equity and the value of its debts. In short: the difference between owning an equity share and owning a corporate bond of the same company is clear if it goes bankrupt or when it makes money. In case of a bankruptcy, the owner of shares loses 100% of its investment whereas the owner of a bond gets the *recovery rate* of the bond (i.e., the remaining value of the company); and when the company makes money the owner of the bond gets no rewards, whereas the owner of equity shares gets dividends (or an increase in the value of one share). Writing the probability of default of a company as a function of the uncertainty of its business, and making the assumption that both investments should have on average the same value for investors established a relation between the value of one share and the value of one corporate bond.

- *Technical Analysis*: It comes from a completely different approach than Fundamental Analysis. While Fundamental Analysis attempts to deduce what should be the market value of a single share looking at whether the company makes sound business decisions, Technical Analysis is rather interested in comparative analyses of similar companies' past stock prices to infer on the future value of a given stock.

    Such analysis comes from a statistical view point, establishing itself on rules and patterns. For instance, *a company's stock price rises for two months, then drops during the two following months reaching the initial level. The stock price then begins to rise in the following week, rising consecutively for the next two weeks.* A technical analyst will apply this rule to all companies which feature such patterns in their stock prices. The field of technical analysis has developed many rules of thumbs to memorize such usual behaviors:

    - Pattern-based behavior: "head and shoulders" or "three Buddhas" are typical names for patterns.
    - Rule-based diagnoses like "point and figure" have been documented too.
    - Moving windows based computations, like "Bollinger bands" are used by such analysts too.

- *Sector Analysis* and *Factor Analysis*: These analysis focus on trying to understand and explain the risks and rewards associated with portfolios. These portfolios can simply be "sectors", i.e., capital weighted indexes of companies of the same sector; they can also be more sophisticated like "value portfolios" or "growth portfolios",[1] based on the aggregation and cross-section of fundamental ratios of companies.

    Sector Analysis emerged naturally from the organization of teams of analysts in a brokerage firm: since macroeconomic and microeconomic events are *a priori* affecting in the same way companies of the same industrial sector, it is efficient to group fundamental analysts working on the same sector in one team, or on one desk. The head of this team should be able to have a good vision of

---

[1]See Chapter 4 for more accurate definitions of these portfolios.

the future of "his sector" as a whole, and can naturally write recommendations and give advice on this sector. At least, it is easier for this team to distribute reports under the umbrella of its sector.

The synchronization of analysts' recommendations is a subtle issue that brokers have to face: what if an analyst believes that Microsoft will make a profit based on an anticipated increase of personal computer sales, and another analyst believes that Apple will lose money based on the exact opposite anticipation? The organization of analysts in sector-based teams is a way to ensure the communication between them so that they can confront their beliefs and converge to more informed conclusions. Factor Analysis is another transverse direction that can help analysts to be consistent: what if an analyst believes a stock price will increase because its *Price to Earning Ratio* is too low, but another analyst believes the price of another stock with a lower Price-to-Earning Ratio will decrease? The more factors are used to ensure the consistency between views on prices, the more reliable these views are.

- *Strategies Valuation*: It is a way to have a look at other risk factors in terms of valuation. Such analyses often emerged under the auspices of equity derivatives brokers, because the best way to give advice on derivatives is to propose strategies involving these derivatives and to "show" that, historically, these strategies provided positive returns. Since the basic way to value derivatives is based on risk replication, i.e., on relying on correlated tradable instruments to build a dynamic portfolio that has the same risk-reward profile, exhibiting such a dynamic portfolio and showing that historically, the pricing of its derivatives is consistent.

All of these ways to provide recommendations will continue to evolve with the cost to acquire and process information. Big data and data sciences are currently in favor of the emergence of the use of alternative datasets or Artificial Intelligence"-based research, using new datasets like satellite images, website traffic, etc and new processing techniques inspired by Artificial Intelligence to provide recommendations. Chapter 6 elaborate in this direction.

Intermediation of capital. The third kind of intermediation operated by brokerage firms consists in putting in touch investors and

companies in need of capital. The chain of market participants needed
to provide capital to companies is the following one:

- An Exchange is needed first, to issue equity shares or corporate
  bonds. The choice of an Exchange versus another comes of course
  from the competition on costs, but also the suite of services provided by the exchange to the company, once it is listed. The company needs to attract the attention of investors, so that its equity
  and its debts are traded on secondary markets at good prices,
  thanks to a buying pressure. Tools to attract investors' attention
  are Fundamental research, as it prevent investors from missing on
  "good decisions" taken by the board of the company, and being
  part of an index. The latter is valuable due to brokers' analysts
  monitoring companies based on the components of indexes; being
  added to an index should increase the number of analysts following the company. It also particularly desirable as Asset Managers
  build funds that are inspired by indexes, or even tracking certain
  indexes: once a company is added to such an index, it guarantees
  a buying pressure and the attention of investors.
- An Investment Bank is needed to obtain advice from a senior
  banker on the best way to structure the capital raising, and the
  book of the bank (or of an affiliated market maker) will be needed
  to guarantee an issuing price. The *book runner* will take care of
  all aspects of issuance, and especially usually accepts to buy for
  its own account a large number of shares (or bonds) to prevent a
  too high temporary selling pressure having bad consequences on
  issuing prices.
- A broker is needed to seek buyers on the primary market (i.e., to
  buy and hold immediately at issuance). Most often the broker is
  affiliated to the bank running the issuance. Of course, its analysts
  will write and disseminate reports on the valuation of the company.
  The more popular the broker, the more attention of investors will
  be attracted. This should guarantee a high buying pressure, that
  could allow the company to raise capital at a cheaper cost.
- Asset Managers are of course the ones that will, at the end of the
  process, provide capital. They intermediate capital coming from
  savings of countries, companies, and households: they require a
  little less liquidity on these savings, and provide exposure to risk
  factors that may need to include in their portfolios equity shares
  or corporate bonds issued by the company.

Of course, the regulator will be involved, to oversee the process and guarantee investors' protection against information or price manipulation. In any case, the broker is in the middle of the process: its analysts will publish reports, its clients may be the first buyers of the created financial instruments (equity shares or corporate bonds), providing capital to the company.

2.2 Organization Inside a Brokerage Firm

2.2.1 Services to corporates

Corporate brokerage. It is of paramount importance for listed companies to understand the identity of its shareholders. Mainly, if an aggressive competitor buys a majority of its shares, the company can be acquired without noticing it soon enough. As a consequence, boards of companies would like to know if such a shift in shareholders is happening to take action in order to prevent them. Brokers, who are key actors in the trading of shares, can potentially see and identify such flows and report it to corporations. To this end, the corporation should have contracted a "monitoring contract" with the broker.

Another type of service available under the umbrella of "corporate brokerage" goes as follows: due to their unique relationship with corporations and deep expertise in trading, brokers are the perfect partners for companies conducting operations on markets: This includes issuing new shares and corporate bonds of course, but also *buying back their own shares*, as well as buying shares of other companies in the case of mergers. Share buyback programs are used by companies to provide equity to their staff,[2] or to redesign the structure of their capital.[3] The format of such programs is similar to the one of new shares issuance: the broker (or a market maker working in association with the broker) agree in advance to buy shares of the company conditionally to the volatility and trading volumes.

Moreover, some brokers are mandated by companies to make the market on their stocks. It is a way to ensure that their equity shares

---

[2]For instance, in the context of stock options programs.

[3]A company having spared cash can choose to "buyback" some of its own shares, and "burn" them. It is a way to affect the debt to equity ratio of the company without issuing any debt.

Table 2.1: Organization of brokerage firms.

Division	Tasks
Sales	Select and distribute the reports.
	In charge of the global sales relationships.
Analysts	Write the reports.
	Get information from CFO of the corporations.
	Discuss with investors' portfolio managers.
Sales-traders	Take investors orders (by phone) via the dealing desks.
	Seek liquidity.
	Select and send flow oriented reports (often written by quantitative).
	In charge of *upstairs trading*.
	Route the remaining orders to traders or trading algorithms.
Traders	Mix manual and algorithmic traded orders.
Dealers	Manage brokers' proprietary books.
AES sales-traders	Receive and monitor algorithmic orders sent directly by low touch.
	Manage the low touch flows.
	Offer execution consultancy to clients.
DMA teams	Monitor DMA orders and operate the help desk.
Middle and back offices	Maintain the relationship with investors.
	Middle and back offices with CCPs.

are always liquid because the market maker will accept to be the counterparty of most buyers and sellers. The potential illiquidity premium[4] that could affect the attractiveness of the stock will hence decrease. Such a service can ignite a self-sustaining virtuous cycle where more liquidity brings even more liquidity. Besides, if a broker is making the market on the shares of a company, he or she will be more informed on flows on this company and be able to provide better monitoring on the composition of its shareholders. The multitude of tasks performed by brokerage firms is carried out by different divisions. Table 2.1 gives an overview of the organization of brokerage companies.

---

[4]An "illiquidity premium" corresponds to the fact that, because they are not sure to be able to sell a stock at the "fair price" due to a lack of potential buyer in the future, investors will not pay its "fair price" today.

> **From a quantitative perspective (10)**
>
> Corporate brokerage needs analytics to monitor, understand and explain to corporates the flows buying and selling the shares of the company. The main goal of such an analysis is to make the difference between *endogenous* and *exogenous* phenomena: are the flows driven by natural rebalancing of large portfolios or are they due to something specific to this company, like the reaction to News, or the premises of an aggressive bid on the company?
>
> Moreover, within the market making services of Corporate Brokerage, dedicated trading algorithms have to be designed. These algorithms have to include specific trading rules, related to the status of this very specific status of such a market making activity. For instance: in most cases such market makers are not allowed to "create a new price" (in the sense that it cannot trade at a price that has not already been traded during the day).

Fundamental analysis: It is also a service to corporates, because it attracts the attention of investors, potentially providing a buying pressure on the equity shares and corporate bonds of the company. In such a case, the company will have a "cheaper access to capital" next time it will issue shares or bonds. Note that a "cheaper access to capital" means that to raise the same capital, the company will either need to issue fewer shares, or to pay a smaller coupon. In the first case, the current shareholders will be less diluted by the next issue of equity, in the second case the company will pay less in coupons to temporarily raise the same amount of money via a corporate bond. In both cases, the company will have to "pay less" to raise the same amount of money.

Dues to potential conflicts of interests and principal-agent issues, the corporate brokerage business is highly regulated.

2.2.2 Services to investors

Remember that brokers are primarily providing trading capacities to investors. Two main reasons support this intermediation role:

the concentration of trading in few places increases the probability to have simultaneous interest from natural buyers and sellers, and fixed costs associated with connection to exchanges are mutualized when a single market participant pays these costs and asks each of its clients a fraction of it. With the rise of electronic trading, this service is now centered around algorithmic trading capacities; providing trading algorithms the ability to split large orders of investors in smaller "child orders" to be send to different trading venues or to be scheduled during the day as to obtain the best possible buying or selling price. Electronification of trading became possible with the natural increase in capabilities to record, store and process information, due to Moore's law. Not only did it unlock the capacity to build decision support systems for trading as well as automating the process; it also lowered the cost to build electronic exchanges, i.e., *trading facilities*. Electronification thus had two simultaneous consequences: partial automation of the trading process and creation of *alternative trading places*. The latter needed modifications of regulations in favor of more competition between exchanges. These regulatory moves have been made almost simultaneously by Reg NMS in the US (2006) and MiFID 1 in Europe (2007).

Section 2.3.2 details the premises and consequences of these regulations; When the number of places to trade increases, fixed costs are multiplied accordingly, and the algorithmic complexity of finding the best combination of venues to answer to the immediate liquidity need of one investor increases too. Brokers have been at the best place to put in place solutions to these two new issues.

"High touch" trading services. The way brokers traditionally took "care" of their clients' orders let them have some degree of freedom in choosing exactly where and when placing child orders to obtain the best possible average price over a period of time defined by the client. Typical care orders are "for the day". The broker, or to be more specific the *sales trader* working for the client, will call some potential counterparties and listen to news surrounding the given instrument. She takes a profit from the "market color" that the desks of the broker (often organized by sector, asset classes and complexity of the instruments) have as they are continuously following, monitoring and probing the market depth. The expression "high touch" means that the client knows that a human keeps an eye on the order; nevertheless with the fragmentation and electronification of markets, they often partly delegate the execution to trading algorithms. There is usually no guarantee of the average price the client will finally obtain, it is a "best effort" relying on the expertise of the broker. The main incentive for the broker to provide good performances is that if she regularly underperforms her peers, she will then stand to lose her clients. This best effort has been formalized by regulators in terms of *best execution*: the broker should be able to prove that it has made the best possible choices. Obtaining a "proof" of such complex decisions is very difficult, hence brokers provide elements at two scales:

(1) First, brokers conduct statistical summaries of their performances and choices, compared to alternative scenarios. Of course, these alternative scenarios are virtual or "paper scenarios" since interactions with the market is a closed loop: nobody really knows what would have happened if this market order would not have been sent, or if this limit order would not have been executed. Double auction dynamics are ruled by game theory, and it is not possible to be really sure of the outcome to "Gedankenexperiment".

The brokers' clients conduct mirror studies, comparing the different brokers they delegated comparable orders to. These transaction cost analyses (TCA) allow the dealing desks of Asset Managers to challenge their broker and compare their skills in order to pick the one with the best chances to deliver them a good execution according to their statistical breakdowns.

(2) Brokers then provide accurate descriptions of atomic events, essentially to be able to provide evidence that when an order has been sent to a particular trading venue, no other venue (at the broker's knowledge) provided a better price for the required liquidity. These detailed proofs are particularly well suited to instantaneous choices, and they are dependent on the overall "execution context", that is partially chosen *ex-ante* by the broker. For instance, the collection of trading venues the brokers decided to be (or not) connected to has a great influence on the sentence *no other venues, at broker's knowledge, provided a better price.*

The "high touch" service gives access to generic "market timing" advice by the sales trader in charge of the client. As the broker's staff follows "morning meetings" as well as analysts' recommendations and reports, they are meant to be able to provide decision support. An asset manager not carefully following markets at a daily scale, would like to sell a large portfolio of instruments as a "block decision" (for instance to face a redemption) may not be aware that certain stocks of this portfolio will be submitted to corporate actions today, or that market participants might be waiting for important news the next day. As a consequence, there could be limited liquidity on these stocks today and it would probably be better to wait a few days before trading them. Dealing desks of large asset managers often keep ongoing relationships with several brokers, to aggregate this information and implement themselves a market timing adapted to the different instructions of their portfolio managers.

Pushed by regulatory demands, brokers improved their information systems to record most of their actions, their Order Management Systems (OMS) and their Execution Management Systems (EMS) are well connected and it is feasible to make different extractions to monitor clients' flows. Initially designed to reduce the operational risk and to answer to regulatory reporting duties, these databases started to be used to export delayed and anonymized information on brokers' flows, and to sell them to other dealing desks. Following the automation of analysts' recommendations that took place around 2005 with the emergence of the TIPS system initiated by Marshall Wace,[5] brokers understood that a modern way to provide recommendations to their clients could be to package them as downloadable files. A few years after the launch of TIPS, several aggregators of analyst recommendations emerged, to provide the raw material for "alpha capture" systematic strategies.

"Low touch" trading services. Low touch services are at the opposite of the spectrum of human intervention: they allow asset managers to access trading venues either via trading algorithms,

---

[5]This large quantitative asset manager asked its brokers to relay normalized recommendations of their analysts, to build portfolios exploiting them, and to pay brokers' research accordingly to the added value of their recommendations in the profits of the portfolio.

designed and coded by brokers, that can be launched on-demand, or via *direction market access*. These services are used by traders or asset managers that have quantitative and programming skills. After 2010, regulators had a tendency to ban "naked access", under which a client could access trading venues as if it were the broker, using its membership but not its risk control devices.

Usually, each member of a trading venue profits from several access points (named SLE, a French acronym[6] for *Serveur Local d'Emmission*), each of them can be parameterized with risk control devices monitoring quantities like the number of messages per second, the total traded amount, and the number of executions. Brokers' clients usually share one SLE, and each broker has, on-premise, a similar risk control system per client. DMA orders are routed to these systems, whereas naked access orders went directly to the trading venue. Since speed became an important parameter for traders, most brokers have colocated[7] their risk control systems in the data centers of the exchanges so that their most latency-sensitive clients can be as close as possible to the matching engine of trading venues when they use low touch services.

While high touch clients have to pay fees corresponding to a human-customized service (from 10 to 6 bp[8] in 2010), low touch clients pay very low fees, in a format named "cost plus": the broker is asked to forward them the exact invoices that the trading venues are charging, *plus* brokerage fees, which are reduced as much as possible (around 1 or 2 bp[9] in 2010).

Algorithmic trading, program trading and (alternative) execution services. In between high touch and low touch services, an offer centered on "automated trading" emerged around 2000. Brokers coded "parameterized trading algorithms", and instead of having to

---

[6]French companies like GL Trade, UL Link or Smart Trade pioneered the business of market access, probably because Toronto Stock Exchange and La Bourse de Paris have been the first exchanges to provide fully automated trading processes.

[7]A software is said to be colocated when it is physically hosted by a computer at the same place as the main server of an Exchange.

[8]As a comparison, the bid-ask spread of a liquid stock of a developed country was between 8 and 4 bps in 2010.

[9]As a comparison, exchange fees were of the same order of magnitude in 2010.

call a sales trader to discuss about a care order to be traded within the day, their clients could, fill some parameters, such as the number of shares to buy or sell, a start and end time, certain limit prices, and a level of aggressiveness on a graphical interface. At the push of a button, the algorithm would then start to trade on their behalf. Section 2.3.5 provides more details on Algorithmic Trading.

It is in particular very convenient to use such machine-driven execution for portfolios; instead of sending the instructions line by line to a broker, and because it would be too heavy (and costly) to have a human taking care of each of the lines on the broker's side, dealing desks can send the full basket of instructions at once to the *Program Trading* (PT) desk of one of their brokers. This service packages a minimal decision support service and algorithmic trading:

- Once the basket of desired instruction is received by the broker, it conducts a *pre-trade analysis* and sends it to the client.

  The pre-trade analysis is a recap of what the algorithm understood of the basket: its breakdown by sectors, currencies, countries, etc., and the expected fraction of the daily liquidity it represents, usually coupled with an estimate of the expected *market impact* of each line and the volatility for the day. Several pre-trade analyses incorporate market context: expected news, corporate actions, or a specific event that could affect the trading on each line. They also recommend an algorithmic configuration for each line.

  Pre-trade analysis can be considered as a risk control layer: if the communication between the broker and its client is not clear or if an operational mistake occurred between the decision of the portfolio manager and its dealing desk, the pre-trade analysis should point out that "something seems to be strange" in this set of instruction. Either the breakdown exhibits an over-representation of a country or a stock, or the expected market impact of a few lines is far larger than the bulk of the portfolio, etc. It is a kind of "last resort check" that the portfolio composition is compatible with what the dealing desk is meant to have sent to the broker.
- At the reception of the pre-trade analysis, the client can adjust its portfolio, accept or amend the algorithmic configuration and send the confirmation to the broker.
- Algorithms are launched on the portfolio; that can be a collection of trading algorithms, each of them "taking care" of a single line,

or a portfolio algorithm, which is aware of the correlations between price dynamics of all lines of the portfolio.

During the execution, sales-traders on the broker side and traders on the client side can make some adjustments or fine-tune the parameters of certain lines.

- At the end of the day, a *post-trade analysis* is ran on the obtained execution: how can the average prices be split between market impact and "fair price dynamics"? Is this decomposition in line with the expectations disclosed in the pre-trade analysis? Did news impact the execution? And so forth.

More than checking if the *ex-ante* expectation of the broker's algorithms have been in line with the observed realizations, the post-trade analyses of all brokers are aggregated by the dealing desk of the asset manager; first to check the consistency within brokers and with independent observations of the dealing desk, second to benchmark brokers in a weekly or monthly Transaction Costs Analysis review.

Some brokers invested in sophisticated pre-trade and post-trade analyses, in conjunction with real-time advisory services. The AES acronym (i.e., Alternative Electronic Services) has been coined by Credit Swiss in the 2000s to define this suite of advanced services associated with electronic trading.

This kind of service gave birth to fully electronic brokers, like ITG. They exclusively provide algorithmic trading, direct market access, and advisory services for execution. One advantage is that they can partner with quantitative dealing desks far better than regular brokers; another competitive advantage is that they are meant to have no balance sheet and hence can claim to have no conflict of interest with their clients.[10]

---

[10] As soon as a broker has a balance sheet, clients can consider that the broker may "front-run" their instruction for its own profit. Having no balance sheet is a guarantee, *per se*, that no such behavior is possible. The real difficulty resides in the complexity for the client to check whether there effectively is no proprietary trading being conducted by the broker. The example of the "ITG Posit scandal" disclosed in 2015 and concerning front running activity held in this company (despite its reputation for not having a balance sheet) during 2009 and 2010, has shown that clients should conduct in-depth due diligence to really know if their broker conducts proprietary trading activities.

From a quantitative perspective (11)

Designing, coding and monitoring trading algorithms is an area dominated by quants. The design of the algorithms needs to model and understand the impact of a transaction (i.e., the *price impact* of liquidity consumption or liquidity provision at the finest time scale) and the impact of a large instruction to buy or sell over few hours and days (i.e., the *market impact* of *metaorders*). The specificities of trading venues in term of liquidity provision have to be assessed too. All this is done using a tick-by-tick database, recording all the transactions and orders sent to trading venues or market makers.

Once the expected impact of providing or consuming liquidity is estimated and captured by models, a notion of "urgency" has to be modelled too. It is often rendered by the mix of the expected volatility (that is a proxy for the uncertainty on the close future price formation process), the remaining quantity to buy or sell (or the current inventory) and a risk aversion parameter.

A trading algorithm can then be defined as the confrontation of the expected impact of trading fast, and the expected risk of waiting too long. Writing this properly from a mathematical perspective ends up with a very natural optimization problem, that can be expressed and well posed in the terms of stochastic control. Such a formulation is the natural backbone of a trading algorithm, around which "tactical" logics can be implemented, based on high-frequency predictions (i.e., when should be the best bid and ask prices in few miliseconds given the state of the liquidity offer?).

Facilitation and central risk books. Chapter 1 made the difference between "pure agency brokers" and market makers or proprietary trading desks. In reality, brokers, typically prime brokers, host at least one desk that can take a position on markets. It can be used in the scope of Corporate Brokerage activities, or to make the

market on illiquid instruments, and also to provide liquidity with a
deep link to brokerage activities. Such is the purpose of:

- *Facilitation*: Under this activity, brokers provide liquidity to their
  good clients. It could be described as a "lazy market making activity": the broker's traders in charge of this activity make a profit
  not necessarily thanks to the profits and losses of their strategies, but also due to a "commercial margin". This margin can
  compensate for the fact that these traders may not have a large
  enough (and especially diversified enough) portfolio of positions.
  They directly ask for a "compensation of the liquidity provision".
  In practice, brokers can offer a discounted price for this liquidity
  to their important clients; should the size be small enough as to
  minimize the impact on their book, they may ask for almost no
  compensation.
- *CRB*: Central risk book is a far larger business. Only prime brokers
  offer this service, which has mostly become a natural post-2008 crisis evolution of proprietary trading activities. Instead of having a
  diverse collection of trading strategies for its own account, some
  desks specialize in one type of the strategies, for example, those
  they provide internally to other desks in the bank, especially for
  derivative hedging, or those they provide to external market participants. This activity is very close to the one of a market maker,
  but rather a market maker who would be specialized in assets and
  flows usually traded by the broker and its clients.

  The focus of CRB is a mix of mean-reverting (or very short-
  term trend following ones) quantitative strategies and techniques
  to avoid adverse selection thanks to a good statistical knowledge
  of flows.

From a quantitative perspective (12)

Managing a central risk book is of course a quantitative job,
it mixes the design of trading and market making algorithms
with portfolio construction. Few of the main questions to
answer from this perspective are: What is the cost of removing

---

(Continued)

(*Continued*)

a "slice" of an existing portfolio?[a] What are the expected moves of the prices given a specific need for liquidity?[b] What is the steady-state need of liquidity associated to an specific intermediation business?[c]

---

[a]For Instance: maintaining a decently low exposure to the market of a portfolio once a subset of it has been used to provide liquidity to a client.

[b]For instance: modelling the level of directional, short-term information contained by the liquidity requests of a given client.

[c]For instance: to be able to provide total return swaps on European names.

Corporate access and research. Corporate access and research, that have been described in the previous section as a service to corporation, are of course consumed by asset managers as "trade ideas", and have been systematically used in the scope of "alpha capture".

One subtle point from the viewpoint of the asset managers is that if corporate access and research is paid only by commercial margins added on top of trading fees; the real cost of this services, and as a consequence, the real value of these services, are thus difficult to measure. In particular, how can it be guaranteed that two clients are paying the same cost for the same consumption of corporate access and research? In Europe, MiFID 2[11] answered to this by a demand of explicit *unbundling* of execution and research services.

2.3 Recent Evolutions of Trading

2.3.1 Electronification

A natural evolution of voice trading. In the pre-electronic era, trading practices evolved around two opposite setups:

- *Bilateral trading*, in which the roles are clearly separated: market makers (or dealers, or banks) only are providing liquidity,

---

[11]Deployed in January 2018.

whereas "clients" (i.e., asset managers) only are consuming liquidity. Moreover, the process is asymmetric in the sense that the client is requesting quotations from different market makers, and then choses amongst the different proposals. In this process, the market makers know their clients by name and can make different prices for liquidity to different clients. Typically, such market-makers conduct *toxicity studies* of their clients, in an attempt to understand the usual cost to provide liquidity to a given client, with respect to a given market context. These studies are meant to identify clients whose orders are more positively correlated to future price changes: such clients should then be "charged" more.

- *Multilateral trading*, during which all participants have a similar role:[12] they can all provide or consume liquidity in a limit order-book (LOB). The mechanism to "match" buyers and sellers is usually based on a price and time priority; each time a new order is declared to the "matching engine", its price is compared with the "resting orders".[13] Two mechanisms emerged for multilateral matching, both inspired by Walrasian auctions

  - *Call Auction* usually implemented for illiquid instruments or before and after market hours as to resolve situations characterized by substantial unsynchronized interests.[14] During a phase of "pre-auction", orders with side, prices, and quantities are declared. An "indicative price" and an "indicative quantity" are disseminated in realtime during this pre-auction phase: they are the price and the quantity that would be matched if the auction was ran immediately. The auction is then ran and the chosen price is the Walrasian price: it maximizes the matched quantity while also providing a price improvement.

    The way prices have been fixed for long in the *pit* in voice-driven markets is exactly as so. A Walrasian price was found by a "trial and error process" implemented by a "quoting agent",

---

[12]With the exception of some market makers who can have special rebates or low fees in exchange for the engagement to provide liquidity on a regular basis.

[13]"Resting orders" are orders previously declared and not matched by now. They are stored in a database named a "Limit OrderBook".

[14]Specific Call Auctions can be implemented for a few minutes towards liquid instruments, around the expiry of a given derivative for which the instruments are the underlying.

exploring prices until he had the feeling of reaching a similar number of sellers and buyers at such price.

- *Continuous auction* is used during trading hours, to have matching in real-time.

  Each time a new order is "declared" to the system, if it is a buy order, any resting sell (resp., buy) order with a higher price is a candidate for matching; amongst them, the ones with the highest prices are matched. The opposite is observed in the case of a sell order. If it is needed to make a choice between resting orders with the same price (for instance if I buy order for 200 shares up to $10 is declared and there are five sell resting orders at $9, each of them for 100 shares), the oldest orders are matched first. The priority thus goes to the price first, then the time (i.e., age).

Bilateral and multilateral trading mechanisms exist for long. They both contribute to two main goals:

- Achieve an equilibrium price that matches the offer and demand: the more buyers, the higher the price and the more sellers, the lower the price. This is the source of *price pressure* and *market impact*.
- Disseminate prices that digested most of the available information concerning the valuation of assets.

Bilateral trading is "protecting" (or giving an advantage) to market makers, while symmetry is preserved among market participants in a multilateral trading process.[15]

Regulation is needed as certain traders or market makers can be tempted to mislead other participants by adopting a fake behavior, like declaring orders they have no intention to execute, even in the opposite direction of their intention, to mimic a "fake price pressure" and obtain a better price.

---

[15]Of course some participants (like High-Frequency Traders, HFTs), who invest in acquiring an expertise of order book dynamics, can have a comparative advantage on other participants.

Negative externalities can emerge from the aggregation of the behavior of participants, regulators have to identify such situations and adjust their response to mitigate these negative effects. A *negative externality* occurs when one participant, in a perfectly rational attempt to maximize its utility, is generating high costs for other participants. The classic example of a negative externality is a cigarette smoker that can affect the health of its relatives who do not want to smoke. This point has been raised during the rise of high-frequency trading: the more HFT in a market, the more data there is to process for other participants who then have to invest in storage and processing capacity, only due to the increase of orders associated with high-frequency activity.

The *electronification of the trading process* is a straightforward transposition of these mechanisms to state of the art software and hardware. It has been part of an effort of regulators towards more tractability of the decisions taken by market participants. In an electronic environment, operators keep track of all declared intentions and traded quantities, associated to the identity of participants. As a consequence, it becomes possible for regulatory authorities to pursue investigations into bad behavior much later down the line.

The natural improvement of the capacity to record, store and process information was required to enable electronification. The practices of Direct Market Access by brokers and the software platforms (especially the OMS) distributed by vendors were preparing market participants, especially dealing desks of asset managers, to electronification. They used different brokers, compared their performances using databases and Excel spreadsheets, started to mix high touch and low touch services. From large asset managers' viewpoint, comparing different brokers and different national exchanges started to be a common practice, hence when the business of exchanges had been widely opened to competition, it was not a huge gap for them to access more than a single exchange per stock.[16]

---

[16]Moreover, the number of stocks having a double listing was not negligible, thus dealing desks of large asset managers had to deal with "competing exchanges"

2.3.2   Market fragmentation

Once regulations facilitated the trading of the same stock on multiple platforms, the first immediate and expected consequence has been the *fragmentation* of liquidity. The exact definition of fragmentation is not clear, nevertheless:

- Necessarily, once a stock is trading on two or more platforms, large liquidity consuming orders have to be *fragmented*, i.e., split into several "child orders", to take profit of liquidity available on all platforms.
- Moreover, a *fragmentation of technologies* happened as well; brokers had to address the specific formats and interfaces of each platform. As soon as the technology allowing access to platforms can be patented (and this is the case), each platform has an interest in developing its own technology, claiming that it is more efficient (essentially faster).
- Liquidity providers[17] have an interest in *fragmenting their quotes* to have access to as much liquidity consumers as possible. In fact, they even have an incentive to *duplicate their orders*, if they are "fast enough": if a market maker duplicates an order on two platforms, she increases the probability that a liquidity consumer, potentially connected to only one of the two platforms, will trade with her.

Fragmentation has been an essential consequence of the implementation of competition between exchanges via Reg NMS and MiFID.

An interesting anecdote is the way the attention of market participants focused on *Smart Order Routers* (SORs), because this component is the software incarnation of an "idealized intermediary"

---

before the fragmentation. Some exchanges already attempted to implement competition, like the London Stock Exchange proposing EuroSETS to trade stocks listed on the Amsterdam Exchange in 2004, but without the support of regulation it failed. Nevertheless, large dealing desks had to start to think about adapted practices to multiple listing.

[17]Liquidity providers are mainly market makers, but large orders of asset managers can provide liquidity too, especially on multilateral platforms.

between traders and exchanges. The term has been coined by MiFID 1 as an essential component ensuring fair competition; each broker had to design an SOR, associated with one (or several) "execution policy", explaining the mechanism implemented in its SOR. In short, the SOR receives an order to send to a trading venue; this order is described like a pre-fragmented era order (a side, a limit price[18] and a quantity), the mechanism inside the SOR decides to split it (or not) to send "child orders" to available trading venues according to an efficiency criterion.[19] Once that is done, the SOR has to take care of any message coming from venues where child orders have been sent to relay consistent information to the owner of the initial order. For instance a "fully filled" message coming from a venue where a child order has been sent is certainly not a "fully filled" message for the original order, but a "partial execution" message. This mapping is not trivial since every trading venue has its own terminology and detailed rules.

A SOR is somehow the "atomic intermediary" that allows its users to overlook the considerations of market fragmentation. The mechanics of the SOR implement an execution policy that is an "informal contract" between the user and the designer of the SOR: what is the list of trading venues eligible for child orders? What is the list of criteria to be used to split the initial order into child orders? And so on. Users pay fees to the designer of the SOR, which can be a broker, a trading venue, or a market maker. The broker sells the SOR as a market access service, the venue as an advantage compared to its competitors, as well as a way to propose Execution

---

[18]Even a liquidity consuming order can be considered having a limit price; in fact, every liquidity consumer should have a limit price. There is no reason for which a trader is ready to pay "any price" to obtain a transaction; there is always a maximum cost (that can be very high) he will not want to pay. A few years after fragmentation occurred, most liquidity consuming orders had a limit price. These orders cannot be strictly considered as "market order" (i.e., to be executed at any price) anymore; they are in practice "marketable limit orders".

[19]This criterion can, for instance, be: "expected average price", or "expected time to full execution", or "minimum exchange fees", etc.

Policies with certain advantages with respect to the venue itself, in exchange for discounted fees. The market maker sells the SOR as a way to propose its clients an additional service at a reduced cost while collecting more information about their flows and trading habits. Dealing desks of certain quantitative asset managers have developed their own SOR, which access trading venues via Direct Market Access.

SORs can be considered as the equivalent to the Google or Bing search engines: they reroute their user to the source of information that should have the highest value for him, while simultaneously allowing their designer to understand the habits of the user. Both a SOR and a search engine need to record and process the informational content of the venues it will route its users to. Much like internet search engines opened the door to *disintermediation* of many services (TV channels, newspapers, restaurants, etc.), SORs opened an era of disintermediation of certain market participants: the first ones being brokers who traditionally were considered to have a human expertise on order splitting; they now have to encode this knowledge into their SOR, and can be challenged by trading venues, market makers or even the more quantitative of their clients on this business. But the SOR has only been the first step towards a large mixing of roles: trading algorithms are more sophisticated pieces of software which can be developed by brokers' clients, away from brokers initial role as one-stop shop for all services of execution. The dislocation of these services is in progress; the dealing desk of an asset manager can partly develop its own algorithms, use the SOR of a trading venue and only use its brokers for DMA or certain specific services.

A standard optimization paradox. With electronification, the different ways to execute the instruction of an asset manager increased, and with software components like SOR and trading algorithms allowing for combinations in execution methods, the number of potential choices dramatically increased. As usual in such a case, increasing the degree of freedom of an optimization problem opens the door to better configurations, but the complexity of identifying the best one increases as well (see Figures 2.1 and 2.2 for

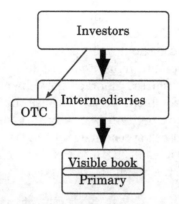

Figure 2.1: Before market fragmentation.

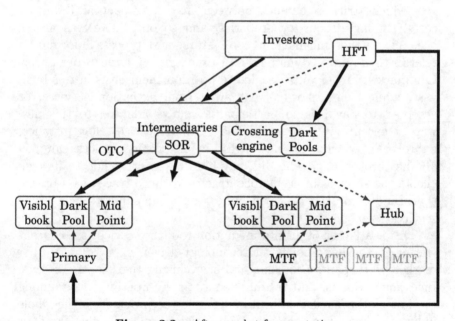

Figure 2.2: After market fragmentation.

two diagrams of the possible flows of orders before and after the fragmentation), and the cost of implementation can simultaneously increase. Nevertheless, should the cost end up increasing, market participants would tend to refuse to adopt such new paradigm. However, the opposite occurred; market participants ended up adapting to this new environment. Partly because the immediate outcome of this increase in competition is a very fast and large decrease in trading fees. The bid-ask spread itself of fragmented financial instruments decreased. As a result, both the explicit trading costs (the fees) and a large part of the implicit trading costs (the bid-ask spread) decreased.

Of course, this new environment demanded new skills and new types of equipment. It required hiring quantitative analysts specialized in market microstructure, in optimal execution (i.e., the field of financial mathematics dedicated to designing trading strategies which strike a balance between market impact and waiting costs), in high-frequency statistics, and so on. There was also a need for further means to record, store, and process information related to liquidity dynamics and execution of large orders. Certain market participants decided to position themselves in this business, while others slowly went away from execution services, or accepted to pay fees to participants who've adapted to this new way of execution as to make use of their services. For instance, a broker B_{old} who did not invest in electronic services can pay another broker B_{new} who did, pay him fees and provide to its own clients the services of this subcontractor with no trace of its brand; the brand of broker B_{old} will appear on all documents and online services.

This is a factor of disintermediation too: the services are concentrating in the hands of fewer technology-driven experts, and other market participants are using and customizing their tools. Brokers, Investment Banks, and trading venues are competing to be among the few platforms that will ultimately be the provider to the whole industry; much like Amazon Web Services and Google Cloud or Microsoft Azure are the main providers of cloud services and packaged Machine Learning and Artificial Intelligence services. Technology has the same effect in all industries: promoting disintermediation of traditional participants (if they do not adapt and invest) and concentrating the core services in a handful of providers. This move goes with a "commoditization" of these services, and a decrease of margins while the associated business goes from a customized "haute-couture-like" model to a mass market. Quantitative analysts have a role to play in this systematization of tools and in the design of customizable but easy to maintain services.

2.3.3 New participants

Indeed, existing participants had to change their business plan; invest towards being part of the small group of core service providers, or use the services of subcontractors. Electronification however introduced mainly two new kinds of participants: first, new trading venues; second, new market makers and proprietary trading firms — the HFT.

New trading venues had a competitive advantage over old historical Exchanges: they did not have to cope with the legacy of decades of IT architectures and relationships with clients. They designed mechanisms which were easy to code as well as to maintain, while their elders had to maintain some complex machinery put in place to respond to layers of client requests and regulators. Nevertheless, certain historical Exchanges invested to renew their infrastructure and to adapt to new behavior. As fixed costs of maintaining highly performing computing systems are considerable, one consequence of this competition has been a consolidation of trading venues under few holdings, with the preservation of a constellation of brands and specific mechanisms. For instance, the London Stock Exchange Group is made of its historical venue, the London Stock Exchange, Turquoise, one of the first European alternative trading venues, Borsa Italiana (the historical Italian Exchange), and MTS (a fixed income market). Euronext, which was originally the Paris Stock Exchange, has been separated from the New York Stock Exchange (the two historical exchanges had merged in 2007) since the former had been bought by InterContinental Exchange (ICE, a US-based alternative venue for Options), and is now made of the Amsterdam, Brussels, Dublin,

Lisbon, Paris, and Oslo historical exchanges, as well as of Bondmatch (an alternative venue for bonds).

It is interesting to follow the successive (stylized) steps of the developments that have been taken place with electronification and fragmentation:

1. Alternative trading venues offered a simplified one-size-fits-all suite of services.
2. Those venues needed liquidity providers to populate their platforms, hence they offered rebate to liquidity providers (i.e., to limit orders). The reasoning is simple: if liquidity is available on a platform at competitive prices with other venues, liquidity consumers with large enough orders will come to trade.
3. Market makers that have invested in technology and quantitative high-tech firms who implemented statistical arbitrage strategies converged towards fast strategies, based on a mix of statistics of order book dynamics (such as short-term mean reversion using sizes at first quantities) and market microstructure expertise (like "scalping", i.e., comparing the liquidity offered on different venues that, if one is fast enough, could almost surely generate profits). A collection of such firms, labeled with the generic HFT name, started to interact with order books, and discussing with trading venues to obtain a good knowledge of their trading rules and the way they have been implemented.
4. As soon as HFTs provide competitive quotes, brokers, via their SOR, immediately re-route liquidity consuming orders to the venue HFTs are populating. HFTs then started to gain traction in the world of trading and market-making.
5. To take into consideration as many events and information as possible, HFTs' algorithms continuously reassess their orders: they cancel or modify them very often. Trading venues and HFTs have to discuss how to align the CPU and memory consumption of the latter with the software and hardware capacity of the former.
6. This sudden increase in complexity (and a lack of understanding) frightened some participants, who suspected that the profit of HFTs was their loss.
7. As a reaction, certain trading platforms offered anonymity features, claiming it would reduce information leakage (birth of Dark Pools).

8. Trading venues provided internalization features, and brokers provided crossing capabilities.
9. High fixed costs and high competition conducted to mergers in all businesses: from brokers to trading venues, and even, some years later, HFTs themselves. Some mixing occurred between these business models; HFTs opened trading venues and bought brokers, trading venues now offer some basic execution services (which were ensured by brokers before), and so forth.

This sequence of events has been observed several times on equity markets and has the advantage to underline the way different intermediaries can compete and transform their offer dynamically. The crucial point is that *fragmentation is the opposite of concentration*, and the latter is meant to be good for price formation. To compensate the creation of new venues, and as a consequence, a decrease of the probability that a buyer meets a seller,[20] *new intermediaries collect liquidity on one venue as to bring it to another venue where the demand would be higher.* HTFs and SORs fill this role; as soon as HFTs make enough money with their trading strategy to provide liquidity transfer at a cheaper price than the fees asked to use a SOR, they operate an "intervenue liquidity arbitrage", a service highly appreciated by the rest of market participants.

Comparing the global cost of using a SOR, taking no risk and paying fees, to the global cost of having HFTs, who take on risks (but earn money on average) but ask for no fees, is a way to understand the essence of financial intermediation.

2.3.4 Reconfiguration of the playing field and potential disintermediation of brokers

The situation described in the previous section is unfavorable for intermediaries. Not only did they have to pay the connection fees to several trading places, but they also had to collect a lot of data and improve their order transmission techniques. Since everyone could create a market, intermediaries decided to create one by transforming some of their OTC trading into a Crossing Engine. They also

---

[20]If you keep the same number of participants, and some of them migrate from traditional venues to new venues, the probability for them to meet at the same venue decreases naturally.

attracted the flow by arguing with investors that their markets banished high-frequency operators, who at the time had a rather bad reputation. Their market share increased significantly to the point of competing with the specialists of trading places. The latter, seeing their margins shrink, invented a new concept, that of Dark Pools; an anonymous order book where the only visible information is the price Bid and Ask. HTFs found themselves embarrassed by the inability to apply their statistical learning methods to Dark Pools and created their own markets where investors could find their inventories. Intermediaries have followed the trend to transform their Crossing Engine into real Dark Pools often of the middle company: think about the yield curve; it is used internally by structurers to price fixed income products, it is used by traders to hedge the associated risk factors in the book of the company, it is used by market makers to make prices and by analysts to value assets, and so forth. Current technologies allow putting in place governance of such a yield curve model: what version, based on which data, it used by every team? Can the software codes be shared? Are the discrepancies between the operating versions identified and understood? etc. Once that is done, developing and offering a version of each feature used by the company to clients in a consistent way with what is done internally is not a big leap. This modularization has different effects, a very interesting one is that clients can choose to consume one service offered by one provider and the other service by another provider: each client can reassemble the collection of services it needs. It can be compared to a restaurant; first, the restaurant proposes a menu hoping to redirect as many clients as possible on the components of this menu and offer plates *à la carte* as a higher margin customized service. If clients can access all restaurant using an application on their smartphone, the designer of the application can recompose a specific menu on the fly for each client that will be the best proposal (especially if it observed a lot of "consuming flows"): the restaurant loses control over flagging a "one size fits all menu". Moreover, in a second step, the designer of the application could even compose a specific menu for each client that will cherry-pick each plate in a different restaurant. Restaurants will not compete as a "one-stop-shop" provider, but on each plate independently. They will lose the capability to manage their margins as a whole but will need to have margin management that will take the flow of consumers very explicitly into account.

Table 2.2: Electronic market development by asset class.

| | | % of trading volume | |
Current state	Products	2012	2015
Fully electronic	Cash equities	72	80
	Futures (eq US Treasury)	90	90
	CDS — index	69	80
	FX — spot	55	70
Significantly electronic	US Treasuries	52	70
	European government bonds	45	60
	Precious metals	40	60
	FX — forwards	40	55
	Agencies	40	50
	Covered bonds	40	50
	FX — options	35	55
	Short-term interest rate trading	30	50
	FX — swaps	30	40
Becoming electronic	Repos	25	50
	Standardized interest rate swaps (IRS)	20	70
	Investment grade v cash	15	40
Largely voice	CDS — single name	10	45
	High yield — cash	10	25
	Bespoke IRS	5	5
	Structured rates/credit	5	5

Source: McKinsey.

Financial markets are going slowly in this direction. The current stage is the formation of large platforms; it is an investment that will be rewarded one way or the other. First having model governance (in this modern sense) in place is useful, even for companies that will mostly consume the services provided by their subcontractors. It allows understanding what is needed, what are the expected features and allows us to evaluate the level of service and the real added value by each subcontractor.

Brokers are at the center of this platformization trend; if they achieve to keep their historical position, they could be the backbones of all the platforms that, for instance, Investment Banks and Asset Managers are putting in place. As shown in Table 2.2, The structural difficulty they are facing is that they are just finishing a cycle of investments corresponding to the electronification of Equity markets, and they are at the start of the investments needed to answer to the electronification of Fixed Income markets (hopefully, if they designed their equity platform smartly enough, they should be able to leverage them in the scope of the electronification of Fixed Income products). Moreover, as brokers are close to idealized intermediaries, they took the habit to make light investments, to be able to adapt to natural cycles of high and low turnovers on markets;[21] they usually tried to have a very light base of fixed cost to be able to face low turnover periods. It may be the occasion to make diversifying partnerships to invest in platform-driven projects, but it is a very new way to manage their business model.

2.3.5   Algorithmic trading

This section aims to give some generic properties of algorithmic trading needed to understand its role in intermediation and the way it could be understood as the first step towards further automation everywhere in the financial system. After all, a transaction is an atomic risk transfer event: when a market participant trades with another one, it incurs a transfer of the risk of holding the position accordingly. The new owner can welcome this new risk exposure, whereas its former owners wanted to part with such risk. For instance, should the new owner have the exact opposite risk exposure, this transaction can be a way to cancel it. Another configuration would be that she is building a diversified portfolio of exposures so that the central limit theorem reduces the idiosyncratic risks and the remaining one (i.e., the systematic risk) can be easily hedged using a Future contract. This is the way risks are traded, aggregated, disaggregated, cut into pieces and traded separately;[22] it is at the center of an understanding of the financial system as a network of intermediaries, which is a very useful understanding for quantitative analysts. Trading is the way dismantled risk circulates in the network of market participants, up to a point it reaches a natural buyer or seller in the real world.

---

[21]Keep in mind that brokers are primarily making money thanks to fees: less trading on markets mechanically implies less revenues for them.
[22]This is exactly the purpose of risk replication: trade the coefficients of the Taylor extension of a nonlinear payoff.

The term *Algorithmic trading* describes a collection of methods to design "automated trading softwares". The main role of these softwares is to take care of a trading process, *once a decision to buy or sell has been taken.* Typically, they emulate the role of brokers receiving instructions to buy or sell a large amount of financial instruments from a client: how to spread this large order, how to split it in child orders to fulfill the objective of the client, what is the nature of the flow consuming and providing liquidity? These questions have been addressed in academic papers since the late 1990s, however the approaches derived from these initial publications are still not widely used in the financial industry. This field continues to be active today, and now covers "Program Trading" and Market Making as well. The field is now advanced enough to feature textbooks that describe the underlying theory while also giving tips and tricks. The basis of the theory of Algorithmic Trading, referred to as *optimal trading*, is about finding the balance between two main components of a utility function

(1) On the one hand, the faster you trade, the more pressure you put on the price which moves in a detrimental way (if you buy the price will go up and if you sell the price will go down); hence, you are penalized by trading fast.
(2) On the other hand, the slower you trade, the further away the price will be from your decision price. This gives you an incentive to trade fast.

These opposite forces naturally give birth to an optimization problem. The way the algorithm controls the trading process is through the trading speed. Different variations of the initial mean-variance optimization have been introduced, such as:

• Nonlinear optimization to account for specific shapes of market impact (i.e., the effect of the price pressure).
• Dynamic, i.e., stochastic, optimization.
• Replacing the speed of trading as control variable, to more direct actuators, like the prices of limit and market orders, or the quotes for a market maker in a bilateral trading system.
• Portfolio trading, taking into account correlations between tradable instruments to hedge on the fly the remaining risk of the traded basket.

- Specific price dynamics, such as introducing mean reversion.
- Taking fragmentation into account, for instance replacing a single trading speed by a vector of trading speed, every coordinate being associated with a specific trading venue.
- Exploiting "trading signals", i.e., short-term predictors of the price, generally based on instantaneous liquidity provision imbalances and short-term liquidity consumption imbalances.
- Last but not least, game theory has been introduced in some framework to account for the anticipated effects of other traders.

Building a suite of trading algorithms that can be used by internal traders and that are offered to clients is an industrial project. It needs a proper recording, storage and processing of market data at high frequency, and of all executed orders. Nowadays, certain engineers and researchers introduce machine learning (a.k.a. Artificial Intelligence) in these algorithms, either to build trading signals, or to solve the associated optimization problem when its dimension is too high for traditional solvers. Engineering such an offer can be considered as building an "execution platform", with associated model and data governances.

Algorithms are executing most of the orders in Equity markets, on Future markets, but their market share on Fixed Income markets is only beginning to raise. High touch traders use algorithms themselves and low touch trading is nothing else than algorithmic trading, including SOR and DMA.

Users of trading algorithms put pressure towards common terminology amongst algorithms providers (i.e., mainly brokers). Essentially, the algorithms are classified according to the nature of the utility function they optimize. It is usually named the *Benchmark* of the trading algorithm. Below is a list of them:

- *Percentage of Volume* (PoV). This is an instruction to follow the volume of other market participants, in real-time.
- VWAP and TWAP, i.e., Volume Weighted Average Price follow the volume that is "usually traded" on a specific day[23] and Time

---

[23]VWAP can be continuously converted into PoV, since if VWAP focuses on "expected trading volume" for today and its prediction for traded volume is perfect, it is a PoV.

Weighted Average Price is a simple linear weighting of the price with elapsed time).

- Implementation Shortfall and Target Close, which are meant to overperform either the entry price of a large order, or the closing price of the day. It is, of course, impossible to guarantee to overperform either the entry price or the close price, but giving this instruction as a benchmark leads to a peg in the aggressiveness of the algorithm on the distance to the entry price or to the closing price.
- Liquidity seeking algorithms chase liquidity on more than one trading platform, they are more sophisticated than SORs. SORs are fully described by their "execution policy", while Liquidity Seekers often include machine learning features, in attempts to estimate in real-time the liquidity available on each platform.[24]
- Other very short-term algorithms, which could be called "trading robots", encode deterministic behaviors. These include for instance, "at close" orders, orders that can be entered in the matching engine anytime during the day, but which will only be activated for the closing auction. Such orders are generally not available on all trading venues. A broker can easily code this kind of order in its EMS and offer it to its clients. Thanks to these small robots, the broker is covering all the trading venues with a "protective layer" that makes them look similar to one another, as to ease the day to day life of its clients. This is a very simple and straightforward function of intermediation between clients and exchanges, associated with a very simple risk transfer: the operational risk that the system of the broker may encounter a bug and as a consequence, the order not participating in the closing auction.
- All these algorithms and robots can be combined conditionally to the market context in the following fashion *start with a VWAP and switch to PoV if the market volume is more than 2 times the ADV.*
- PT algorithms are dedicated to portfolio trading. They take care of synchronization of the portfolio's lines, taking into account their correlations in the computation of the market risk associated with

---

[24]Online liquidity estimation is easier for algorithms of brokers which have a lot of clients as they can aggregate (in an anonymous way) all the attempts to consume liquidity on a lot of platforms. The more often trading venues are "scanned" by algorithms of the broker, the more reliable are its liquidity estimates.

the fraction of the order not executed. Moreover, PT has synchronization features making sure that at any point in time of the execution, the remaining portfolio keeps, for instance, its cash exposure or its market exposure (or the beta with respect to a well-defined risk factor).

These "benchmarks" are easy to understand, and can be immediately associated with a specific requirement. For instance, keeping a cash exposure of a portfolio can be useful for a long-only fund with a very low cash pocket, or targeting the close is adapted to synchronize positions during index rebalancing days. Some benchmarks reflect users' beliefs in what will occur during the execution: PoV can be appropriate if a trader knows he has to trade a given stock on a day during which news impacting it are meant to be reported, with the trader being unaware of the outcome of the news. The PoV will follow the other market participants' rhythm, probably with a very slow trading speed before the issuance of the news, to then accelerate right after it is known. It can be considered as a way to "follow the liquidity" of the stock in real time. Nevertheless, it is also dangerous as it can contribute to a "snowball effect", or a "hot potato game" which can be very detrimental to the price formation process, like during the May 2010 Flash Crash on US Equity markets.

This list of benchmarks can be split into two categories: short-duration ones, that in some way ease the day to day life of human traders in an electronic (and hence high frequency) environment (Liquidity seekers, trading robots and Implementation Shortfalls are, for instance, in such category); and long-duration ones, which are more concerned with taking care of "market timing" at the scale of the decisions of asset managers. Almost all the trading algorithms can have a very long duration version of themselves; it makes sense to consider an Implementation Shortfall, a VWAP or a Liquidity Seeker over days, or even weeks to trade illiquid instruments or very large positions.[25]

The mechanisms driving a trading algorithm clearly have two layers: a strategic layer, taking care of the medium term balance between market risk and market impact, and a tactical layer, using some degree of freedom given by the strategic layer to take profit

---

[25]It took weeks to unwind Jerome Kerviel's positions.

from prices or liquidity opportunities. The parameters tuning the behavior of a trading algorithm are hence of two kinds: long term ones, driving the strategic layer (like a generic level of aggressiveness, some liquidity and prices limit to be respected over the life of the whole execution) and short-term ones driving the tactical layer (like the list of venues to consider, the way to interact with the order book — typically fraction of liquidity consuming orders, dynamic limits taking correlated instruments into account, and so on).

Trading algorithms are designed by dealing desks of asset managers when they are sophisticated enough, by investment banks for hedging purposes, or by brokers to be used internally by their sales traders or by clients. Brokers are the largest providers of trading algorithms; their clients pay fees to access to these algorithms via a remote interface. These algorithms are a "best effort"; the brokers are not guaranteeing any prices, it is instead the responsibility of the user to fine-tune the parameters of the algorithm to obtain a good average price at the end of the day. If a client wants a guaranteed price, he should rather go to a market maker or a "prime broker" with a Central Risk Book (CRB) (see Section 2.2.2 for more details about CRB).

Pre- and post-trade analysis, TCA consultancy. The fact that the user is in charge of taking adequate "meta decisions", such as the choice of the algorithm benchmark and the tuning of the parameters, puts the emphasis on Transaction Cost Analysis as well as pre- and post-trade analysis. Section 2.2.2 already exposed the main principles of pre- and post-trade analysis and of the logic beyond TCA:

- Pre-trade analysis is a way to share an understanding of the list of large orders to be executed sent by a client. It allows to obtain advice about which benchmark to use for each of them.
- Post-trade analysis is a way to check that the *ex-ante* expectations have been met.
- TCA is a regular review of the quality of the obtained execution conducted by the dealing desks of asset managers to rank their providers (and in particular their brokers). Transaction Costs Analysis is also conducted in the scope of the continuous improvement of decisions taken by the dealing desk.

TCA started to be formalized (especially in academic papers) in the early nineties, whereas algorithmic trading started in the late nineties. The way these two domains are connected follows the very wide principle stated in the forties by the French Institute of Statistics (INSEE): *compter pour comprendre, comprendre pour agir* (i.e., "count to understand, understand to act"). TCA is the "count" part of this mantra, whereas algorithmic trading is the "act" part of it. The "understanding" of the efficiency of a trading process is a never-ending one: all market participants are exploring it and are sharing part of their knowledge, either during private meetings, during industry conferences, or thanks to the intermediation of academic publications. Brokers developed consultancy services to help their clients fine-tune the execution services they offer. This is of course not a naive offer: in a world where execution is becoming a commodity, having a high-level consultancy service develops "stickiness" of clients.

2.3.6   Market microstructure

Market microstructure is the academic field covering phenomena discovered once you go further than considering financial markets as a place where sellers are corporates issuing shares and bonds, and buyers are asset managers. Understanding how financial markets work needs to take into account intermediaries and hence to understand the relationships between them. One step further in this direction comes the need to consider the "financial system" as a whole; and in modern markets, the simplest way to identify the different roles and relations is to put the emphasis on *intermediation*. It is exactly the purpose of this book, with a focus on what can be useful for quantitative analysts, or "quants". Market microstructure is thus of importance for this book; nevertheless, we will put the emphasis on some macroscopic aspects, refereeing to another book, Lehalle and Laruelle (2018), for details.

The previous chapter and previous sections already describe the market participants and how they fulfill intermediation roles, and especially how they intermediate risk. The following chapters will continue to elaborate in this direction. As far as microstructure is concerned, the focus comes to the way the structure and the rules of markets influence price formation. Intermediation practices most certainly also have an important influence on price dynamics. The next section thus deals with price formation. As a consequence, it is enough to list there why and how each participant has to worry about market microstructure.

- Brokers (the agency sell side) are probably market participants that are, with regulators, confronted the more to market microstructure. The part that they are focusing on is the influence of trading rules (such as the *tick size* or fee schedules) on price formation, but more than that, on liquidity formation. Their position puts them in a situation to explain to other market participants what are the expected consequences of new features as the access to a trading venue is needed to be a member of this venue, and members of the venues are essentially brokers and market makers. They incorporate their knowledge of microstructure in their trading practices and in their trading algorithms. They give advice using their understanding of microstructure via their execution services. Some of them publish reports, similar to analysts' research, on microstructure, since this is a natural way for brokers to disseminate their knowledge to their clients.
- Market Makers are of course following closely evolutions in market microstructure, since a change of rules can demand adaptation of their liquidity providing strategies. High-frequency market makers are very sensitive to evolution of trading rules and regulation because if they misunderstand a point, the error they can make will be reproduced thousands of times, i.e., at high frequency, during the day, and can thus end up incurring large losses or lawsuits.[26] Market makers also partly shape market microstructure, since they are in some markets the main liquidity providers. In bilateral trading, they issue the rules that have to be followed by market participants, and in this respect, they have a similar position to trading venues.
- Market operators and vendors have different positions towards microstructure.

---

[26]The penalty of 5 million Euros handled down by the French authority, the AMF, is a good example of how a misunderstood rule could have large consequences for HFT.

Exchanges and other trading venues are in fact *part of the micro-structure*; their rulebooks (i.e., the rules that have to be fulfilled by their members) are the atomic elements of market microstructure: the tick size (i.e., the minimum allowed price change between two consecutive prices), the fees, the mechanisms of auctions, the sequences of priority of liquidity providing orders waiting for a liquidity consumer, trading hours, and so on. All these fundamental elements of microstructure are written by Exchanges and trading venues. If each one of them is writing its own rulebook, the conjunction of all their rules is the outcome of the way they compete,[27] nobody really controls it except regulators.

On their side, technology vendors try to follow (and sometimes anticipate) the evolution of market microstructure to update their offer. For instance, "best execution proofs" demanded some evolution in OMS and EMS.

- Regulators are the gatekeepers of the integrity of market microstructure, or at least they try to demand, accept and refuse changes so that price formation occurs in a smooth and orderly fashion. They are themselves affected by (unexpected) microstructure changes, such as how the emergence of high-frequency trading demanded that they learn how to monitor, store and process terabytes of data, whereas they formerly had top deals with small databases and simple monitoring tasks.

- Asset Managers (the buy-side) are primarily concerned with liquidity. Their investment decision has to take into account the liquidity premium of tradable instruments they are buying and selling. As a consequence, if they are not aware that an instrument is now more liquid, or that another instrument is less liquid, they will take bad decisions, or a least their decision will cost them more than expected, impacting the revenues of their investment vehicles. Their dealing desks are continuously speaking with their brokers as to be well informed. Moreover, asset managers contribute to the public debate; for instance, when BlackRock published in 2014 white papers on the importance of standardization of corporate

---

[27]The "tick size war" during June 2009 in Europe is a typical outcome of such a competition.

bonds and suggested changes in the way these instruments could be traded, pushing towards more electronification.

- Investment Banks are impacted by the cost of trading to hedge their exposure to different risk factors. The more frequently the hedge and the more factors they neutralize, the more they trade. They are informed on the impact of microstructure changes via their brokers or one of their subsidiary that is a brokerage company.

  They are specifically concerned by macro-prudential rules (see Section 1.7), that are in fact part of market microstructure. If the capital requirement of Investment Banks increases, they will have to trade more, in some specific (risky) directions; this will mechanically put pressure on liquidity in these directions.

- Structurers are essentially impacted by the rules governing the issuance of financial products, and the requirements for the distribution of these products. 3 elaborates in this direction, listing, for instance, some consequences of the PRIIPS European directive on structurers' business.

All market participants are impacted by market microstructure, and most of them influence the microstructure themselves. Either because they are fixing some of its rules (like trading venues), or because their flows are large enough to modify trading habits (like Investment Banks). Since they provide access to trading, brokers, in particular, inform other market participants of the expected evolution of the microstructure, and on possible consequences. Regulators monitor the outcome of this large corpus of rules and habits, and take decisions to level the playing field, to ensure that there aren't too many negative externalities or that no participants are paying unfair costs. Their main objective is that the resulting prices dynamics are correctly informing on the value of financial instruments and goods.

2.4 Basics of the Price Formation Process

We have seen in Section 1.6, that price moves are mainly due to information and flows. In brief: on the one hand, new information affects the future value of assets, and tradable instruments' payoffs are linked to the value of underlying assets at maturity; on the other hand, flows generate a pressure on the balance between offer and demand that changes the price of tradable instruments offered for trading.

Intermediaries are affected by, and contribute to price movements. Since intermediaries are buying and selling risk exposures, and because they are aggregating and splitting risks according to their business model and their capabilities, it is expected that their influence on prices is *natural*. That is, it is expected that the way price pressure follows intermediaries' flows increase the price of crowded risk factors, while decreasing the price of neglected ones. Moreover, as it is easier to intermediate a risk factor while its price does not change, it is expected that the faster an intermediary is able to find a counterparty to unwind a position, the cheaper it values its role as an intermediary, and hence the cheaper the liquidity provided by this intermediary is.

The example of market makers. Market makers provide very simple examples of this relationship between price moves and the value of liquidity. Making the market on an instrument which price does not change is not a difficult task: if the fair price is at $10, a market maker can provide quotes at $9 and $11. As soon as a buyer enters the market, it will buy at $11 and when, after a while, a seller will come, it will sell at $9. Making such a market with bid and ask quotes at $9–11 is lucrative because each couple of transactions will bring a reward of $2. Nevertheless, different events can change this idealized configuration where the role of the market maker is simply to synchronize buyers and sellers, who, otherwise, will never match (especially if the time between two arrivals is long):

- The balance between buyers and sellers can be biased: instead of having balanced sequences of buyers and sellers coming to the market makers, a large number of participants in only one direction may come to her. Say, for instance, that only buyers are coming such that the market maker accumulates a short inventory of 15 times the average trade size.

  In such a configuration, the market maker will have to hedge herself now short directional position. The easiest way to do so is to buy the instrument, but as this market is not liquid enough to operate without a market maker, it is impossible. Another way is to find a positively correlated instrument and to buy it (or a negatively correlated instrument and the sell it). This will *propagate the price pressure of the market makers' clients to correlated instruments in a natural way.* In any case, the market maker will lose money while she is hedging her short inventory; a good practice is hence to anticipate such one-sided flows, i.e., to "predict" short-term flows. A market maker equipped with such a predictor will adjust its quotes on the side of the flow: if a large number of buyers (respective sellers) is anticipated, the market maker will adjust its quotes to a higher ask price (resp., a lower bid price).

• Another possible issue is that the market maker has a small inventory, for instance, a long inventory of two average trade size, then information is disclosed that changes the value of the traded instrument. If it is "good news" for the company that issued the instrument, the market maker will have to make profits; if it is "bad news" for the company, the market maker will have to make losses.

Every market maker tries to anticipate price changes, to "predict" future price moves, which can be due to information. In any case, to protect herself against such sudden price moves, the market maker can rely on the volatility of the prices. The volatility, being a proxy to uncertainty in the price formation, it is exactly reflecting the probability that an unexpected price move leads to losses for the market maker. To compensate these potential losses, she will ask for more potential profits (made of the bid-ask spread): volatile instruments will have a larger bid-ask spread, and hence have a higher liquidity cost.

This simple example shows that intermediaries will propagate their expectations to the cost of liquidity: the more uncertain, the higher costs for both buyers and sellers; the more pressure on one side, the higher costs for participants coming to trade this side. Other parameters affect the cost of liquidity, such as the average time between the arrival of traders: the smaller this inter-trade time is, the lower the cost of liquidity; simply because the market maker expects to be able to unwind her position sooner.

Another lesson from this example is that price pressure and information propagate to the correlated instrument via intermediaries, due to their natural hedging practices. A chain of intermediaries can hence be formed when a market maker on an instrument hedges her position using another instrument, where another market maker will have to face this flow. Either this second market maker will have an opposite inventory, and he will absorb this flow, or he will, in turn, be exposed to a large imbalance of inventory, and propagate it via its own hedging process until the risk exposure finds a natural counterparty.

The third message of this example is that intermediaries try to build predictors of information and flows, and in any case, they try to be aware of new information and incoming price pressures as soon as possible.

2.4.1 When information moves prices

Section 1.6.1 already discussed the way information could (and should) move prices. First of all, "information" on the real economy is one of the key elements that changes the value of assets. If a medical company just invented a new drug and patented it; it will make more profits and hence the value of one share of its Equity will see its value increase accordingly to the anticipated success of this drug. If it will need 1 year to put the drug on the market, some uncertainty may be associated with waiting for this time to come (will the company makes the right decisions to achieve its goal of launching the drug in production in 1 year? will its competitors discover a molecule having the same effects? and so on); a discount rate then has to be applied to adjust the anticipated value of this new asset so that it can be taken into account today. Nevertheless, this news will influence the price of its Equity shares, and probably its future access to capital in a favorable way. It may also influence the price of the shares of its competitors in the opposite direction. It is not always as simple; say that a company manufactures products in plastic and the price of crude oil increases because of a pipeline issue somewhere around the globe. If this company has already bought a financial product protecting it, at least partially, against crude oil upward price moves, this company will not be that affected. But if it did not, the price of its Equity shares will be affected in a negative way. It is hence needed to have a good understanding of the balance sheet of the company (has it bought financial products? does it have reserves of plastics? and so on) to be able to draw a conclusion from the news. Nevertheless, information has the capability to move prices; some news influence the idiosyncratic part of price movements (if the news is very specific to a company), others instead influence, at least partly, the systematic part of price moves (if it affects an industrial sector, for instance).

A quantitative analyst will easily observe that news is affecting traded volumes and volatility of prices, but the direction of the associated price move is rarely straightforward to guess without reading and understanding the content of the news. Progresses made in the mid 2010s in Natural Language Processing (NLP) help to associate an expected direction to news as soon as it is issued, but it is a painful exercise. Some technology vendors developed expertise in NLP and are selling pre-processed news feed, tagged with a "sentiment score", taking values between -1 and 1. A quantitative analyst will also note that the influence of news on traded volumes and volatility follows the correlations structure of tradable instruments: highly correlated instruments are all submitted to these increases of trading activity.

An example of pure information and surprise. On January 8, 2008, the French President Nicolas Sarkozy announced during a speech that advertisements were to be banned from public TV channels.[28] Nobody expected the French President to make such an announcement, which was not discussed with stakeholders and was not on the agenda of the French government. It had been a very interesting "experiment": new and unexpected information, during trading hours (around 10:35 am Paris time).

The straightforward anticipation is that private French TV channels will get more revenues from advertisements, since companies will spare the budget that they were currently allocating to public channels, and they will try to keep a good coverage of their products. Hence, the price of one Equity share of the first TV channel (TF1) immediately jumps upward. Figure 2.3 shows its price move, along with the traded volumes and an intraday estimate of the volatility.[29] The increase of volatility is a natural consequence of price moves,

---

[28]In France, a part of TV channels are public institutions, in an effort to guarantee some diversity and culture in the programs. They are partly financed by taxes. The idea supported by President Sarkozy was that they should be fully financed by taxes to be sure they cannot be influenced by lobbies.

[29]The Garman–Klass estimate of volatility is used with 1 min time bins.

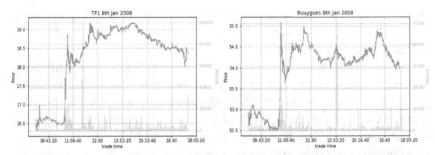

Figure 2.3: Intra day price change on news. Here the president Sarkozy (France, 2008) unexpectedly announced that the advertising will be banned from the public TV channels; the value of the private TV channels changed immediately. Propagation by correlations: the same day Bouygues price moved in a similar way.

it mainly gives a measure of the intensity of the slope of price movements. It is clear on the chart that traded volumes are synchronous with price moves; the price is moved by liquidity consumers who are dynamically adjusting their estimate of the future profit of TF1, with a discount rate corresponding to an unknown exact date for the entry into force of this decision. It seems that the consensus went first to €18 for one share, before stabilizing around €19. The main price jumps came with high traded volumes. During price oscillations, it is obvious that some market participants obtained inefficient prices: just after the main jump, some buyers bought at much higher prices compared to what they could have obtained a few minutes later, and after a while, buyers and sellers could have been both frustrated. These oscillations are clearly not efficient. Price jumps have not been large enough to trigger the *circuit breakers* that are in place on trading venues. To avoid these inefficient oscillations after large price jumps, circuit breakers halt trading, wait few minutes, and reopen with a call auction. Call auctions avoid these large price fluctuations: all traders contributing to the price formation during a few minutes have the exact same price.

Propagation via correlations. Simultaneously, the price of an Equity share of Bouygues exhibited the same kind of jump, but with a smaller amplitude. It is clear in Figure 2.3 that price–volume patterns are similar for TF1 and Bouygues. The explanation is as simple for a fundamental analyst as for a quantitative analyst: the former will notice that Bouygues owns a lot of shares of TF1, hence when the price of TF1 appreciates, the one of Bouygues follows mechanically; the latter will rather observe that price moves of TF1 and Bouygues are usually correlated. The mechanism of propagation could either be buyers having the same analysis on TF1 and Bouygues, and buying the two stocks in adequate proportions; or it could also be that market makers are "hit" on TF1 and use Bouygues to hedge their overly short position. In such a case, intermediaries propagate price movements in an "efficient direction": when TF1's price goes up, Bouygues' one follows, and it has a fundamental explanation.

Propagation of price moves along correlations is very common in financial markets, the exact way it occurs is not always clear; it can be via natural buyers or sellers, or via intermediaries, such as in the explanation of the TF1 — Bouygues example.

Zooming out: Long-term sectorial effects. However, when zooming out on a daily scale, the observed price changes are not resilient: the price of TF1's stock was, in fact, decreasing during the month of January 2008. Figure 2.4 shows how TF1's prices followed the media sector for a while, which had been bearish in 2008 as the start of the financial crisis affected advertisement budgets very early on. In the long run, this sectorial effect dominates the instantaneous impact of the news.

Again, the sectorial effect influenced TF1's price several ways: fundamental analysts' anticipation of revenues due to advertisement decreased, and market maker or other intermediaries hedged the downward price moves on the European media Futures by selling baskets of its components, including TF1.

This example illustrates several facts of price formation; when a piece of information hits an isolated company, the price of its stock changes in the following way:

1. It changes almost immediately, with large volumes, oscillating to reach the new "fair value" of the stock.
2. The prices of related (i.e., correlated) companies move as well.
3. Sectorial moves generally dominate the price movements of its components, which are slowly following it.

If information simultaneously affects a large number of stocks, for instance, a whole sector, the sector "moves first", especially if Future

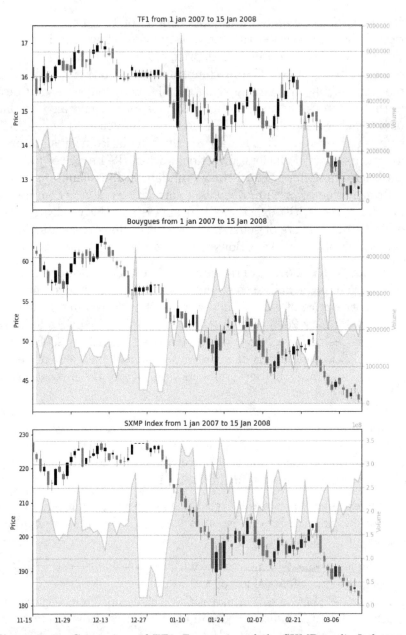

Figure 2.4: Comparison of TF1, Bouygues and the SXMP media Index at a daily time scale.

contracts are available. Futures are generally "cheaper to buy" than individual stocks: their bid-ask spread is smaller than the ones of the components of the equivalent basket. Hence, certain market participants will tend to first directly adjust their position on the Future, and some other market participants are simply using the Future to hedge their evolving positions driven by coherent price moves all over the sector. Once again, this illustrates how intermediaries are contributing to form prices thanks to the way they intermediate risk. Without any risk limit, a market maker would never propagate the imbalance of flows "hitting" it. It is because they need to hedge the imbalanced positions that intermediaries propagate in a consistent way; i.e., along with the correlations between tradable instruments.

2.4.2 When market makers can read information

The previous examples insisted on the fact that market makers act as liquidity providers. All the given explanations of price formation have been based on the "old view" that market makers are providing liquidity and other participants are consuming liquidity. It is mainly true for bilateral trading since the relationship between both sides[30] is asymmetric: the participant who asks for a quotation will consume liquidity, whereas the one who answers will provide liquidity to him. Nevertheless, the roles become ambiguous as soon as trading is hosted by limit order books; in such trading venues, everyone can send limit orders that will provide liquidity.[31] Providing liquidity is meant to be cheaper than consuming liquidity; for one, when a limit order is executed, it "spares" the bid-ask spread, since to be executed at the exact same time with a liquidity consuming order (i.e., a market order or a marketable limit order), one would have to "cross the spread". But it is more complex than that because adverse selection is "paid" by limit orders; given that a limit order is executed when the price is going into its direction (i.e., down for a selling limit order and up for a buying limit order), what if the limit order would be been canceled just before its execution and reinserted few cents further away from

---

[30]To understand price formation, knowing who buys and who sells is not enough, it is also needed to understand who provides who consumes liquidity.

[31]Brokers often claim that more than half of the child orders of their trading algorithms provided liquidity.

the last traded price? There are good chances that its owner could
have obtained a better price. Measuring this "hypothetical gain", and
labeling it as adverse selection is a common practice among market
makers, to understand if they do not provide overly cheap liquidity.
Moreover, academic studies conducted by the French regulator (who
have access to a lot of information about owners of the orders), have
shown that modern market makers (i.e., high-frequency ones), are
far from acting solely as liquidity providers. They consume liquidity
as well, probably to hedge their inventory or to take profit from flow-
driven opportunities.

The way prices form in case of unexpected idiosyncratic information can be observed when such information is disclosed during an
order book-driven trading session. Intraday Earning announcements
are perfect configurations of this kind of event. Figure 2.5 shows two
days during which, on two different stocks (Ericsson and Nokia),
earning announcements have been delivered. Reading the news publicly released just after the announcements, it can be seen that the
information on Ericsson the REF:DAY was very easy to understand,
while the information on Nokia the REF:DAY was far more complex.
As a consequence, price dynamics were very different:

- When the news release was easy to read (even by a computer),
  Figure 2.5 shows that prices primarily moved because liquidity
  providers adjusted their quotes.

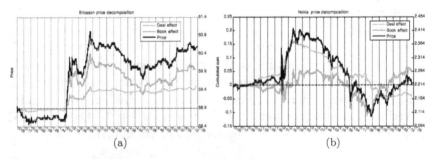

(a)   (b)

Figure 2.5: Thanks to the decomposition of price moves in two components;
driven by liquidity consumption or driven by liquidity provision, one can make
the difference between two configurations. (a) Decomposition of intraday price
moves of Ericsson the REF:DAY? (b) Decomposition of intraday price moves of
Nokia the REF:DAY?

- While when the news was difficult to understand, Figure 2.5(b) shows that, not only did the price oscillate more (it seems that analysts did not transpose the consequences of this news on Nokia's Equity value very easily), but the price moves were also driven by liquidity consumption.[32]

The exact way information influences liquidity providing orders, hence market participants acting as market makers, has evolved a lot with the availability of computing power;[33] the consequences are that it is needed to reconsider the "old way" of thinking about the role of liquidity consumers and liquidity providers in the market. While liquidity consumer are meant to detain a privileged information showing their understanding about stocks behaviour, liquidity providers are exposed to adverse selection because they cannot process information. They however protect themselves by inferring information from trading flows. Nowadays high-tech liquidity providers can take a lot of fundamental information into account, from texts to balance sheets of the companies (that have for long been available in an electronic format). One of the consequences is that prices can "move" solely because liquidity providers understand fundamental information, cancel their quotes to reinsert them at the adequate (i.e., "information aware") new price. It is no more needed for liquidity consumers to exercise pressure on the quotes, provoking adverse selection on the liquidity providers so that once this price pressure is detected by the latter as a proxy of information, quotes are finally canceled and both sides (liquidity providers and consumers) reach an agreement on a new price.

2.4.3 When flows are moving prices

The previous subsection underlined that prices can move due to an early understanding of new information by liquidity providers, because liquidity consumers exercise a price pressure on quotes so that this information is first incorporated in trading flows, and

---

[32]The exact way to split price move into liquidity provision and liquidity consumption parts are described in detail in REF:Besson:L.

[33]The level of linguistic complexity of "a text that is easy to read with a computer" is changing each year thanks to progress in Natural Language Processing.

only in a second step, in price levels. But there are also examples
of flows moving the prices without any new information. A very
good illustration of this phenomenon is the unwinding of Jérome
Kerviel's position by Société Générale Investment Bank. In January
2008, SocGen discovered that this rogue trader had accumulated a
huge position, essentially in Future contracts on European indexes
(REF:find:numbers) that was not only far beyond authorized limits,
but which was also at a terrible loss. The bank had no other solution
than liquidating this position, mixing over the counter blocks and
executing on trading venues.

This is important to understand that this huge collection of very
large sell orders on European equities (directly or via Future contracts), had no fundamental reason: SocGen's traders were not motivated by following new information, they just had, because of this
very rare configuration of a rogue trader, a large position to liquidate,
using as many means as possible to find market participants to sell to,
and fearing information leakage. Figure 2.6 shows the impact of this
liquidation on price formation: this non-informative selling pressure
clearly moved the prices down with a simultaneous increase of traded

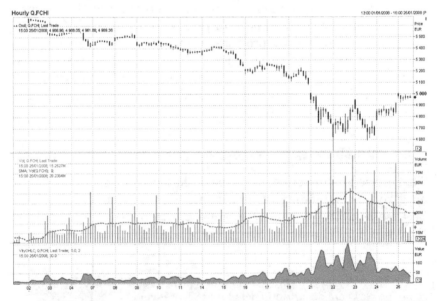

Figure 2.6: Market impact generated by the unwind of Jerome Kerviel's
position.

volumes and volatility. It is remarkable to witness two main downward moves of European prices, probably because SocGen's traders waited for the prices to *relax* a little bit before exercising, two days later, further selling pressure on them. It is also interesting to observe that prices seemed relaxed back to their initial levels a few days after this exceptional pressure.

Summary of an example of price dynamics. Up to this point, a few different configurations of price moves have been illustrated by examples:

- The "French private TV channel" example illustrated that information moves prices, not always in a very straightforward way, since fundamental analysts need time to adjust their estimates of the long-term value of tradable instruments consecutive to the new information. It has shown that information "follows" correlations: it propagates price movements to related instruments. Moreover, price moves are not driven only by idiosyncratic news; systematic ones (such as the health of sectors, countries, etc.), are contributing to prices in a similar fashion.
- The "Nokia and Ericsson" examples illustrated that there is not a simple separation between, on the one hand, liquidity consumers who process and understand fundamental information, and on the other hand, liquidity providers who are exposed to adverse selection and use their private observation of flows to attempt to avoid it. Nowadays all participants exploit all the possible information: fundamentals and flows can be processed by anyone who invests in the adequate skills and technologies.
- The "Jérome Kerviel" example illustrated that buying or selling pressure can, on its own, move prices. It gave the occasion to observe how prices relax after this kind of not informative pressure.

Explaining these phenomena gave occasions to explain how intermediaries take part in price formation: their hedging practices contribute to propagating price moves to correlated instruments. The more active[34] they are, the more consistent prices are.

---

[34]Their activity is driven by a lot of parameters like transaction costs: the more expensive, the less they trade.

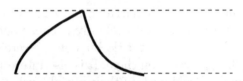

Figure 2.7:   The way market impact impacts the price: first prices are moving up a quasi-linear way, but after a while, it starts to be more difficult to push prices that are reacting in a concave way. Once the pressure stops, the market impact reached a maximum that is usually called the "temporary market impact", and the effect of this pressure starts to decay.

2.4.4   The market impact of large orders

If information primarily moves prices, the example of the liquidation of the large position of a rogue trader has shown that a "mechanical" buying or selling pressure on prices can be enough to move them. The way such a pressure moves prices is called *market impact*. Numerous empirical studies have shown that even relatively small pressure moves prices in a very structured way. Figure 2.7 is a stylized view of the way such a pressure moves prices, it corresponds to the buying of a large amount of shares or contracts that is executed via child orders at an almost constant trading speed:[35]

1. At first the prices react in an almost linear way to the pressure: it most likely corresponds to a period during which other instruments are not really impacted.
2. Then it is more difficult to move the price, as a consequence the shape starts to be concave. This is can be due to the fact that some participants, presumably market makers or some short-term asset managers, are starting to hedge the position they take on other correlated instruments. It allows them to simultaneously provide more liquidity and to propagate this market impact to these correlated instruments (keep in mind the TF1 — Bouygues example).
3. When the execution of the large order ends, i.e., when the trader or the algorithm stops to consume liquidity, the market impact has reached its maximum, which is called the *temporary market impact*.

---

[35]This means that to buy a large volume V of shares during T hours, the trader or the algorithm will target to obtain $V/T/6$ shares every 10 minutes.

4. After this peak, the price relaxes, this is often call the *decay* of the impact.
5. After a while, this decay stops to stabilize at the level of the *permanent market impact*.

These effects can only be observed empirically once enough large "metaorders" (i.e., a large order that will be split into a collection of child orders issued by an asset manager or a trader) are aggregated. The methodology is very simple: observe the price $P_k(t)$ on the tradable instrument number k and renormalize time such that $t = 0$ is the start of a metaorder and $t = 1$ is its end; then track $p(t) = \epsilon_k \cdot (P_k(t) - P_k(0))/(P_k(0) \cdot \sigma_k)$, where σ_k is the volatility (or the bid-ask spread) of the instrument number k, and ϵ_k is the sign of the considered metaorder (i.e., $+1$ for a buy and -1 for a sell). Empirical studies have shown that the temporary market impact $P(1) - P(0)$ is proportional to the volatility of the instrument times the *square root* of the traded quantity (i.e., the size of the metaorder) renormalized by the daily traded quantity on the instrument.

Putting all the pieces of price formation together. This "market impact shape" has to be superposed to information-driven price moves, since the market impact is only concerned by the isolated effect of a large meta order. In short, price moves are made of market impact, plus the mechanical effect of flows of other market participants, plus informational effects, plus the influence of other correlated instruments

$$\Delta P = \text{MI}(V) + \text{Flow} + \text{Info} + \text{Correlated}.$$

Figure 2.8 puts the emphasis on the effect of the flow of other market participants on the trading costs, seen from the viewpoint of a specific trader or trading algorithm. The three curves correspond to three configurations: either the flow of other participants is in the same direction as the one of the considered metaorder (solid line), or it goes in the opposite direction (dotted line). The dashed line corresponds to a configuration where the flow of other participants cancels close to zero (i.e., the buying and the selling pressures are close to being equal). It is clear that trading "in the direction of the flow" costs more than trading on an instrument when the pressure is balanced; trading against the flow can even be rewarded by *negative costs*.

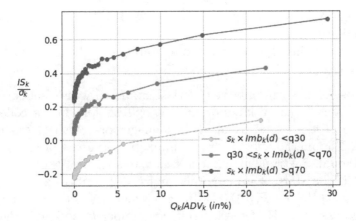

Figure 2.8:   Effect of flows on the trading cost.

The *trading costs* are measured as the difference between the average price obtained for the metaorder and the price at issuance of the
metaorder. This cost naturally encompasses the four effects: market
impact, flow, information, and correlated instruments. Nevertheless,
since it is averaged on a lot of metaorders REF:how:many?, the informational part and the part due to correlated instruments most likely
cancel out. The two effects captured by Figure 2.8 are hence the market impact and the flows; it shows that such flows are dominating
the market impact.

In terms of vocabulary: market impact and flows can be said to
contribute to *price formation*, while information can be said to be the
driver of *price discovery*. In this sense, price formation is a progressive mechanical effect while price discovery is "targeting" to reach
the "anticipated fair value", seen from the viewpoint of all market
participants. The effect of correlated instruments is mixed and can
be seen as a "consistency term", avoiding the dislocation of prices.

Mitigating the cost of metaorders. It has been seen in Section
REF:algo:trading that to design a trading algorithm, it is needed to
choose a cost function (i.e., a utility function[36]) to be minimized,
once penalized by a term corresponding to a waiting cost (or to the
risk that the average price would be too far away from the decision

---

[36]This utility function is called the "Benchmark" of the trading algorithm.

price if the execution of the large order lasts too long, this term is called the *risk aversion* of the utility function). This means that there is an "optimal trading trajectory", that is not at a constant trading speed during the life of the metaorder, such that the trading costs are cheaper than the other trading profiles.

Going back to our symbolic decomposition of price moves during the execution of a large metaorder (i.e., market impact plus flows plus information plus related instruments), one can ask which terms are optimized by a trading algorithm. The answer lies in two elements:

- On the one hand, the trading speed can be adapted to the shape of the way the market impact progressively goes from zero to the temporary market impact: if this shape would be linear, and when the risk aversion term of the utility function is set to zero (to enable a simple reasoning) it would be optimal to trade linearly (i.e., at a constant trading speed). But the shape is concave, hence it is probably better to trade slower at the start and faster the end (when the risk aversion is zero).
- On the other hand, the risk aversion puts the incentive to trade faster at the beginning and slower at the end. Ideally, the risk aversion term has to be adapted to the anticipated flows, information and correlated effects for the day; if the flow is expected to be in the opposite direction, the algorithm can afford to trade slower, mitigating market impact. If the algorithm anticipates that there will be a new release on the traded instrument at the beginning of the day, then either the associated anticipated price move is in the same direction than the metaorder (i.e., upward for a buy order or downward for a sell order), and in such a case it will be optimal for the algorithm to trade fast; but if the anticipated price move is in the opposite direction, the algorithm will trade slower. It is straightforward to deduce in a similar way what is the optimal strategy as a function of the anticipated correlated effects.

To summarize: the more accurate anticipations on the "market context" (i.e., the flows, the information, and the correlated effects) during the trading are, the less the market impact will dominate the optimal trading strategy. But when nothing is known in advance, one could say: *if the algorithm is agnostic on the market context for the day, the market impact is the primary driver of the trading strategy.*

2.5 Risk Transfer and Liquidity Provision

This chapter puts the focus on brokerage; indeed, since brokers are the main access to trading for all market participants, understanding the way they provide intermediation services allows them to have an overview of most of the trading activities. Moreover, several sections of this chapter addressed the way market makers intermediate liquidity. Structurally, when a broker provides access to two trading venues over three in a fragmented market, market makers will "take" liquidity on the third one and "bring" it to the other two, while clients of this broker will put pressure on the two other venues. The mechanism is straightforward as the exact same instrument is offered to trading on the three venues; there is no specific cost when a share bought on one of the venues is sold on one of the two others:

- Assuming there is no specific flow of information (or price moving events on correlated instruments) for this day on the traded instrument; before the considered client starts to send buy child orders (on the two available venues) of his meta order, the prices are similar on the order books of the three venues — say that the best bid price is at \$9 while the best ask price is at \$11 on all of them.
- When traders or trading algorithms will start to push the price up following the market impact curve of Figure 2.8 that has been commented in the previous section, both bid and ask prices will start to increase on these two venues. There is, for now, no reason for the bid and ask to move on the third venue.
- As soon as the ask price will be larger than \$11 plus the associated trading fees say \$11.01, a market maker is rewarded when she provides liquidity at \$11.01; she can sell shares at this price and then buy them back instantaneously at \$11 on the third venue. The profit per trade is \$0.01 minus transaction costs.
- This process will create a liquidity consuming flow on the third venue; it will thus move the ask price on this venue up to \$11.01.
- Now the three venues have the same best ask price; and if the client will continue to buy aggressively, he will push the price higher, directly on the two venues he has access to, as well as via the market maker: *this liquidity consuming flow will be intermediated to the third venue.*

A first remark is that if the broker demands more than \$0.01 to provide access to the first venue, it is cheaper for its clients to implicitly use the services of the market maker.[37] This action of taking liquidity on venue C to transfer it to another participant on venue A and B is a very basic form of risk intermediation: the exchanged risk factor is the price movement of the traded instrument during the transfer, i.e., probably few milliseconds on Equity shares of liquid companies. This is a very small risk, and even if the operational risk associated with this transfer were to be added, this risk would remain minimal.

The same story can be told on two tangible instruments and can be easily extended to an ETF or to a Future. In these two last cases, the two instruments to consider are the ETF (or the Future) and the associated basket of securities, they both have a bid-ask spread, even if one of the baskets has to be computed using a weighted average of the bids and asks of the basket's components.

Derivative hedging as risk intermediation. It is in fact not far more complicated in the case of a nonlinear derivative.[38] The payoff of a Call Option being the minimum between the spot price at maturity and the strike of the Option (both being known at creation of the Option), if it is a plain intermediary,[39] the counterparty of the buyer of a Call at \$12 (i.e., the market participant who will have sold this Call) will have to hedge it. The hedging process of this Option is simple: when the spot price will go up she will buy some shares (to have them when the owner of the Option will claim his payoff at maturity), and when the spot price will go down she will sell some of her shares. She will initially have to buy a number of shares corresponding to the probability that the owner of the Option will claim the payoff, multiplied by the number of shares that will have to be delivered. The exact parameters of this hedging process first depend on the time to maturity, since the smaller it is, the more

---

[37]Strictly speaking, other types of market participants can put in place this liquidity transfer. For instance, short-term hedge funds or proprietary trading desks.

[38]Futures are linear derivatives, because their payoff is a linear function of the underlying, while options, i.e., calls and puts, are nonlinear derivatives as their payoff is a non-linear function of their underlying.

[39]The seller of this Option can have different reasons to not hedge it: she may want to take on this exposure, or she may already be exposed to the exact opposite exposure.

certain the payoff becomes, and on the volatility of the underlying share as it measures the typical amplitude of its price move during a unit of time. It is also a function of the exact mechanism chosen to implement the hedge: from the closed-form Black and Scholes formula to more sophisticated modeling that will be solved using Monte-Carlo simulation or backward numerical schemes.

The important point here is that the risk bought by the owner of the Option (i.e., the payoff at maturity) will have an influence on the price moves of the underlying since the intermediary will generate a trading flow via its hedging process that will, as it has been already explained earlier, push the price. The mechanisms are clear:

- The buyer of the Option transfers a risk[40] to the seller of this Option.
- Since the seller acts as a pure intermediary, she will hedge this risk as soon as it will be too large with respect to its capital that can be put in risk.
- The hedging process will generate a pressure on the asset every day, corresponding exactly to the probability, seen from today, that the risk will materialize itself.

This means that the intermediation of this risk has exactly the sense that one could expect: the more Options are bought from intermediaries, the more the price will move in the same direction as if the associated risk would have been bought, but mitigated by the probability that this risk realizes.

In practice, either the risk circulates because the intermediary found a buyer of the exact opposite risk (or a seller of this risk), otherwise, it will be transformed in the most basic form of risk transfer: a buy or a sell on a trading venue. Maybe another intermediary will have sold the same risk but doesn't have the capability to trade directly — over the counter — with the former intermediary. In such a case they will both hedge their risky positions. The magic of the hedging will allow these two intermediaries to *match their hedging trades* (one will be a buy of the underlying whereas the other will be a sell of the same underlying security) on public trading venues;

---

[40]This is the exact definition of risk provided in the previous chapter: a future payoff.

they will, in reality, match their risk, but will never have to share information about their exposures, nor about the appetite of their clients. The hedging process is a way to anonymize flows and positions of intermediaries on many risk directions, linear or not. Last but not least, this process naturally matches risks coming from different products with different payoffs, provided that they have the same underlying. Via the effect of price pressure on the correlated instrument, risk can be matched between non-linear Derivatives having correlated underlying assets.

Factor investing as risk intermediation. Similarly, when an Asset Manager provides an investment vehicle that is exposed to a given factor, say for instance the *low-volatility factor*, she is intermediating this risk. To understand how it works, first some details on what is a low-volatility vehicle: this is a portfolio made of Equity shares of companies. Compared to the market portfolio, in which shares are weighted by the capitalization of the company that issued it (like for the S&P500, the Russel 1000, the CAC40 or the DAX), a low-volatility portfolio will put more weight on the stocks having the lowest volatility of their returns, and less on the more volatile ones. To be able to maintain the exposure of the portfolio to the low-volatility factor, the Asset Manager will periodically buy and sell stocks to maintain its target weights: when the price of a low volatile stock increases, some of its shares will be sold; conversely, when the price of high volatile stock goes down, some of its shares will be bought. This is exactly the hedging process associated with having sold the future returns of the low-volatility factor. The effect is again one that could be expected: the more buyers of one traditional Investing Factor (like low-volatility, Size, bet-against-beta, Momentum, etc.), the more pressure on stocks that are needed to build the associated portfolio.

Synthetic Factors or synthetic[41] ETFs are not that different: instead of hedging the payoff associated to the Factor, the intermediary will hedge it only when the exposure to the risk kept in its balance sheet or its book is too high with respect to a regulatory or

---

[41]Synthetic products are investment vehicles using a return swap: there is no guarantee that the portfolio associated to the vehicle exactly reproduces the risk Factor, but the returns of this Factor are due.

best-practice-driven metric. Minor changes will probably not trigger hedging trades; trades, and hence price moving flows, will be triggered only conditionally to the risk-management-driven threshold of the intermediary. These synthetic products allow intermediaries to merge their inventories on a set of products before considering to hedge their exposure; it is somehow similar to implementing only one hedging process for a large set of vehicles. This has the advantage that it decreases the trading costs, but it links the products together(if one of them suffers from huge losses, not only the associated vehicle may go bankrupt, but other vehicles that are in the same "set of products" may follow the same path, simply because they are all linked to the solvability of the same intermediary), adding some counterparty risk to the products, and maybe a little bit of operational risk as well.

Risk intermediation everywhere. The vision developed in this section on risk intermediation is probably one of the most unifying ones for a quantitative analyst working in modern markets as this reasoning can be extended to all kinds of risk transfers. Even a basic risk transfer done by banks when they issue loans is hedged via their Asset Liability Management processes.

From a quantitative perspective (13)

Financial mathematics have been built on the idea of risk management. Portfolio construction, derivatives hedging and optimal trading have as their core engine a risk model: how to build a portfolio under a given level of risk? how to maintain the risk in the book of an investment bank structuring derivatives at a decent level? or how to minimize the risk of an open position while time lapses? More recently, counterparty risk management, emerging after the 2008 — 2009 Global Financial Crisis, gave birth to a lot of quantitative models too.

Issues raised in these areas are usually modelled and sophisticated via quantitative teams working for market participants, having practical concerns and up-to-date datasets,

(*Continued*)

(Continued)

and academics knowing how to properly translate these open problems in mathematical terms and then working on a qualitative understanding and on numerical scheme to them. These implicit and explicit collaborations maintains a good rate of processes and innovations to always reduce the risk taken by each participant in the financial system. One of the next quantitative challenges is to enable communication between these different fields, to provide to market participant with an integrated view of their current level of risk, and different ways to reduce their exposure to risk factors.

Of course from an operational perspective it is always better to split a large problem into smaller problems and to solve each of them independently; but it is suboptimal. Moreover, it is very difficult to "split" the influence of the level of liquidity to distribute it to smaller problems: liquidity is a *mean field* in the sense that it is a medium that propagates back and forth to all areas of the financial system. Any problem is influenced by the state of the liquidity in the considered tradable instruments, and any solution to a problem requires to provide or consume liquidity on correlated tradable instruments. The recent theory of Mean Field Games seems to provide an adequate mathematical formalism to describe the way liquidity interacts with the actions of market participants.

2.6   For More Details

Brokers are the perfect instance of intermediaries on financial markets, it is important to take time to understand their role and the kind of intermediation they operate. The book (Lehalle and Laruelle, 2018) contains a lot of information about their role and their practices, and about smart order routing, fragmentation and algorithmic trading. Information about the flash crash will be found there too.

Algorithmic trading has been developed in other books than Lehalle and Laruelle (2018, Chapter 3); Guéant (2016), Cartea *et al.* (2015), and Guo *et al.* (2017). It is important to understand that optimal execution, initiated by the seminal paper of Almgren and Chriss (2001), is now a very mature field. It is more than a toolbox of economic models, because it is made of very practical recipes that are followed by brokers, banks and market makers when they design trading algorithms. Because of this, it is now possible to build more economic models in which agents are not modelled by equations but in which each agent really follows the same recipes as real algorithmic designers. Modelling a collection of agents and their interactions is difficult, but recently Mean Field Games theory started to provide a mathematical framework to address the complexity of these interactions. See, for instance, Cardaliaguet and Lehalle (2018) and references therein; it contains an application to algorithmic trading.

To breakdown the design of a trading algorithm into its main two dimensions (i.e., intraday risk of an open position and market impact due to the pressure of trades on liquidity), good entry points in the literature are Gatheral *et al.* (2018) and Bacry *et al.* (2015). It may be good to come back to the qualitative paper of Kyle (1985) and then follow its advances up to the great (and more mathematical book) of Çetin and Danilova (2018).

There is surprisingly not a lot of academic papers on intermediation of risks, but Greenwood *et al.* (2015) can be a good entry point as research on systemic risk from the viewpoint of the balance sheet of an investment bank, for instance starting with Hurd (2018).

References

Almgren, R. and Chriss, N. (2001). Optimal execution of portfolio transactions. *Journal of Risk*, 3:5–40.

Bacry, E., Iuga, A., Lasnier, M., and Lehalle, C.-A. (2015). Market impacts and the life cycle of investors orders. *Market Microstructure and Liquidity*, 1(02):1550009.

Cardaliaguet, P. and Lehalle, C.-A. (2018). Mean field game of controls and an application to trade crowding. *Mathematics and Financial Economics*, 12(3):335–363.

Cartea, Á., Jaimungal, S., and Penalva, J. (2015). *Algorithmic and High-Frequency Trading*. Cambridge University Press.

Çetin, U. and Danilova, A. (2018). *Dynamic Markov Bridges and Market Microstructure: Theory and Applications*, volume 90, Springer.

Gatheral, J., Jaisson, T., and Rosenbaum, M. (2018). Volatility is rough. *Quantitative Finance*, 18(6):933–949.

Greenwood, R., Landier, A., and Thesmar, D. (2015). Vulnerable banks. *Journal of Financial Economics*, 115(3):471–485.

Guéant, O. (2016). *The Financial Mathematics of Market Liquidity: From Optimal Execution to Market Making*, volume 33. CRC Press.

Guo, X., Lai, T. L., Shek, H., and Wong, S. P.-S. (2017). *Quantitative Trading: Algorithms, Analytics, Data, Models, Optimization*. CRC Press.

Hurd, T. R. (2018). Bank panics and fire sales, insolvency and illiquidity. *International Journal of Theoretical and Applied Finance*, 21(06):1850040.

Kyle, A. S. (1985). Continuous auctions and insider trading. *Econometrica: Journal of the Econometric Society*, 1315–1335.

Lehalle, C.-A. and Laruelle, S. (2018). *Market Microstructure in Practice*. World Scientific.

Chapter 3

Intermediation of Risks Via Structured Products

3.1 Structured Products: A Risk Packaging Tool

Chapter 2 introduced the way market participants interact within the financial system. This chapter goes beyond a simple definition of "structured products": it focuses on the activity of the firms, and more often describes the activity of teams that are structuring such products. It is not straightforward to make the distinction between roles of *brokers, investment banks*, and *structurers*, because a "Prime Brokerage company" is often hosting teams involved in brokerage (i.e., providing access to tradable instruments), financing, and designing and building products themselves (i.e., *structuring* products). The link between the three activities is often the balance sheet of the mother company: if a firm goes beyond the business of pure agency brokerage, it then needs an inventory and owns a book, hosted in a balance sheet, to maintain such inventory. This inventory of tradable instruments has more chances to be balanced if it is bundled with the activity of financing because financing projects of corporates (via loans, or bonds and equity shares issuance) will allow an investment banks (and its prime broker) to own instruments that are not very liquid (because the firm will have access to the primary market). This will allow its market makers to provide liquidity on these instruments (or other instruments sharing risk factors with them) to other market participants.

147

Here, we define a "structuring" team as *a team designing financial products, using a mix of traditional asset classes, such as stocks and bonds, and derivatives to design a certain risk-return profile.* The goal of such a team is often to design a product for the need of a specific class of client (typically an asset manager, an insurance company, or an agent outside of the financial system). As such, the chapter will cover, for instance, the design of Exchange Traded Funds, as well as of derivative products like Call and Put Options, and naturally of "structured products" (i.e., a bond with a variable coupon indexed on a financial payoff). This chapter focuses on "structured products" more than on other derivatives, and the type of organization that we call structurer is focused on the role of the *arranger* as it is at the core of the structuring business.

According to our definition, the difference, as far as hedging is concerned, between structurers and investment banks is that structurers study the hedging process of each product they design, while investment banks hedge the corresponding exposure. We will see that often a third entity, usually a bank (that can be different from the investment bank), is really issuing the debt on which the structured product is based. In practice, the investment bank takes the risk associated to the coupon in their book (i.e., of their balance sheet) and hedges it. The structurer, who we will often call the *arranger* to underline the fact that it has the idea of the product, packaging together the coupon, the swap with the investment bank to hedge it, and the need for financing of the other bank issuing the underlying bond (this will be detailed in Section 3.4). The structurer values the products they design, hence controls the value of the commercial margin it adds on the top of the product. It owns the intellectual property (IP) of the product. Moreover, it has been already explained in the former chapters that investment banks, thanks to their global hedging strategy, net a lot of exposures and hence reduce the effective cost of replicating the risk via trading, lowering transaction costs. In the scope of structured products, it is natural that they are in charge of providing the swap corresponding to the coupon of structured products: they add their exposure to risk factors, and with chance it will allow them to net it with other exposure they already have. The arranger sometimes try to design a products that simultaneously answers to the need of a client who will buy it, but also to the exposures of investment banks.[1]

Structured products are a very specific class of financial product as they are packaging together different types of risks: counterparty risk, exposure to the yield curve, and exposure to a formula (payoff) for the calculation of the coupon or the redemption amount.[2] Thus, understanding their role in risk intermediation is very instructive.

From a quantitative perspective (14)

In this book, "structurers" are in essence financial engineers, inventing new payoffs for which other market participants can have some appetite, and designing processes to hedge the associated risk. We make a clear difference between the activity of designing the hedging process of a coupon (that is in the hands of the structurer) and implementing it (in the hand of an investment bank) as nowadays fixed costs associated with the implementation of hedging are high enough so that only a handful of investment banks worldwide can afford to implement it in a cost-effective way. Many structuring teams are in practice using an investment bank in a "back to back" fashion to have it implement the hedging on a day to day basis.

3.2 From Derivatives to Structured Products

Structured products embed a risk transformation process, where the seller agrees to give to the buyer insurance against a risk factor, as well as a promise of a future gain called the payoff, in exchange for a risk premium. This feature of structured products is inherited from

---

[1]As a consequence the swap will be cheaper if it remove exposure than if it adds exposure to some risk factors. Section 3.3.2.3 explains how Credit Linked Notes fullfil exactly this role of reducing exposure of investment banks to Credit Default Swaps.

[2]The coupon or the redemption amount can, for instance, be indexed on returns of a portfolio of equities.

their derivative components used as building blocks to design the expected risk/return profile for each product. In this section, we will focus on derivative products, how they come to play in the financial markets, the risk of the optionality they provide to both sides of the deal (buyer and seller) and what are some standard hedging strategies used nowadays to neutralize their risk.

3.2.1   Role of derivative markets

The tale of a future contract on silk.   *Consider a silk merchant who buys silk in India to resell it in France. Let's say, for example, that it takes two months between the time silk is purchased in India and its availability in French markets. When the merchant delivers his silk in Paris, two months after the goods have been shipped, he is not sure that he will be able to sell it at a price that will allow him a profit. This would imply a selling price higher than the price of purchase plus transportation costs and the insurance price against any contrarian event. The effective price could be much higher than the one expected. But as long as there is the chance of having a pleasant surprise, there are as much chances to have the depressing news of not being able to sell higher than the minimum bearable price and to suffer a cost. The merchant can take on this risk, but may prefer it to be deterministic (know in advance), even if it means reducing his expected profit. There is a stock exchange in Paris that lists silk. On this stock exchange, standardized baskets of silk, in quantity and quality, are traded daily and the prices are publicly known. The series of past prices in itself provide valuable indicators for evaluating the risk of prices. For example, it allows the calculation of past silk price volatility (that is reflecting the level of uncertainty on price formation), but also the analysis of possible correlations between silk prices and other economic indicators (like weather). Once again, we see the advantage of organized and centralized markets, compared to bilateral trading, in terms of information asymmetry. As soon as a stock exchange lists a well-defined basket of a commodity, it usually pushes other exchanges to list the same Future contract, and competition between buyers and sellers, including market makers, stabilizes the price around a* fair value. *This faire value reflects the collective anticipations of this continuum of market participants on the future price of this basket, at expiry. This way, the Stock Exchange* *quotes daily contracts for immediate delivery* Spot market *and for future delivery. These contracts, called* Futures, *stipulate that the seller of the contract commits to deliver at a future date the well-defined basket of goods (or tradable instruments) to the buyer of the contract, at a price fixed at the signature day. These contracts can be traded on the exchange(s), which allows an active secondary market to take place. Naturally the transactions of this contract very close to maturity are made at a price that is very close to the spot market.*

In the case of our merchant, if he finds that the spot price of silk in Paris is 100$, *whereas the 2-month contract costs* 95$, *he will interpret this difference as the fact that the participants on the silk futures market anticipate a drop in silk price in the next 2 months. Fearing such a negative trend, the merchant decides to be cautious. As his business continues to be profitable at* 100$ *but no longer at* 80$, *he sells 20 contracts at the price of* $20 \times 95 = 1,900$$. *If the effective price on the spot market when he receives the goods after 2 months is* 80$, *the contracts he previously sold also cost* 80$ *at their expiry. He can then buy back these contract for a benefit of* $20 \times 95 - 20 \times 80 = 300$$. *His total income will be* $1,900 = 1,600 + 300$$ *that is, the sale of silk plus the gain of the protection on the futures market. It is said that the merchant was long on the physical silk, therefore averse to the downward risk of price movement and short on the futures market. This is a legitimate hedging strategy against market risk; that is, taking opposite positions of the same amount on futures and physicals.*

All natural agents long silk on the physical market are risk-averse to the downside movement of prices and seek to hedge it on the futures market. For the sake of the price formation process on the derivative market, we find as counterpart all natural short silk agents, such as manufacturers who use silk as a raw material, averse to the upward price movement. As we've seen before, natural opposite stakeholders have low probability to meet one another on the market at the same time and with the same amounts. The market also features market-makers and speculators, lacking any stakes on the physical market but willing to take a risk on the derivative market in the hope of making a profit. They rely on their own anticipations on any factor affecting silk price.

The Grossman–Stiglitz paradox explains that the opportunity to be rewarded from correct anticipations is the only way to motivate efforts in processing information such that this information will reflects into prices: if prices are always correct, nobody will be rewarded to gather information and hence the prices cannot be correct.

The risk transfer that derivative markets provide is not restricted to futures; it is present on other categories of derivative instruments too, such as options and swaps. These categories give a different risk-return profile and hedge for their traders. There are two types of options: Calls giving the right (but the not the obligation) to buy on a future date the underlying instrument at a fixed price. Puts follow the same logic but to sell the underlying asset in the future. Therefore, by buying a put option, the long silk merchant buys protection against a falling price without depriving himself of a potential profit if the price happens to rise. A short silk manufacturer will buy a call option to protect himself against the risk of a rise in the price, while at the same time conserving the possibility of a profit if the price falls. This involves far less capital that buying or selling Future contracts.

Derivatives markets are therefore markets where different sources of risks are exchanged between market participants. Some natural risk takers outside of the financial system (like our silk merchant) and market participants are exchanging risks up to the point that investment banks and market makers have a large unbalanced inventories. To unwind their exposure to some risk factors they will "replicate the risk in the market", i.e., hedge it on exchanges thanks to tradable instruments correlated to the corresponding risk factor. Today, derivatives exist not only on commodities, i.e., standardized goods, such as oil and refined products, metals and agricultural products, but also for standardized services such as sea freight and, last but not least, for most financial instruments: bonds, interest rates, equities, equity indices, and the major currencies: dollar, euro, yen, and so on. The efficiency of agreeing on a two-way contract with very clear terms has led to derivatives being sometimes used in place of direct investments, to the extent that in general the global market for derivatives is larger than the market for underlying instruments.

3.2.2   Hedging of derivatives

A derivative product, in contrast to traditional instruments, is any financial security that derives its value from another financial product called the underlying asset or benchmark. The most common underlying instruments for derivatives are stocks, bonds, commodities, currencies, interest rates, and market indexes. The value of the underlying instruments can usually be determined easily since they are commonly traded on exchanges. It is important that the price of the underlying instruments of a derivative can be observed by the buyer and the seller of the option, otherwise the information asymmetry is usually in favor of one of the two sides of the trade.

A derivative product is also a contract between two or more parties. Thus, even if the derivative product derives its price from fluctuations in the underlying asset, it also has its separate price formation process defined in turn by the supply and demand on this single contract. The derivatives price, which is also the risk premium of guarantee on the underlying, gives insight on market expectations of future levels of the underlying. Thus, price movements of the derivative and the underlying are interlinked and allow to design hedging strategies of the derivative risk by imputing the exact opposite sensitivity to risk factors on the spot markets. These factors are assessed using the *sensitivities*, or *Greeks*.[3]

These sensitivities corresponds to the variation of the value of the derivative seen from now when some risk factor changes. The natural risk factors are the price and the volatility of the underlying, the interest rate, etc. If the considered risk factor is tradable, it means that to be protected against a change in this factor, it is enough to sell the corresponding sensitivity.

For instance: the Delta (with notation Δ) is the change in the value of an option when the price of the underlying changes, i.e., when the price changes by δS then the value of the option increases by $\Delta \, \delta S$. As a consequence, the value of a basket made of one option and $-\Delta$ underlying instrument will not change with the price of the underlying. Each Greek provides a perfect hedge if it is possible to buy or sell the corresponding instrument and put it in the same basket as the option.

In practice, if an investment bank owns two derivatives A and B, one having respectively a Delta of Δ_A and Δ_B with respect to the same factor F, a basket made of 1 contract of A and $-\Delta_A/\Delta_B$

---

[3]The sensitivities of derivatives are named "Greeks" because Greek letters as used as a notation. Nevertheless, some sensitivities have fake Greek letters, like *Vanna* that does not belong to the Greek alphabet.

contract(s) of B has no more exposure to the variations of F. This *netting* of contracts enables to reduce the exposure to a factor by simply selling or buying contract in adequate proportions. Either it is done on exchanges, either simply via sales of such contracts to agents outside of the financial system.

Of course the sensitivities are not static: they change with market conditions, this means that an ideal mix of 1 and Δ_A/Δ_B has to be rebalanced every day, or even every hour, or even faster if markets are under stress (i.e., when the levels of risk factors change quickly). The process of continuously adjusting the Greeks is what derivatives traders are doing all day long. Il is often called hedging or risk replication. Since it is impossible to really adjust the exposure every millisecond, they take temporary risk inside an envelope decided in agreement with their risk department.

Basic valuation of vanilla options. In the following, we define the main *Greeks* to illustrate the mechanism of replicating the risk associated to different factors (Table 3.1). We give formulas in the context of the simplistic method of the Black–Scholes–Merton model. The advantage is that the sensitivities have a closed-form formula within this model. Beyond the Black–Scholes–Merton dynamics, one

Table 3.1:   Main greeks and their definition.

Greek	Symbol	Measures	Definition
Delta	δ or Δ	Underlying exposure	Change in option price due to underlying price
Gamma	γ or Γ	Convexity of payout	Change in delta due to underlying price
Theta	θ or Θ	Time decay	Change in option price due to time passing
Vega	ν	Volatility exposure	Change in option price due to volatility
Rho	ω or Ω	Interest rate exposure	Change in option price due to interest rates
Volga	λ or Λ	Vol of vol exposure	Change in vega due to volatility
Vanna	ψ or Ψ	Skew	Change in delta due to volatility

always needs a model to estimate the sensitivities of an open derivative position. This model will specify

- the different risk factors that will be taken into account, their dynamics and their relationships;
- the nature of the uncertainty (typically supported by a Brownian motion for Black–Scholes–Merton, but it is usually extended to a Levy process, i.e., Brownian plus Poisson-like jumps), and their dependencies (i.e., correlations).

Once it is done, different approaches are possible to estimate the Greeks: boiling down the dynamics to a system of (backward) PDE when possible and solving them using a numerical scheme like the Euler scheme, or simulating a large number of trajectories via a Monte Carlo like approach. In the end, the method relies on a finite-difference like method since the sensitivity is the partial derivative of the payoff with respect of the considered risk factor. Its discrete equivalent is the variation of the value of the contract while the considered risk factor changes by a unitary amount. Section 6.3.2 of Chapter 6 mentions the way machine learning approaches, based on the efficient computation of partial derivatives, can be reused for the computation of sensitivities. In practice, any model (even a data driven one), can be used to price an option. The main limitation is the computing time.

The following formula can be found in any textbook on derivative pricing

$$\text{Call option price} = S \cdot N(d_1) - Ke^{-rT} \cdot N(d_2)$$
$$\text{Put option price} = -S \cdot N(-d_1) + Ke^{-rT} \cdot N(d_2),$$

where T is the time to maturity, r is the risk-free rate (minus the dividend yield if any), σ is the volatility of the underlying (expressed in the same unit as the time to maturity), S is the spot price and K is the strike (the price at which the option can be exercised: to buy for a Call option or to sell for a Put option). The intermediate variables d_1 and d_2 are defined as

$$d_1 = \frac{\log \frac{S}{K} + \left(r + T\frac{\sigma^2}{2}\right)}{\sigma\sqrt{T}}, \quad d_2 = d_1 - \sigma\sqrt{T}.$$

$N(z)$, the cumulative density function of the normal distribution, arise because the main assumption of the Black–Scholes–Merton is Brownian. For reader familiar with probabilities, d_1 is clearly linked with the probability that the spot price reaches the strike since $\log(S/K)$ is the log-distance between them, $r + T\sigma^2/2$ is a trend, and $\sigma\sqrt{T}$ reflect the "time to maturity" at the speed of this Brownian motion.

DELTA Δ measures underlying exposure. The most commonly examined Greek is delta, as it gives the underlying sensitivity of the option (the change in the option price due to a change in the underlying price). Delta is normally quoted in percent. For calls, it lies between 0% (no delta sensitivity) and 100% (trades like the underlying). The delta of puts lies between -100% (trades like the underlying) and 0%. If a call option has a delta of 50% and the underlying sees a 1 Euro increase, the call option will then see an increase of 0.50 Euro in value ($=$ Euro $1 \times 50\%$). Note that the values of the call and put delta in the formula below give the underlying sensitivity of a forward of the same maturity as the option expiry. The sensitivity to spot is slightly different. Moreover, it is to be noted that there is a (small) difference between the probability that an option expires ITM (In The Money: The optionality won't be executed) and delta.

$$\text{Call delta} = N(d_1),$$

$$\text{Put delta} = -N(-d_1) = N(d_1) - 1.$$

GAMMA Γ measures convexity (the amount earned by the delta hedge. Gamma measures the change in delta due to a change in the underlying price. The higher the gamma, the more convex is the theoretical payout. Gamma should not be considered a measure of value (low or high gamma does not mean the option is expensive or cheap); implied volatility is mostly the measure of an option's value. Options are most convex, and hence have the highest gamma, when they are ATM (At the Money: S=K) and also about to expire. This can be seen intuitively as the delta of an option on the day of expiry will change from 0% if spot is just below expiry to 100% if spot is just above expiry. A small change in spot causes a large change in the delta, hence the gamma is very high.

$$\text{Gamma} = -\frac{N'(d_1)}{S\sqrt{T}\sigma}.$$

THETA Θ measures time decay (cost of being long gamma).
Theta is the change in the price of an option for a change in time to
maturity; hence, it measures time decay. In order to find the daily
impact of the passage of time, its value is normally divided by 252
(trading days in the year). If the second term in the formula below
is ignored, the theta for calls and puts are identical and proportional
to gamma. Theta can therefore be considered the cost of being long
gamma.

$$\text{Call theta} = -\frac{S\sigma \times N'(d_1)}{2\sqrt{T}} - rKe^{-rT}N(d_2),$$

$$\text{Put theta} = -\frac{S\sigma \times N'(d_1)}{2\sqrt{T}} + rKe^{-rT}N(d_2).$$

VEGA measures volatility exposure (average of gammas).
Vega denotes the sensitivity to the volatility of the option price. Vega
is normally divided by 100 to give the price change for a 1 volatility
point (i.e., 1%) move in implied volatility. Vega can be considered to
be the average gamma (or nonlinearity) over the life of the option.
Since Vega has a $\sqrt{T}$ its the formula, power vega (vega divided by the
square root of time) is often used as a risk measure (to compensate
for the fact that near dated implied volatilities move more than far-
dated implied volatilities).

$$\text{Vega} = S \times \sqrt{T} \times N'(d_1).$$

RHO ρ measures interest rate risk. Rho measures the change
in the value of the option due to a move in the risk-free rate. The
profile of rho with respect to spot is similar to the delta, as the
risk-free rate is more important for more equity sensitive options (as
these are the options where there is the most benefit in selling a
stock, replacing it with an option and putting the difference in value
on deposit). Rho is normally divided by 10,000 to indicate the change
in price for a 1-bp move.

$$\text{Call rho} = KTe^{-rT}N(d_2),$$

$$\text{Put rho} = -KTe^{-rT}N(-d_2).$$

VOLGA measures volatility of volatility exposure. Volga is short for VOLatility GAmma and is the rate of change of vega due to a change in volatility. Volga (or Vomma/vega convexity) is highest for OTM options (approximately 10% delta), as these are the options where the probability of moving from OTM to ITM has the greatest effect on their value. For more detail on the Volga, see the section How to Measure Skew and Smile.

$$\text{Volga} = \frac{S\sqrt{T}d_1 d_2 N'(d_1)}{\sigma}.$$

VANNA measures skew exposure. Vanna has two definitions as it measures the change in vega given a change in spot and the change in delta due to a change in volatility. The change in vega for a change in spot can be considered to measure the skew position, as this will lead to profits on a long skew trade if there is an increase in volatility as spot declines. The extreme values for Vanna occur for c15 delta options, similar to Volga's c10 delta peaks. For more detail on Vanna, see the section How to Measure Skew and Smile.

$$\text{Vanna} = \frac{-d_2 N'(d_1)}{\sigma}.$$

From a quantitative perspective (15)

It is important to read these sensitivities as the "unit of intermediation needed for a possible variation of an underlying risk factor". The risk factors considered here are the price of the underlying for the Delta and the volatility for the Vega, etc. When an investment bank sells a derivative, it is immediately exposed to risks in a lot of directions: it accepted to take in its balance sheet the risk corresponding to the payoff of the product at maturity. It is clear that this bank does not want to wait for the last minute to discover that it has to deliver this amount of shares or cash. At any point in time, it has to measure the probability that such an event occurs, and to be prepared. Being prepared allows to measure how much the risks taken are adding up or cancelling themselves. It allows also to start to get the shares or the cash in advance, to avoid

(Continued)

(Continued)

to pay not only what it has to deliver, but also the market impact associated to a very large immediate buy order.

If one looks carefully at formula of a *Call Delta*: it is the probability that the issuer will have to deliver a share of the underlying: it is natural that when the price moves towards the strike of the option, this probability increases (and it decreases if the price goes in the other direction). What is the best action from the viewpoint of the intermediary that issued this contract? It is, naturally, to buy in advance shares in proportion to the probability increase or decrease. Each formula of sensitivity can be read as the amount to be delivered at expiry times the probability that the delivery has to be done. This is the natural way for intermediation: another market participant buys a risk exposure (corresponding to the payoff of the derivative), the investment bank is now left with the opposite exposure. As an intermediary, it will buy-back these risks smoothly,[a] in line with the increases or decreases of the probability that the risk will realize at maturity. Either the seller of this smooth version of the risks exposures is another intermediary, if by chance it would correspond to its own replication of some risk taken against another client then the exposures are "netted". If it is not another intermediary, this seller is then a natural risk taker, and the risk exists of the financial system.

An advantage of sensitivities (or greeks) is that they come from a Taylor expansion, and hence they allow to write the value of the uncertainty of the payoff at maturity as a sum of coefficients (the sensitivities) times the dynamics of each related risk factor (like the price or the volatility of the underlying).

This linear property of Taylor expansion allows to sum the sensitivities of all the products sold by a given market

---

[a]This smoothness reflects the slow evolution of the probability of occurrence of a future event, that is of course not the case if the factors change abruptly.

(Continued)

(Continued)

participant: if an investment bank sold n_A contracts of product A with a delta of Δ_A and n_B contracts of another product B with a delta of Δ_B, then the Delta sensitivity of the portfolio $n_A A + n_B B$ is $n_A \Delta_A + n_B \Delta_B$. This is very useful because this investment bank needs to buy or sell only the remaining delta: this Taylor expansion in greeks allows to "net" internally the risks. In short: an intermediary with a book of contracts corresponding to future payoffs, i.e., risks, can confront each contract to a collection of risk factors (again, here "risk factors" are typically prices, volatilities and correlations of underlyings or components of the yield curve) by estimating its sensitivity to each factor. Then, it is enough to organise them in a large table where rows are the contracts and columns are the factors: the cells of the tables are the sensitivities of each contract (row) to each factor (column), the sum of each column is the net sensitivity to each factor; only this remaining exposure has to be hedged (a.k.a. replicated, i.e., traded on markets or OTC) to decrease the risk embedded in the book.

Of course, since this methodology relies on a Taylor expansion, it is important to choose well the risk factors (regulations, like Basel Accords, are listing some important factors) and it is crucial to check that the remaining term is really negligible.

3.3 The Structure of Structured Products

Structured products are tailor-made investment solutions designed to provide a specific risk exposure for a specific expected return. The purpose of this exposure can be hedging (a company having a nonlinear exposure to a complex mix of economic variables can use derivative products), risk transformation (a firm that would like to transfer a specific risk to a willing third party in exchange of a premium), or simply speculation (i.e., an investor believing in a specific complex economic scenario would like to have a cost-effective way to bet on it). They are usually built from basic bricks (zero-coupon bonds, options, swaps, etc.), hence structured products often provide a mix of:

- *guaranteed capital*, having in mind that the drawback of guaranteed capital is counterparty risk or formula based redemption,
- *fixed or variable coupons*, indexed on a formula that is, in fact, a recurrent payoff,
- *exposure to specific market factors* via the coupon and the counterparty risk.

The financial flows involved in a structured product are the following:

1. It starts like a bond (most often issued by a financial institution): the buyer of the product will provide capital for a given *duration* to the issuer in exchange for a periodic coupon.
2. The formula to compute the value of the coupon is a payoff, i.e., it provides a risk exposure to the buyer of the product. Periodically, a predefined index is computed according to its position with respect to some thresholds; the value of the coupon is fixed and delivered to the buyer.
3. At the end of the duration (i.e., *at maturity*): a fraction of the initial capital will be given back to the buyer of the product. This fraction is again the outcome of a pre-defined formula.
4. Moreover, some structured products have an early redemption feature: under pre-specified conditions, they can be terminated. In such a case, no more coupons are issued and the fraction of the initial capital to be delivered to the buyer is computed according to a pre-defined formula.

In terms of basic bricks, such a product is a combination of a bond, a derivative for the coupon, and a derivative for the payment of the capital at expiry (maturity or early redemption).

3.3.1 Structured products components

The bond component. Depending on the investment objective of the structured product, the interest paid by the bond component is used to set up the "derivatives" part to either provide the capital guarantee, or to improve the return on a non-capital-guaranteed product. The guarantee or the protection of the capital is ensured by the issuer or its guarantor. In case the issuer defaults, initial capital is no longer guaranteed. It is therefore essential to check the quality of the rating assigned to the issuer by rating agencies.

The derivative component of the coupon. The derived strategy, usually composed of options, is essential in the construction of a structured product. It is what determines, most often, the level of performance. The choice of derivatives will depend on: the desired level of risk for the product (capital protection or not), the preferred investment horizon, and the desired risk-reward with respect to market conditions. All structured products, from the simplest to the most complex ones, rely on derivatives, most often in the form of options.

The underlying for the coupon. The concept is simple. Consider a product that aims to repay the initial investment at maturity plus a coupon linked to the performance of an underlying asset, for example, the Euro Stoxx 50 Index, over five years. For €100 invested:

- €80 is used for the repayment of the initial investment at maturity. With a locked interest rate over 5 years, it ensures the repayment of the initial investment. (This example is based on a high interest rate environment compared to the rates observed in recent years for the euro.)
- €15 are used to buy financial instruments (derivatives) that provide the performance element. This performance is variable and unknown before the expiry of the contract.
- €5 is the cost of structuring the product augmented by the fees as a margin of the business activity of the product issuer.

The performance element will determine the final return: if the performance of the underlying is positive at maturity, then the investor will receive part of that performance in addition to the initial investment. Otherwise, only the principal will be refunded.

Asset classes of the underlying. To allow product coverage, the underlying of the structured product must be tradable. Conversely, insurance products are not built on tradable assets. Structured products allow investors to complete their range of investments on assets they know how to manage and for which they have been granted limits (Figure 3.1). The underlying is an index or a price that can be jointly computed by the buyer and the seller. Under the European Benchmark Regulation (BMR), any index on which a financial product is based has to be calculated by an independent organization to guarantee transparency and avoid any manipulation like it has

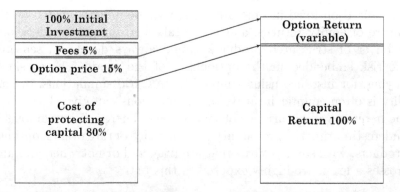

Figure 3.1: Guaranteed capital structured products schema.

been done in the past with the Libor.[4] Here is a list of underlyings that are frequently used to base structured products on:

- *Index*: Equity indexes, such as CAC 40, S&P500, etc. or Dividends Yield indexes, Volatility Indexes like the VCAC, or VIX.
- *Interest rates*: Short rates: Euribor (fixing from 1 month to 1 year) or Long rates: rate Constant Maturity Swap (CMS).
- *Credit/loan*: The default risk of the issuer is the underlying of the product.
- *Exchange rate*: Spot, forward, deliverable, undeliverable.
- *Commodities* prices or indexes, like oil or wheat.
- *Climate indexes* or *Energy indexes*.

When a coupon is computed on one of the above underlyings, the structured product is a mix between a fixed income component (on the bond part) which duration can be modified by the level of the index, and returns that are not from the same asset class. It can be useful for some institutions that have "good practices" in terms of split of their investments between equity and fixed income products. Structured products being based on a bond issued by a bank, we can consider that it belongs to the class of fixed income products, nevertheless, its returns can be indexed on equities or commodities. Is allows to asset managers to have access to returns of another asset class if they prefer. Of course, the caveat is that these managers,

---

[4]The Libor scandal shocked the financial community: before the Global Financial Crisis, banks manipulated the price of the Libor to make profits.

specialized on fixed income products, may be undereducated on the nature of equity returns, and hence take bad investment decisions. A buyer of structured products should always develop a sense on the risk embedded in the optionality of the product he or she is buying, for instance using simple Monte Carlo simulations; optionality is often counter-intuitive and simulations can give clues about the frequency of occurrence of some events. There is a human bias in underestimating the probability of occurrence of rare events, optional products, with some returns that are triggered or not when an index crosses a level, are highly exposed to this bias.

3.3.2 Main ways to package risk

3.3.2.1 Autocall

Definition. Autocall is the abbreviation for automatically callable. It is a bond that can be ended in anticipation when certain market conditions are met. Early repayment is the trademark of Autocalls. The duration of the investment is thus unknown at the beginning of the deal. The maximum duration is however known. More often, the underlying used to compute the coupon is an equity index. Autocalls are highly recommended for investors seeking a minimum level of performance stability when uncertainty on the market is high.

Mechanism. Here is a typical example of an Autocall: A Bond with a 10 years maturity; the equity index is the EuroStoxx50. As a consequence, each year, the note ends if the EuroStoxx50 returns have been more than 5% and in such a case the investor receives

- His capital increased by 7% per annum if the index is greater than 105% of the initial level.
- His capital increased by 3% per annum if the index is between 80% and 105% of the initial level (a safety airbag).
- His capital if the index is between 80% and 65% of the initial level.
- The value of the investment in the index if the index is less than 65% of the initial level (a loss of at least 35%).

Product risk exposure. Autocalls are a way for investors to get exposed, in a limited manner, to equity risk in a fixed income logic (getting coupon and potentially the capital at maturity).

- The cost of the nonlinear exposure to equity risk is partially compensated by the uncertainty on the repayment date.
- Volatile markets allow paying higher coupons in exchange for a higher risk exposure.
- Limited exposure to equity risk:
  - Early redemption on upward scenarios, which caps the potential gains from equity exposure.
  - Capital guaranteed for moderate backward scenarios, plus potential coupons accumulated during the product's life period.
  - Risk on the investment in case of large backward scenarios.

3.3.2.2   Equity linked swap

Definition. An Equity Linked Swap (ELS) is an OTC transaction to exchange at fixed dates cash flows representing the performance of an Equity (a stock, a basket or an index) either against a fixed or floating rate (equity swap) or against the performance of another equity asset ("out-performance swap").

Mechanism. An ELS can be *total return* arranged to pay dividends or *price return* where the dividends are implied in the spread. The total return swap implies 3 legs as described in Figure 3.2(a): the index performance flow, the index dividends flow, and the rate flow. The Price Return Swap implies only 2 legs: the index performance flow and the rate flow, here described in Figure 3.2b(b).

There are three types of indices according to dividend treatment:

(1) **Price return (PR) index:** It behaves like a stock meaning that the theoretical spot price drops at the ex-dividend date by the number of index points corresponding to the dividends paid by the companies included in the index.
(2) **Gross total return (GTR) index:** The provider reinvests into the index 100% of dividends paid by the company. The divisor is adjusted to compensate the dividend detachment; therefore spot cum and spot ex are identical.
(3) **Net total return (NTR) index:** The provider reinvest into the index a net dividend after deducing taxes.

Product risk exposure. Since an ELS synthetically replicates the value of the underlying equity asset (stock or indices), it is a way to

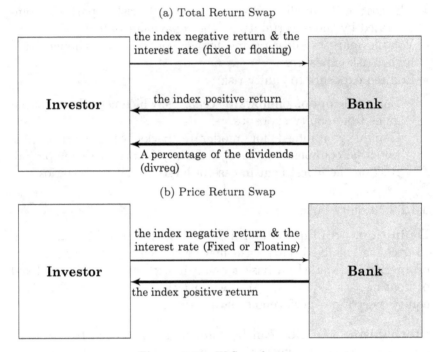

Figure 3.2: ELS mechanism.

get a linear 1-to-1 exposure to the equity risk without mobilizing capital at inception. ELS allows for the following risk exposures:

- Getting exposure to a broad range of equity underlyings and strategies without operational constraints such as high trading costs, corporate events, time to market, long or short, single stock vs basket, dynamic vs fixed, and so forth.
- Diversifying a portfolio exposure while complying with asset allocation regulations or funds' prospectus.
- Hedging an exposure by implementing a short strategy without having to sell the stocks directly.
- Generating leverage: to refinance long positions or to get exposure to the underlying without buying it generates leverage on the portfolio.
- Getting exposed to the credit risk by implementing a lending strategy (buying the shares, buying the swap and lending the shares).

3.3.2.3 Credit linked note

Definition. The Credit Linked Note (CLN) is a bond (or note) issued by a financial issuer having the following characteristics:

- In the absence of a credit event on the selected reference entity (corporate, other banks); the client receives coupons during the life of the product (could be fixed or variable) and receives at maturity the initial invested capital.
- In the case of a credit event on the selected reference entity; coupon payments stop from the credit event. At maturity, the client only receives the recovery rate on the reference entity multiplied by the notional.
- Like any bond, in case of bankruptcy of the issuer, the investor can lose its investment.

Mechanism. Let's take the example of a bank lending money to a company, XYZ. When it does so the bank holds on its balance sheet the credit risk of XYZ going bankrupt before paying back the loan. The bank could decide to transfer the credit risk to investors by issuing CLNs. Investors will ask for a return on investment proportional to the credit risk of the company XYZ.

In practice, the bank will place the funds raised from issuing CLNs on less risky bonds.

- If company XYZ is solvent, the bank pays the CLNs' premium to investors (pays the notes in full).
- If company XYZ goes bankrupt, the note-holders (i.e., investors) suffer a capital loss.

Product risk exposure.

- A CLN exposes the investor to double credit risk: The credit risk of the issuer of the CLN (the bank) and the one of the underlying reference (the company) in exchange for a higher yield compared to an equivalent bond.
- CLNs allows banks to recycle the credit risk taken against CDS buyers (credit protection buyers).
- They give investors the possibility to get exposure on a credit reference for which certain maturities or certain currencies are not available on the bond market.

3.3.2.4   Convertible bonds

Definition.   A convertible security is a corporate bond that gives the holder the right to convert or exchange the bond for a fixed number of ordinary shares. It is a hybrid security with debt and equity-like features. Under normal circumstances at maturity, they are worth either their cash redemption value or the market value of the shares into which they are convertible, whichever is the greater.

Mechanism.   The standard contract of a convertible bond goes like this. Consider a Company XYZ bond with a $1,000 par value that is convertible into Company XYZ common shares with a 6% annual coupon and a conversion ratio of 20 (the number of shares that the investor will receive if he chooses to convert the bond into shares). This is equivalent to purchasing 20 shares of Stock XYZ at a price of $50 per share ($1,000/ 20 = $50).

   Every year during the contract the bondholder receives $60 interest payment. At maturity,

- If the stock price of XYZ is higher than $50, let's say the stock price has risen to $75 per share, the investor will choose to convert his bond to 20 shares of stock and now his investment is worth $1,500.
- If the stock price of XYZ is lower than $50, the investor will receive back the bond notional of $1,000.

Product advantages.   The product has a double exposure to equity and debt. The main risk exposure is:

- A positive exposure to the upside movement of the underlying with protection from downside movement.
- The appealing asymmetric profile of convertible bonds is justified by the credit risk the investor accepts to take by financing young, or distressed, augmented by the liquidity risk.
- When a stock has already outperformed, the product behaves as a call option: Getting protection from a downside event while getting part of positive performance. Thus, it reduces exposure to stock market risks.

3.4 The Business Model of Structured Products

A structured product full team involves a lot of skills which are listed by Table 3.2. The core activity is done by the "Financial structuring" group, which is not only evaluating the products via quantitative methods; but it is also communicating with clients and the Sales team to have ideas for products that will interest clients at a reasonable price. This team, while being in communication with sales, maintains a direct link with the trading desk, to have a better understanding of the practical hedging and trading issues, and of hidden costs. It has been underlined in the introduction of this chapter that the trading desk can be outsourced "back to back" with a large investment bank. In such a case, the "Trading and Management team" is smaller, it oversees and monitors the work of trading desks of the investment banks that are implementing the hedge. Outsourcing is costly in term of fees, but a well organized large investment bank can lower its trading and hedging costs far more than what an independent structurer could do (essentially due to the netting of different positions across this large bank, either directly when it is allowed, or via "technical trades" thanks to transparent and well-priced transactions). The legal workaround of structured products is very demanding because such products have a lot of optionalities and their regulation have evolved a lot; especially in Europe with MiFID 2 and PRIIPS. The importance of the compliance echoes to the legal workload, and risk control is very important since the day to day life of these products can encounter unexpected market contexts or options that have to be addressed as soon as possible, and not at expiry (Table 3.2).

From a quantitative perspective (16)

Quantitative analysts will certainly be involved in the financial structuring as well as in risk control. For the Financial structuring, a good knowledge of derivative products (valuation, Monte Carlo simulation, and hedging) are needed, while the risk control will require more extreme risk measurements (like Value at Risk) and a good understanding of risk models (see Chapter 5) and operational risks. The interactions with

---

(Continued)

(Continued)

Sales teams and with clients demand a good understanding and solid intuitions on the main sources of costs of any structured product in order to be able to draft payoffs that will answer to requests which are not yet fully specified.

Table 3.2: Organization of structuring desks.

Team	Tasks
Sales teams	Responsible for identifying customer needs and selling the offer. Customers can be categorized by type and geographic area. • Retail: Distribution networks, private banks; • Institutional: Banks, insurance, pension funds, sovereign funds, asset managers; • Corporates: Large companies, SMEs, local authorities.
Financial structuring	Define the financial characteristics of the products, determine the price of the offers (starting from the cover price ensuring the desired profitability by the bank). They can also carry out certain risk related measures (CVA, FVA, etc.).
Trading management desk	Implementation of the operation, management of the hedge, monitoring of the life cycle and the result. They are usually divided by asset class and by underlying.
Legal structuring	Define the legal contract documenting the operation.
Product marketing	Implement the commercial supports by integrating, in particular, the financial advantages of the products.
Risk control	Check that the products put in place comply with the market, operational and counterparty risk limits.
Compliance	Compliance with regulations for products, their management, and marketing.

3.4.1 The consumers of structured products

The first and largest consumers of structured products are by far institutional investors, via investment vehicles that are mainly distributed to retail investors. Institutional investors manage the wealth of different classes of the population with various profiles and AUM levels; they are constantly in need of new investment solutions, customized to each fund's profile, cost-efficient, and diversified across asset classes. In France for instance, €3 billion of assets under management were invested in structured products in 2018. Insurers take the lead with life insurance contracts, followed by private banks then pension funds and mutual funds. Sovereign funds come after depending on the type of diversification they would like to achieve, and the level of capital they would like to guarantee.

Institutional investors seek performance on one or more asset classes. While they could invest directly in the underlying they prefer structured products for different reasons: The nonlinear nature of the payoff and to some extent the guarantee they offer in terms of capital is seducing. Besides, in an environment of low yield for fixed income products, such vehicles can provide equity-like returns, and in an environment of low equity returns, the coupon can be designed to be driven by fixed-income factors. Structured products constitute tailor-made solutions that can be adjusted according to market conditions by combining customer-specific parameters (strategy, risk-return profile, maturity, and nominal) and a wide range of underlying assets — equities, indices, commodities, foreign exchange, interest rates. Their repayment formulas are almost unlimited, beyond the simple dividend payment of an equity share or the simple coupon of a bond.

The second important consumer of the structured product are corporates. Not as investment tools for enhanced performance but for hedging purposes by creating a precise protection on investments or risks already borne.

The third biggest consumers of structured products are retail investors seeking capital guarantee with a potential of performance. Regulation has made it a key objective to protect this category of investors. Specifically, products should only be offered to investors with the necessary financial knowledge to understand the associated risks. Products need to have clear, accurate statements of the

investment's objective and of the potential investment risks, as well
as of transparent costs and fees. Products should also meet some
minimum liquidity requirements to lessen the burden of the leverage
effect and hedge on the underlying market. However, less complex
products, employing transparent underlying indices should find no
difficulty to meet the regulatory requirements.

3.4.2   The motivations of structured products suppliers

As is the case for the majority of financial services, structured
products are provided by the sell-side. In the first place, we find
investment banks since structured products are complex risky assets
involving several sources of risk. There are at least two: the credit
risk due to the bond component and the market risk because of the
derivative component. So who is better equipped to monitor market
risk and credit risk at the same time than banks present all along the
value chain from conception to selling, through replication and market risk hedging. The creation of structured products indeed requires
a variety of skills.

3.4.3   The life-cycle of structured products

Structured products are available on various investment vehicles such
as Euro Medium-Term Notes (EMTN), and certificates, all issued
mainly by financial institutions. Structured products involve the
following flow exchanges:

- The bond component supports the initial and terminal flows (i.e.,
  the capital is transferred from the buyer to the seller at emission
  and goes back to the buyer at the expiry of the product) and the
  principle of a coupon.
- A derivative component is attached to the coupon: the way the
  coupon is computed is a payoff written on an underlying that is
  often an index.
- Another derivative component can be attached to the expiry: when
  does the product end and how much of the initial capital goes back
  to the buyer of the product.

These three components provide different risk exposure: a counterparty risk (supported by the buyer of the product), a nonlinear exposure to the risk factor supported by the underlying of the coupon, operational risk all over the life-cycle of the product.

A structured product transaction is an agreement between the issuer, most often a financial institution seeking new ways to raise capital and finance projects, and the buyer who accepts to be exposed to the risk packaged in the product.

This means that the buyer has views on the risk associated with the product: typically, an investor having directional views on the future movement of the underlying which would make the realized yields of the coupons more attractive. Moreover, the issuer has financing needs at different time maturities and looks to raise capital and diversify the nature of its bond buyers at the same time. The issuer values in a martingale way making the uncertainty attached to the payoffs risk-neutral. As a result, the transaction takes place at a common price.

In between the issuer and the buyer, two other participants act as pure intermediaries: the arranger and the trader. They are risk-neutral and make their revenues with commissions and fees. They do not have views on future market movements, but they simply value them at their replication cost. They are pure intermediaries between the issuer and the buyer. One of their talents is to be involved in as many transactions as possible, as to make more fees. The best way to do so resides in understanding and anticipating the appetite for risk of the buyers and the life-cycle of capital needed by issuers,[5] to then transfer client appetite for risk to the market while answering to issuer's need of funding.

Figure 3.3 explains the process of the creation of standard structured products and how different market participants are involved at different stages of the life-cycle of the product. The numbers from 1 to 5 correspond to exchanges of cash flows happening at issuance, during the operation and at maturity:

---

[5]The duration of the products and the type of guarantees has to match the needs of the issuers in terms of Asset and Liability Management (ALM).

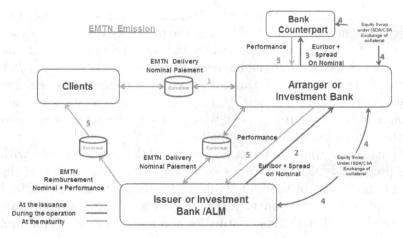

Figure 3.3: Structured product issuance.

1. The client buys the structured product from the arranger.
2. The issuer issues a bond with a coupon (Euribor plus a certain spread depending on the issuer's credit risk) that is bought by the arranger.
3. The arranger will use this coupon to pay for the derivatives, the coupon, and the optional expiry: it will allow the arranger to provide the buyer of the product with the expected more sophisticated coupon.
4. During the life of the product, the arranger can host the trading or he can pay a larger investment bank to hedge the derivatives. Thanks to this, the trading investment bank delivers the payoff to the arranger who then delivers it to the buyer of the product (through the issuer).
5. At maturity, the derivative pays the required performance. The arranger channels it to the issuer who will add it to the reimbursement of the initial capital and deliver the total amount to the client.

This is a very good example of sophisticated intermediation of risk-taking place in financial markets. Several participants are involved, each of them having a specific need and thus takes care of a specific mix of risks. At the end of the process, a bank raised capital to fund projects in the real economy, and investors or corporations obtain the exposure they asked for. Of course, it demands that the buyer of such

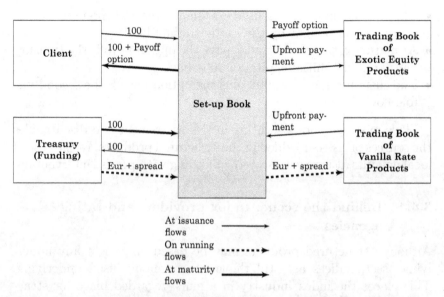

Figure 3.4: EMTN cash flow when the arranger, the issuer and the trading desk are hosted by the same investment bank.

products are educated enough to understand the exact nature of the risks they are exposed to, instead of being focused on the (optional) yield that is written in the contract.

Since investment banks are present all across the value chain of structured products, we find the same flows within the same investment bank where the issuer, the arranger and the trading counterpart are different desks of the same entity. In such a case, the visible flows (from the outside world) are limited to the ones going to and from the buyer of the product. All the other flows are internal and transit through a set-up book via technical trades as detailed in Figure 3.4.

- The customer buys the product at 100\$ at the start of the deal, which is the first visible flow at the issuance of the product.
- This amount of cash is placed in the treasury (ALM — Assets and Liabilities) desk of the bank for the period of the deal. This desk plays the role of the issuer; in exchange for funding, it pays the inter-bank rate plus a spread (Euribor + 5bps).
- The Euribor + 5bps flow is paid to the vanilla rate trading book on running basis in exchange for the premium of the vanilla option paid upfront at the start.

- The upfront payment is used to finance the risk premium of an exotic option bought by the exotic trading book.
- At maturity, the exotic trader pays the option payoff, the treasury hands out the initial capital of 100$ back.
- The customer receives 100$ plus the option payoff, the second visible flow.

This montage allows scrutiny in risk assessment and disentangles the sources of risk embedded in the structured products. In the case of local defaults, it is easy to stop the bleeding with precise intervention.

3.4.4 Behind the scene: Index providers and rating agencies

Although structured products may be based on almost any underlying asset, indices are still the most commonly used underlying. This places the index industry in a much-regarded place for structured products, as index providers exchange important flows with issuers before the creation and during the life-cycle of the structured product.

First of all, the index industry is no more than a branding business. Each index (i.e., CAC 40, FTSE100, S&P500, etc.) is a registered trademark that can not be used or replicated without the explicit permission of its creators. Therefore, if the arranger chooses a certain index as an underlying he will need to agree in advance with the index provider on the right to use the name of the index, in exchange for licensing fees,[6] on top of the cost of subscribing to index-related market data commercial packages that include continuous index levels, historical components, weights, number of shares of index constituents and additional metrics used in the calculations.

Arrangers could use traditional "Blue-Chip" indices as underlying for structured products. However, the client's needs evolve rapidly to seek exposure to alternative sources of risk premia. Therefore, new indices are tailored at the arranger's request to achieve the desired risk-return profile. Since the index performance and the structured

---

[6]Licensing fees could be either a fixed amount paid upfront, a variable percentage of the invested amount in the structured product, or a combination of both.

product attractivity are structurally interlinked, there is a risk to manipulate index levels to yield high returns for the products. That was the case for the Libor calculation during the subprime crisis, where some banks contributing to the interbank rate were reporting false rates to hide their credit exposure, giving the market the impression that they were more creditworthy than they really were. In response to the Libor scandal, and to avoid any future price manipulations, a new regulation, the European Benchmark Regulation (BMR), came into force on January the 1, 2018 to define new requirements for index providers and the corresponding sanctions if those are not met. In the wake of the BMR regulation, index administrators are held responsible for the calculation and dissemination of the indices they design even if a third party is involved in the calculation. Some structured products issuers have the BMR accreditation and still factually maintain the possibility to issue products on their own indices. However, it is seen as a good practice to entrust the index calculation to a third party. The introduction of the BMR brought on a high fixed cost for small players to enter the business, favoring the development of big franchises such as MSCI or FTSE Russel; MSCI alone manages more than 160,000 indexes.

To continuously meet the rapid pace of structured product innovation, index providers need to invest massively on research (either internally or externally by partnering with rating agencies and alternative data providers) to design indices with exposure to special thematics such as Smart-Beta, factor investments, reputation risk, energy transition, or ESG — E (environmental), S (societal), G (governance) by only picking assets with a certain risk-return profile. Index providers are driven by the demand of investors via structured products teams that are often hosted in investment banks or are discussing with investment banks and are themselves good clients of investment banks. Again, there is a risk of one way market there: if the regulation, or the risk departments, or the risk replication process forget a risk factor, then the product will be incorrectly priced (because the cost of replicating the risk in the direction of this factor, or the cost of the capital that should be needed to be put in from of this risk, is not paid by anyone until this risk materializes and most market participants along this long chain of dependences lose a lot of money. This issue can be labelled as a "model risk" and is largely developed in Chapter 5.

3.5   Risk Intermediation Via Structured Products

3.5.1   Risk valuation starts at issuance

There is a common misconception that if the hedging of structured products goes wrong then the investor's promised payout is at risk, whereas subject that the issuer is solvent at maturity, it guarantees the payment of the agreed payoff amount. Thus, promised payout delivery is a risk for the bank, and the hedging represents the issuer's best practice for a long-lasting business.

The risk replication paradigm states that the value of a product is the expected cost of its replication, from issuance to expiry. Therefore, in order to evaluate the price of the financial instrument, the bank must first be able to evaluate the structuring cost of the product and model the evolution of the product according to the underlying. This will allow it to put in place hedging instruments to minimize the risks generated by the instruments sold to customers. For instance, in the case of stock options sold to a client, the bank will hedge the sensitivity to interest rates, delta shares, share price volatility and potentially stock dividend, equity, loan-to-equity, financing cost. These hedges are made by trading in the instruments available on the interbank market. Hedging products will be built by creating an opposite sensitivity to the customer exposition. The major problem of these hedging products is that the purchase of a protection requires payment of a premium by the investor, for which he is rarely willing to pay at the start of the transaction. In most cases, this protection is financed by giving up a potential capital gain (in case of favorable market conditions) of the investor's initial exposure. The main hedging instruments are as follows:

- Listed shares, futures contracts on equity indexes.
- Future contracts on bonds or interest rates.
- Options on stocks and indices.
- Interest rate swaps — floating index versus fixed rate.
- Dividend swap.

The sophistication of structured products is the exact nature of the payoff allowing a nonlinear exposure to a risk factor. Structured products are tailor-made transactions (OTC contracts). Nevertheless, they follow a standardized legal framework put in place by the International Swaps and Derivatives Association (ISDA). At the issuance of the bond, the financial stability (debt level) of the issuer is documented by its issuance program. The contract allows also to define the flows of products, the obligations of the parties (calculations, information) and especially what would happen if parties were to be confronted with certain special events, such as abnormal market conditions or credit events. Beyond market risk, the main risk of structured product portfolios is life-cycle management. This includes tracking product adjustments (securities transactions, mergers, acquisition, exceptional dividends, takeover bids/public offer of exchange), and tracking product events (maturity, barrier activation). These events and their treatments have to be taken into account with accuracy in a risk replication framework, to reflect the expected value of the contract at inception.

Let's take the example of a bank being short delta on the underlying stock. This sensitivity is hedged by an equity loan and a sale in the market. The bank carries a loan–loan risk that it accepts under normal market conditions. In the event of a sudden large increase in the cost of loan–loan, it may negotiate the establishment of a compensation clause on the loan–loan to a certain level (or an early termination clause in the case where the asset is no longer borrowed). One of the main challenges in risk hedging during special events is the difficulty of observing prices. The less liquid an instrument, the more difficult it is to be able to trade large amounts at the current market price: the market impact of a large trade increases the cost of replication. The issuer must estimate these additional costs in order to charge them to customers at the implementation of the transaction.

In principle, the value at issuance should reflect all these uncertainties: the randomness of price moves are considered as the *known unknown* by hedging desks, while the subtleties of rare cases and the gap in the description of the resolution of possible events are rather seen as an *unknown unknown*. The value at issuance should be equal to the expected value of all these possible events, weighted by their probability of occurrence. For nonlinear payoffs, the expected value is not risk-neutral anymore as it includes a fraction of the risk. In that sense, structured products are tools for *risk intermediation*. Once the product is live, the trading desk implements the hedge, and slowly the expected cost becomes realized profits or losses: profits if the realizations of unknowns are in favor of the issuers, and losses they are in favor of the buyer of the product.

3.5.2   The hedge is not free of charge

The principal profitability of a structured product business stems from the commercial invoicing carried out at the issuance. Obviously, the hedging price is increased by a safety margin to face part of the uncertainties. The goal of the teams managing the products is to immunize the portfolio of products sold to customers against the numerous sources of risk. This protection is achieved by setting up hedging instruments based on a valuation model. The rule of the model is to project the risks on the sensitivities of the hedging instruments, assuming that they behave in line with the model used in their evaluation. Several episodes of model failure proved to professionals that models are mere simplifications of the complex and continuously changing reality. As such, when models are inadequate and some important parameters are missing, the hedge is incomplete, which exposes banks to huge risks. *Model risk* and its implication are covered in more details in Chapter 5.

The implementation of these hedges is done by paying a spread with respect to the market value used to calibrate the model (cost of bid/ask). Since the instruments sold to customers are complex in nature and therefore cannot be bought back on the market, the hedge is dynamic: the distortion of the product's sensitivities over time and the movement of the market parameters are not identical to the evolution of the sensitivities of the market. A complete model should, therefore, assess these additional costs.

In most cases for "complex" products (i.e., different from a vanilla option), the coverage of sensitivities to the implementation of the operation is not sufficient. Indeed, with the evolution of the underlying, the sensitivities of the product evolve differently from the hedging portfolio. The introduction of these additional hedges generates a cost (mainly a bid-ask spread charged by the market). It is possible to model the evolution of the hedging on the available instruments and integrate these additional costs. However, certain aspects and mainly the evolution of the market liquidity are difficult to anticipate. Therefore, large trading desks have the advantage of size over small ones. A trading desk being large enough[7] to hedge several products of different types of payoff, both in terms of the nature of exposure and the duration of risk (i.e., very diverse market conditions), will on average have a book less exposed to uncertainties, as some source of risks will cancel out. On the contrary, a small structuring firm would rather not hedge its own positions itself and instead ask the services of a bigger investment bank to delegate the risk of uncertainties. Financial intermediation is structurally in favor of the creation of large participants in between ultimate buyers and sellers, it is in their books that a large part of the idiosyncratic risk gets diversified and transaction costs decreases.

3.5.3 Effect of structured products replication on prices formation

We have seen in Section 2.4.4 of Chapter 2 that flows could move prices, via the market impact, and in Section 2.5 of Chapter 2 we have seen that the process of hedging a derivative could move prices thanks to the exact same mechanism: the delta hedge of a vanilla option corresponding to the opportunity to buy at expiry (i.e., the hedge of a sold Call Option) requires to buy an estimate of the number of shares that the intermediary would have to deliver if the price goes below a certain level called "the strike". It is roughly the number of shares to be delivered multiplied by the probability of the option to be called. As a consequence, the market impact corresponds to a "conditional pressure" that one could expect. In brief, the more probable it is for the shares to be delivered, the more the price pressure moves the price of the underlying via market impact in the direction to deliver the shares (this increases the price moves, and thus can be qualified of "self-fulfilling prophecy"). This mechanism is aggravated when the underlying instrument is less liquid. The market impact of a large trade is detrimental to the price of the trader initiating the trade.

---

[7] "Large enough" means here that this desk has a lot of clients, for a lot of products.

In addition, structured products are tools that allow investors to express their directional views on future movements on the underlying assets, and since the payoff is nonlinear the exposure to risk factors is most of the time leveraged. As a result, shocks on the structured product's trading diffuse into the price formation process of the underlying asset at a higher magnitude through the hedge.

From a quantitative perspective (17)

Derivative products and structured products are typically a natural way to mix risks: the issuer accepts to take on its book the opposite exposure to what its clients need. Concentration of the intermediation allows participants having a lot of clients to net the exposure to common risk factors via the estimation of sensitivities (most often using Monte Carlo simulation or numerical schemes); the more clients they have, the higher the probability to be able to net exposures (if the configuration is not a "one way market": all clients — and other market participants in general — want to consume the same risks). The more standard the products, the higher the probability to net the exposures too. This mechanism of netting requires quantitative analysis to: estimate the exposures (sensitivities), breakdown the exposure into meaningful factors, monitor the exposure and build some analytics to guess of the market is not "one way", and to estimate the remaining risks and the accuracy of the Taylor expansions used to hedge the risks.

3.6 For More Details

Ekeland *et al.* (2013) is a good reference to understand how market participants interacts around Future contracts from a theoretical viewpoint. To stay on the theoretical side of financial markets, it is important to read some textbooks in financial mathematics like Karatzas *et al.* (1998) or Shiryaev (1999); mathematics captures the proper way to formalize sciences in general. It is also the case for problem born in financial markets: only a proper formulation of derivative pricing or portfolio construction allows to go further.

Then it is possible to use this well specified model to design Monte Carlo simulations or a finite difference scheme, or any optimization involving future payoff. For advanced methods for Monte Carlo simulations, have a look at Bouchard and Touzi (2004) and Pagès *et al.* (2004). It would be a mistake to shortcut the mathematical writing of a problem to solve, especially when probabilities are involved.

It is known that one big issue in modeling price dynamics of derivatives is the lack of enough tradable instrument corresponding to the risk factor the derivative is exposed to; for a recent book on derivative pricing using the mathematical tools, known as the "incomplete markets problem"). Probably pushed by the success of data sciences and by the maturity of the field[8] (that started in the 1980s with for instance El Karoui and Rochet (1989)), a new trend in financial mathematics is driven by linking mathematical modeling between different financial domains and confronting them with data. A good example is the "rough volatility model", developed in Gatheral *et al.* (2018).

On financial markets, the uncertainty is so large compared to other sciences that it is important to revisit often the solutions that have been put in place. It means that the components that have been used for a mathematical writing have to be questioned, and probably new ones have to be added after few years of evolving economic conditions. Typically, liquidity issues raised during the Global Financial Crisis now have to be taken into account in most financial problems. Liquidity is difficult to formalize in a proper way because it involves the actions (and flows) of all market participants. Mean Field Games theory provides a nice way to formalize how agents interact via an anonymous "context" (i.e., a *mean field*). It is probably one of the interesting way to model liquidity: no isolated agent can drive the market liquidity but all of them are contributing to the state of the liquidity and each of them is influenced by it. It is the definition of a mean field addressed by MFG; for more detail, read the two fascinating volumes written by Carmona and Delarue (2018).

---

[8]Practitioners, and especially heads of quantitative teams of investment banks, recently published books reflecting their modeling practices, see Bergomi (2015) and Kettani and Reghai (2020).

Beyond this specific theory, it is important to model a problematic with as much accuracy as possible and not being attracted by an existing model one is already familiar with. This bias often leads to blindly dealing with always the same family of models. Diversity of modeling angles is important, hence interdisciplinary teams are always welcome by leading market participants. Very early in the development of finance, Grossman and Stiglitz identified that it is important to work hard and to not ignore his or her homework; any detail that does not seem to match with evidence is important to follow up on. This is one of the sense of the Grossman–Stiglitz paradox developed in Grossman and Stiglitz (1980).

References

Bergomi, L. (2015). *Stochastic Volatility Modeling*. CRC press, New York.

Bouchard, B. and Touzi, N. (2004). Discrete-time approximation and Monte Carlo simulation of backward stochastic differential equations. *Stochastic Processes and Their Applications*, 111(2):175–206.

Carmona, R. and Delarue, F. (2018). *Probabilistic Theory of Mean Field Games with Applications I-II*, volume 84. Springer, Cham, Switzerland. https://link.springer.com/book/10.1007/978-3-319-58920-6.

Ekeland, I., Lautier, D., and Villeneuve, B. (2013). A simple equilibrium model for a commodity market with spot trades and futures contracts. In *30th International French Finance Association Conference*, p. 33.

El Karoui, N. and Rochet, J. C. (1989). A pricing formula for options on coupon bonds. University of Paris. Working Paper.

Gatheral, J., Jaisson, T., and Rosenbaum, M. (2018). Volatility is rough. *Quantitative Finance*, 18(6):933–949.

Grossman, S. J. and Stiglitz, J. E. (1980). On the impossibility of informationally efficient markets. *The American Economic Review*, 70(3):393–408.

Karatzas, I. and Shreve, S. E. (1998). *Methods of Mathematical Finance*, volume 39, Springer, New York.

Kettani, O. and Reghai, A. (2020). *Financial Models in Production*. Springer, Cham, Switzerland. https://link.springer.com/book/10.1007/978-3-030-57496-3#about

Pagès, G., Pham, H., and Printems, J. (2004). Optimal quantization methods and applications to numerical problems in finance. In *Handbook of Computational and Numerical Methods in Finance*, pp. 253–297. Springer.

Shiryaev, A. N. (1999). *Essentials of Stochastic Finance: Facts, Models, Theory*, volume 3, World Scientific, Singapore.

Chapter 4

Asset Management as an Intermediary Between the Investors and the Real Economy

4.1 The Role of Asset Management in the Financial System

4.1.1 The contact point between the financial system and the real economy

We have seen in Section 1.5.1 that the *Buy Side* is composed of asset managers, but their role and their functioning have not yet been explained. The aim of this chapter is thus to detail their role in the financial system and to describe their business and the way they process.

Asset managers, corporations, and banks are all agents operating on the border between the financial system and the "real economy". When corporations express the need to raise capital, banks help them to do so by either providing them loans or by redirecting them to the financial markets where they can either issue bonds or equity shares. These basic financial instruments are of paramount importance to asset managers and retail investors looking for to invest and to diversify their risk. Asset Managers can buy these financial instruments either on the primary market, directly from the issuer, or on the secondary market, "on Exchanges", from a potential seller. They can in turn sell them back on exchanges to buy other assets to adjust their portfolio risk exposure at the cost of a "liquidity premium" (i.e., paying transaction costs).

Corporates consume investment vehicles to keep their assets and liabilities balanced through time and for future maturities and to manage their exposure to macro-economic changes, captured by risk factors. Retail investors consume these products to protect their savings against different economic factors, and to synchronize their savings with their financial goals, typically, buying a house, paying the university tuition for their children, or keeping money for their retirement. They can either go on their own to the market and buy, "on exchange", tradable instruments or buy investment vehicles packaged by asset managers.

Asset managers provide a clearly defined service. For instance, pension funds offer the ability to spare money for retirement. Other asset managers offer specific investment vehicles with specific exposure to specific asset classes, such as private equity, real estate, equity markets, fixed income markets, and more recently providing exposition to equity factors or themes, like Value, Growth, or ESG. This industry adopted a common vocabulary of *risk factors* or *rewarded factors* following decades of *ex-post* decomposition of investment strategies returns. These factors have initially been *characteristics* of companies (countries, sector, size, dividend yield, etc.), but soon have been pre-packaged in tradable instruments in the market, such as Exchange Traded Funds (ETFs) and P-Notes.

Passive investments. In terms of financial flows, the role of asset managers is clear: retail and corporate investors could always bury their savings in a shoebox, but in such a case they would be exposed to inflation in a very general manner. Instead of keeping these savings at home, they can invest them in order to achieve a list or sequence of *investment goals*. For instance, if someone wants to buy a house in 10 years and has some savings, buying a small apartment with these savings somewhat ensures that this amount of money, which can buy 100 square meters today, will be worth the same surface 10 years later. Qualitatively, to be protected against inflation in the same way that buying a flat of 100 square meters and keeping it ensures you to have the value of 100 square meters in the future, whatever the variation of any other economic factors, a more generic investor should buy a fraction of any existing asset. In theory, if one succeeds to invest in all assets in proportion of their value today and hold them, he will find the "equivalent value" of this initial investment in the future. This passive view on investing makes sense if you do not want to make any bet, but would like to preserve the intrinsic value of your wealth. A bet would be to buy more real estate than its current proportion of the existing assets; thus, over-weighting real estate in the initial portfolio. It is a good bet if the real estate market returns more on investment through time than other asset classes, and of course, it is a bad bet otherwise.

On paper, such a passive investment strategy seems very safe, as long as economic value creation comes from assets that can, at least partially, be acquired. Unfortunately, the life cycle of value creation is more complex. It is always very difficult to buy a fraction of the most innovative businesses, especially at their early stage. When, as an investor, could someone have bought shares of Amazon or Facebook? Probably very late, until these companies were listed on an exchange an investor would be interested in investing in corporations in their private equity stage, or even earlier, in some projects financed by loans. Moreover, it is not always possible to estimate the correct fraction of a listed company required to implement a purely passive investor viewpoint. The concept of *free float*, that is the fraction of the capital that is open to public investors, is used by index providers like MSCI, FTSE, and Euronext to provide reference lists of investible capital. But an investment using only the free float as a reference would miss part of the value created by this company. These simple examples show that a fraction of the economic value and in fact of the economic growth will always escape to a purely passive investor. In financial studies, we always consider passive investments returns as benchmarks. However, the benchmark is never fully representative of the real economic growth but is rather a proxy of it. In any case, the notion of benchmark, or reference universe, is complex to define too.

There are investment bets everywhere. Let's not forget the regional aspect too. An investor based in a certain country would probably like to invest in assets located in other countries, as to capture the global economic growth. But the list of countries to include is not straightforward. If the investor decides not to include some countries, she is making a bet similar to an investor over-weighting the real estate sector against other sectors. But, including all countries is cumbersome. Some countries, like China, prevent foreign investors to buy shares of all local companies. Last but not least, should the investor decide to buy assets of other countries, he will have to acquire them in their local currency, thus a currency effect takes place. In this case, he will be exposed to an exchange rate when he sells the assets (which may or may not be favorable), or he may buy protection against the future exchange rate by using financial instruments. In the latter case, he will have to finance this protection and therefore accepts to get exposed to the yield curve.

These short paragraphs show how investments are made of a sequence of decisions that can be explicit, like over-weighting a sector or a country, or implicit by not hedging the currency risk. In all cases, investors will have to take risks that can be expressed in terms of risk factors (such as sectors, countries, currencies, growth companies, etc.). It is extremely important for investors who wish to gain exposure to such risks to be aware of the correlation between these factors and the additional risks involved. For example, the fact that correlations between factors are a function of market context. It is easy to see that under conditions of market stress, correlations increase, simply because most assets fall simultaneously. An important factor in investment decisions is the risk-reward profile of a portfolio; since the reward of a bet increases with its risk, it is important to look for maximum returns within a risk envelope (this is the foundation of modern portfolio theory).

Towards active investment strategies. As a consequence, a good addition to passive investing are riskier investments, aimed at capturing returns to compensate for the opportunities that the passive portfolio will miss. These riskier investments can be real estate, private equity, or any other bet on uncertain projects that may become the future Amazon or Google. Such riskier investments are usually called "active investments" because they require more monitoring and resources. Once again, the Grossman–Stiglitz paradox is lurking here: the act of actively seeking out rewarding risky projects is a mean of disseminating information about these projects into prices, and it is only if the information is not already in the price that the task of identifying it incorporates it in the price.

Diversification is key. The difficulty is to target investment sources that are not too correlated, because having assets that are too correlated in the same portfolio means that they will have both good and bad returns simultaneously, and thus such a portfolio will have a greater risk (in the sense of "greater probability" of performing poorly). It is preferable to have two investments that not only perform well, but also are as uncorrelated as possible. The success of using risk factors in investment strategies lies in the fact that these factors cover all possible investment worlds; they provide a vocabulary for describing a portfolio of bets. However, the success in risk-factor investing lies on the stability of their risk-reward profiles (i.e., at least weakly stationary in the statistical sense) and the correlations (or dependencies)[1] must also be stable.

From a technical point of view, one could seek to "build" investment strategies that are independent of the most common risk factors. And since the most common risk factor is an aggregation of all tradable assets, corresponding to the most natural passive investment strategy (i.e., buying and holding an equity index) a good start would be to build portfolios independent of this passive portfolio, which is usually referred to as "the market". To do so, some hedge funds have quickly understood the interest in building "cross-sectional portfolios", i.e., to rank the invested assets on the same day (or week, or month, or quarter) according to a "characteristic" and to buy those that are at the top of this list and sell those that are at the bottom. Such a portfolio is likely to have a low correlation with the market portfolio and can have decent returns if the characteristic is well-chosen. Years later, Fama and French popularized this approach, the difficulty however being in choosing the right characteristic. They proposed the size of the companies in the portfolios, or their price/earnings ratio, while other authors proposed the beta of stock returns relative to the market factor, etc. This growing "zoo of factors" and its pitfalls are discussed in Section 4.4.4.

Leverage and financial risks. Building such long–short strategies (i.e., buying and selling simultaneously) is very different from blindly and passively buying and holding assets for many reasons:

- Firstly, a sell-short position has a potentially infinite loss whereas this is not the case with a buy-long position (you can't lose more

---

[1] In statistics: *dependence* is the nonlinear version of *correlations*.

than the price at which you bought an asset, but if the price sky-
rockets, you can lose gigantic sums if you sell it),
- In a world without a financial system, it is impossible to sell an
  asset if you have not previously purchased it.

The financial system, and in particular investment banks, using their
balance sheets, can provide ways to sell an asset that one does not yet
own. Doing so is called "short selling". In practice, the investment
bank already has this stock on its balance sheet, or borrows it. The
investment bank then lends it to the investor, who is now allowed
to sell the stock without having acquired it first. Of course, another
investor have bought it, but he didn't intend to sell it at that particular time in the future. In most cases, the owners of these borrowed
shares are long term investors: they plan to hold their shares for a
very long time and can afford to lend them out for a few weeks or
months, to boost their portfolio earnings.

There is a lot of side activities around passive investing that are
done with market participants to make a little more money. ETF
structurers, who build investment vehicles that are structurally very
passive, are often associated with investment banks to loan parts
of their portfolios in exchange for revenues, which provides a small
boost to the performance of their vehicles. Other ETF structurers
directly build synthetic vehicles, partnering with an investment bank
to obtain a total return swap corresponding to the returns of their
desired basket; this is a way to directly delegate to the investment
bank all this financial engineering: instead of owning the portfolio
and loaning part of it to banks on demand, the capital is transferred
to one bank that delivers the returns of the components of the ETF
and keeps for itself the potential advantage of having some stocking
in its inventory (i.e., on its balance sheet). The bank can then use it
as collateral or lend it to short sellers.

Stock lending is a business by itself and it is of course more rewarding to lend rare stocks (i.e., of emerging countries or with a small free
float), than very liquid ones. This activity is not without any risk
as seen with the Gamestop "short squeeze" of January 2021, or the
Volkswagen one in October 2008. Sometimes market participants who
lent the stock of a company have to buy it back because the ultimate
owners do not want to lend it anymore. The market impact of this

massive buy back can push the price to very high levels without any fundamental good news on the underlying company.

Coming back to long–short strategies, it is clear that they create leverage: While the investor physically buys some stocks (or instruments) and short sells others, his gross exposure is about twice his long exposure, and his net exposure is close to zero. The cost of borrowing can change from day to day (or month to month). Another way to implement market-neutral strategies (i.e., portfolios that are as little correlated to the market portfolio as possible) is to short sell a sufficient number of future contracts to negate the market factor exposure of a long portfolio. This again creates leverage, and the investor selling futures contracts must meet an initial margin requirement at the initiation of the short sale and must then make maintenance margin calls.

Other investors buy protection against market stress by selling derivative contracts whose price increases with volatility, so that under conditions of market stress, as volatility increases, they will make money to compensate for their loss on stocks. All these examples show that financial engineering and thus financial intermediation are part of the asset management industry; asset managers and investors are consumers of financial instruments provided by market intermediaries. They consume brokerage services, of course, but also structured products, and they interact with the balance sheet of investment banks to align the risk-return profile of their portfolios (or investment vehicles) with their needs or with their investment thesis. This allows them to adjust the profile of their portfolios so that they are as correlated as possible to the risk factors they are seeking and uncorrelated to the risk factors they are trying to avoid.

Back to the real economy. Keep in mind that while the previous paragraph focused on the financial ecosystem, there exists another perspective on active investing, which goes further than simply redirecting household savings from the bank accounts into riskier portfolios. Investing in corporate bonds and stocks provides capital to companies that are trying to create value for their customers, and the information extraction that drives financial flows to one company over another is simply meant to reflect (or predict) those that are successful at doing so. Instead of holding onto their savings, the investor, whether it is an individual or an institution, provides capital to successful companies or individuals to enhance their growth and reward their efforts. All being well, this creates more jobs and therefore more savings, which in turn will become productive in the same fashion. The bet of capitalism is that this investment cycle creates more welfare than keeping money in a shoebox.

4.1.2   Intermediation by asset managers

Asset managers act as intermediaries between savings (from individuals and companies) on one side and economic projects that need capital on the other side. Their investments:

- Finance projects in the real economy by allowing the savings of the population to access loans, bonds and shares of companies;[2]
- Provide investment solutions and hedging tools to investors, following a clear "investment thesis" so that their vehicles can be simply understood and combined.

The role of financial education is crucial in this process, as both points assume that asset owners (i.e., individuals, companies, or countries with savings) have sufficient information about the investment instruments being offered and sufficient financial education to understand the associated risks, enabling them to make rational decisions. In addition, investors need to be able to assess the adequacy of the risk/reward profile of the proposed products to their investment objectives. Therefore, regulation comes into play to enforce *transparency* and information disclosure in this business line as a key measure of investor protection.

Asset managers provide expertise in financial products. Nevertheless, some complex investment vehicles require a high level of financial literacy, which is why the regulator only allows professional investors to purchase highly complex products. Naturally, the *financial advisory* profession is highly regulated, with a particular emphasis on fiduciary duty: they must act in the best interests of

---

[2]We do not differentiate here between government bonds and corporate bonds.

their clients as they serve as intermediaries between the investment vehicles provided by asset managers or investment banks, or individual investors.

In terms of money flows, asset managers act as intermediaries between, on one side, retail and corporate investors that have limited knowledge of financial markets and on the other side, the wide variety of investment vehicles and tradable products. In terms of risk, asset managers also act as intermediaries: On the one hand, they combine tradable instruments and thus the risk factors to which their clients wish to be exposed to, and on the other hand, they consume products designed by structurers, sell-side and investment banks. These intermediaries recycle (by hedging or replicating) these risks either to agents in the real economy, or to other asset managers, and so forth.

Asset managers provide hedging instruments. Hedging is at the heart of the asset allocation business. It allows asset owners to reduce or eliminate their exposure to an identified risk. For instance, an investor who owns real estate in a country may not want to have additional exposure to the wealth of that country's economy. He may then use ETFs and/or futures contracts to reduce or eliminate that exposure. Another typical example is that of an expatriate who is paid in the currency of a given country but who lives or has the majority of his expenses in another country, thus in another currency. This person may then be interested in hedging the exchange rate risk between the two currencies.

We have seen in Chapter 3 that structured products can be used to hedge more sophisticated risks. While investment banks are the main providers of customized products for hedging purposes, asset managers also offer some of these products, albeit in a less complex manner.

Asset managers package risks too. The primary role of asset managers is to build investment vehicles dedicated to the needs of a broad class of asset owners. Some asset managers, such as hedge funds, themselves provide investment vehicles to other asset managers, such as pension funds, with continuous inflows. The asset manager ecosystem is diverse; some players build products that they sell, others serve as intermediaries between certain niche asset managers (and the derivatives or structured products provided by investment banks) and end clients. The constellation of asset managers is itself a network of intermediaries, each with expertise either in creating a specific type of product or in approaching a specific type of client. The former has expertise in synthesizing and packaging specific risks, while the latter knows the risk/return profile of end clients and their preferred products. Their common goal is to build investment vehicles that are in line with the demand for risk, at a cheap price (i.e., in line with the supply of risk).

In this process of matching supply and demand, risk management is of paramount importance, as risk that is not properly priced will appear cheaper than it actually is. This can lead to a transfer of risk to the end customer or one of the asset managers in the production chain, who will have to bear the consequences of the unmanaged risk if it materializes. Poor risk assessment usually results from overlooking a link to an economic factor, or not properly assessing the liquidity of the factor chosen to summarize the risk.

4.2 Overview of the Asset Management Industry

In this section, we define in detail and distinguish between the different types of asset managers: pension funds, wealth managers, mutual funds, hedge funds, sovereign wealth funds, endowments and insurance companies. They are generally referred to as institutional investors because they are mandated to invest their clients' money for various purposes.

It is important to underline that the baby boom[3] played a role in the development of asset management. When this population began to work, pension funds were the natural way to invest their savings; this led to a steady stream of inflows of liquidity into the equity and bond markets of Europe and the United States, and thus stimulated economic growth in those regions. The previous section gives clues as to how the asset management industry is a way for capitalism to create future growth with current savings. This is exactly what happened in the 1980s and 1990s in Europe and the United States. The creation of pension funds in China, accompanied by an increase in the place of capitalism and free markets, is part of the reason

---

[3]The increase in the number of annual births after World War II.

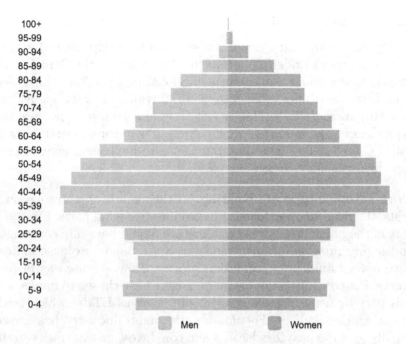

Figure 4.1: The population pyramid of Spain in 2016.
Source: Wikipedia.

why global investment banks have been trying to open subsidiaries in Asia since the turn of the millennium, and why China is trying to prevent Chinese savings from leaving the country.

The life cycle of savings, in conjunction with age pyramids (see Figure 4.1 for example), is a source of business cycles. If an individual begins by spending most of his or her income during the first 10–15 years of his or her working life, he or she then begins to save and invest for the future: living as a couple, the share of fixed costs in his or her spending decreases, and he or she will need money for his or her children's college education, and later for his or her own retirement. This cartoonish spending cycle for an individual if applied to the entire population of a country gives pension funds and asset managers the opportunity to play the role of intermediation between the current population, current projects and ventures, and future outflows. Again, the main objective of the population is not only to be protected against all forms of inflation, but also to benefit from the value creation they co-finance through the asset managers.

4.2.1   Pension funds

Partly due to the baby boom, these funds have experienced steady growth in assets under management. According to the 2015 OECD report, assets under management in global pension funds increased from US\$15.8 trillion in 2008 to US\$25.2 trillion in 2014, equivalent to a 60% increase in capital in just six years. Pension funds are the typical example of long-term investors. Their common strategy is called Core-Satellite investing, but they also implement endowment-type investments (see Section 4.2.5).

Core-satellite type of investing. As the name of this strategy suggests, the resulting portfolio is divided into two main parts. First, the core of the portfolio is invested in mature, liquid blue chip companies and highly rated government and corporate bonds. Because indices have a very fluid price formation process, they are used as benchmarks. For cost mitigation, asset managers have chosen to implement this part by using passive investments (such as ETFs) which track major market indices. Fortunately, the index industry has grown rapidly over the past few decades and core investing can track certain market anomalies such as value over growth, momentum or alternative weighting procedures. In addition, this slow-moving asset under management can be optimized and generate additional revenues through securities lending and transaction costs mitigation, using cross-functional dealing desks to optimize its predictable rebalancing.

The remaining portion of the portfolio, called satellites, is allocated to actively managed investments with higher expected returns but also higher expected risks. The goal is to select investments for which a portfolio manager's skill provides an opportunity to earn higher returns than those generated by the passive part of the portfolio. In a very broad sense, satellites are expected to provide alpha, or at least not provide high beta relative to the returns of the core portfolio (see Section 4.2.3 for a short discussion about alpha vs. beta). Satellites can be implemented in a variety of ways, but they generally have the following characteristics: they invest in less liquid or riskier assets, such as debt and emerging market equities, and they are intended to be active strategies.

Pay-as-you-go pension system. Unlike pension funds (that is, workers contributing money each year, the sum of which is then invested and its returns are to be used to pay their pension when they retire), pensions in some countries are based on redistribution.[4] In such a pay-as-you-go pension system, the money of workers who contribute today is used to provide pensions to former workers who are at retirement. It is very easy to understand that in such a system there is no need for financial intermediaries, and therefore savings do not participate in the financing of the economy as they would if invested in pension funds. It is also easy to understand that there are bad configurations of the age pyramid for this redistribution scheme: if there are far fewer workers contributing today than there are retirees, the pension mechanism will have difficulty meeting its commitments. However, a large age imbalance can also be detrimental to pension funds due to a long-term impact on the market: when there are many workers, pension funds invest massively in the economy via financial instruments. As a result of this large inflow, prices rise and remain so as long as this flow of workers is maintained. due to a long-term impact on the market. This phenomenon can create a type of inflation: for a dollar invested in the first phase (large inflows), one gets fewer assets than for the same dollar 50 years later in the second phase. Once again, since the financial system is made up of a sophisticated network of intermediaries buying and selling risk factors on different time scales, it is rarely possible to reason in isolation, and the Latin formula *caeteris paribus* is rarely applicable.

4.2.2　Mutual funds

Mutual funds, such as SICAV or FCP in France and mutual trusts, have grown very rapidly, in part because of the evolution of employer-sponsored retirement plans from defined benefits to defined contributions. Both concepts are shaping the asset management industry, as the contract between the client and the fund must be clearly defined:

Defined benefit: The employer guarantees the level of benefits already specified in the agreement, most often based on the employee's salary

---

[4]Most countries have a pay-as-you-go pension system, but its share of pensions is larger in certain countries like France, and much smaller in others such as the USA.

and seniority. These plans can be managed internally or externally; however, they are disappearing in favor of defined contribution plans, as companies feel that the risk for this type of liability had become too great.

Defined contribution: The employer agrees to pay regular contributions to a management organization, which, together with the income generated by their investment, will be paid out in the form of an annuity to retired employees. The amount of this pension is the result of the management of the plan by a third party. The employer does not provide any guarantee on the level of annuities paid.

Moving from a defined benefit to a defined contribution plan means that retirement plans have shifted from a result-driven engagement to a means-driven commitment. This exposes clients to issues such as the market impact of the population age pyramid described in the introduction to this chapter.

The principal–agent problem in asset management. An important issue in asset management is related to what economists have called the principal-agent problem, following the work of Bengt Holmstrom and Paul Milgrom in the late 1980s. This problem arises when one person (the principal) delegates to another (the agent) a task, and in particular a task related to the management of an asset belonging to the agent himself. In theory, the principal should let the agent do his or her best, and the reward of the resulting gain should be shared between the two;[5] but since the agent usually has fixed costs that are difficult to observe, the principal must reward his agent with a fixed and a variable portion. However, as the agent's efforts are also difficult to observe, the agent might simply not work at all and receive the fixed part of the reward at a negligible cost. To avoid promoting this lazy behavior, the principal will begin to set observable indicators and analytical criteria, and index the agent's reward (usually with a mixture of fixed and proportional rewards) to these criteria. The main problem in doing so is that the principal will impose constraints on the agent (who will have to work on these ad hoc and very specific requirements instead of working hard for

---

[5]The typical example is that of a landowner (the principal) and a farmer who farms the fields on his or her land (the agent).

the principal objective), which can be detrimental to the efficiency of the work, notably within the sphere of asset management. This is especially true when innovation is required: the principal is certain to never have anticipated what is required to achieve successful innovation, and so its indicators will essentially prevent the agent from thinking outside the box.

This problem arises very often in the field of asset management: the asset owner would like to have observables to index the reward (i.e., the fees) of his managers. How does one explain the difference between the few basis points of compensation for structuring an ETF and the 2/20 compensation system of hedge funds?[6] Defining the correct performance indicators will determine the relationship between asset owners and asset managers, as well as other intermediaries: the "asset consultants" who pool the assessment of asset managers in the hope of providing more information to asset owners and putting in place the right analysis to effectively measure their performance.

4.2.3 Hedge funds (or alternative investments)

Hedge funds are a special class of asset managers in the sense that they use more financial engineering tools than other types of funds. They are meant to provide "alpha" rather than "beta". This alpha vs. beta terminology comes from the standard notation of linear regressions and relies on the CAPM: a regression of the returns of a fund R minus the risk-free rate R_f with respect to the market factor R_m.

$$R - R_f = \alpha + \beta R_m + \epsilon. \tag{4.1}$$

Thus, a fund provides *beta exposure*[7] when its *alpha* is zero. On the contrary, a fund is supposed to provide alpha when the β coefficient of this regression is not statistically different from zero. According to the mechanics of the linear regression, portfolio returns must not be significantly correlated with known factors such as the market factor.

---

[6]Hedge funds are often remunerated with a 2% management fee and a 20% incentive fee (i.e., based on a "high watermark" indicator).

[7]When factors other than the market factor are used in the regression, some may argue that the fund provides beta exposure if, again, the resulting *alpha* is zero.

Table 4.1:   Top 10 hedge funds in the US, in 2017.

Manager	Location	Year established	AuM (bn $)
Bridgewater Associates	US	1975	161.9
ASR Capital Management	US	1998	106.2
Man Group	UK	1983	57.9
J.P. Morgan Asset Management	US	1974	49.0
Renaissance Technologies	US	1982	47.9
Millennium Management	US	1989	34.3
Standard Life Investments	UK	1998	33.2
Och-Ziff Capital Management	US	1994	31.8
Elliott Management	US	1977	31.4
Two Sigma Investments	US	2002	30.4
Baupost Group	US	1982	30.0
Winton Capital Management	UK	1997	29.3
Marshall Wace	UK	1997	28.4
Davidson Kempner Capital	US	1990	27.9
Adage Capital Management	US	2001	27.7
BlackRock Alternative Investors	US	2005	27.6
Citadel Advisors	US	1990	27.0
D.E. Shaw & Co	US	1988	26.0
Farallon Capital Management	US	1986	23.8
GAM	UK	1983	20.7

Table 4.1 lists the top 10 hedge funds in the United States. We note that some hedge funds are, or were, subsidiaries of intermediaries, including investment banks and mutual funds. This characteristic allows them to make extensive use of other financial institutions; they often need to short certain risk factors or company stocks, and thus use nonlinear products such as derivatives (as nonlinear dependencies often do not appear in the beta of a linear regression).

A good way to avoid being correlated to aggregate risk factors is to specialize in a niche. For example, certain hedge funds study pharmaceutical companies submissions to the FDA in the US and, alongside a team of medical doctors and pharmacologists, they aim to anticipate whether the government will approve the drugs, taking long or short positions to exploit this knowledge.

Another method is to use statistical arbitrage strategies to identify persistent statistical relationships between financial instruments (from stock returns to derivative Greeks) and bet on the fact that they will return to normal when they no longer match the identified expectations. These strategies can be considered to be similar in nature to market making, as these hedge funds take positions in a way that prevents long-term statistical relationships between instruments from drifting too far apart. These strategies are intended to provide liquidity to other market participants.

Consider the example of two companies whose stock returns are generally correlated because one of them is the other's main supplier: when the customer company does well, its supplier does well too. A statistical arbitrage strategy may have identified this relationship without an analyst having examined the fundamentals and supply chain of these companies, but through statistical analysis of the correlations between their returns. If the customer company delays its orders by one or two quarters more than usual, the supplier company may suffer for a few months, so the hedge fund will bet on better returns from the supplier over the medium term. Of course, there is a risk in doing so: the client company may be in the process of changing its supplier, so betting on the fact that the usual supplier will have more orders in a few months in this case is a mistake.

In general, statistical arbitrage strategies involve more than just two instruments, in order to take advantage of diversification. If the statistics are right "on average", it is a good idea to make the same statistical bet on as many configurations as possible, so that the identified statistical relationship come true sufficiently enough to make a profit. If one bet that flipping a coin without bias will result in 50% heads and 50% tails, it is better to do it on 500 trials than on 2 trials.

To come back to the example of the supply chain providing investment opportunities, the increased availability of data on the real economy (satellite images, credit card bills, factory production, patents, etc.) opens the door to further strategies for hedge funds, as they often employ high-level experts (either scientific experts, or statisticians, or field experts) who can deal with these very original datasets often called *alternative data*. Chapter 6, and in particular Section 6.3.3, deal with this new trend in information sources for investment.

Another notable type of strategy used by hedge funds focuses on the macroeconomics. Originally referred to as Commodity Trading Advisors (CTAs), these hedge funds make long-term bets on the usual relationships between macroeconomic variables.

4.2.4   Sovereign funds

Table 4.2 lists the world's largest sovereign wealth funds. Most of them, such as the Norwegian fund or the Abu Dhabi Investment Authority, derive their allocations from surplus revenues from the oil sector. Sovereign funds are similar to endowments in that they aim to provide dividend-like income to their host countries. They are very long-term investors and can therefore theoretically bear more risk than other types of investment structures.

They often adopt a strategy close to the core-satellite model, where the core is invested in the global economy in liquid assets and the satellites are less liquid, or riskier types of investments, sometimes investing in their home countries to stimulate growth. Recently, certain sovereign funds have moved toward socially responsible investments, excluding companies for ethical reasons and paying greater attention to environmental, social and governance issues.

4.2.5   Endowment funds

An endowment is a donation of money or property for a non-profit organization such as a church, university, or hospital. Endowment funds manage these savings and pay dividends to the organization or contribute to investments, most often focused on infrastructure, for the organization.

The amount under management is referred to as "the principal" or "the corpus". The endowment logic consists of generating enough real returns to meet the organization's yearly expenses while preserving the real value of the principal. This means that the returns generated must cover annual withdrawals and increase the principal to offset inflation.

The largest US endowments, held by top-ranked universities such as Yale and Harvard, know exactly how to achieve these goals. Because their outflows are highly predictable, endowments can afford to invest in illiquid assets, agreeing to freeze some of their assets for

Table 4.2: Largest sovereign wealth funds Feb 2021.

Sovereign wealth fund name	Country	Assets US $ billion	Inception	Origin
Norway Government Pension Fund Global	Norway	1,273.54	1990	Oil
China Investment Corporation	China	1,045.72	2007	Non-commodity
Abu Dhabi Investment Authority	UAE-Abu Dhabi	579.62	1976	Oil
Hong Kong Monetary Authority Investment Portfolio	China-Hong Kong	576.03	1993	Non-commodity
Kuwait Investment Authority	Kuwait	533.65	1953	Oil
GIC Private Limited		453.2		
Temasek Holdings	Singapore	417.35	1974	Non-commodity
Public Investment Fund	Saudi Arabia	399.45	2008	Oil
National Council for Social Security Fund	China	372.07	2000	Non-commodity
Investment Corporation of Dubai	UAE-Dubai	301.53	2006	Non-commodity

Source: Statista.

the very long term in exchange for better returns. Yale's endowment illustrates the weight of these illiquid strategies; in 2008, Yale's endowment had a 14% allocation to US securities, while the remaining 86% was spread across foreign equities, private equities, real estate and absolute return strategies. As a comparison, while market growth between 1985 and 2008 averaged about 12% (taking the S&P 500 performance as a proxy), Ivy League university Harvard generated 15.23% and Yale 16.62%.

Table 4.3: Key figures on the development of wealth management in $trillions, grey rows are percent changes.

Region	2014	2015	2016	2021E
North Am.	52.2	53.3	55.7	73.0
		2.0%	4.5%	5.6%
Latin Am.	4.7	5.0	5.4	7.5
		6.3%	8.7%	6.7%
West. Europe	38.3	39.2	40.5	48.1
		2.4%	3.2%	3.5%
Est. Europe	3.2	3.4	3.6	4.7
		7.2%	4.7%	5.5%
Middle East and Africa	7.4	7.5	8.1	12.0
		1.9%	8.5%	8.1%
Asia-Pacific	31.2	35.0	38.4	61.6
		12.3%	9.5%	9.9%
Japan	14.5	14.7	14.9	16.2
		1.8%	1.1%	1.7%
Global	**151.4**	**158.2**	**166.5**	**223.1**
		4.4%	**5.3%**	**6.0%**

Source: BCG June 2017.

4.2.6 Wealth management

Certain individuals, such as high net worth individuals (HNWI), have so much savings that commercial and investment banks started to provide them with specific investment vehicles. These individuals have no urgency for outflows, or these are highly predictive, hence they can afford to invest in illiquid assets like endowment funds do. Table 4.3 shows the increase in the asset under management for this category of investment.

4.2.7 Insurance companies

There has been an important influx of interest towards insurance assets ($25 trillion). Contrary to other institutional investors, their core business is not related to money allocation but to risk transfer and management. Hence, by selling insurance contracts, they take on their clients' risk in exchange for a premium plus fees and margins. They also need to either transfer such risk to another counterparty with the exact opposite risk or to dilute it on the financial markets. The risk netting is not always immediately achieved, some products require netting through time. Not surprising that their strategies are based on asset-liability strategies (ALM). Moreover, regulatory authorities pay close attention to risk issues and have tightened the solvency requirement as well as accounting standards.

4.3 Concentration of Assets Towards a Few Strategies and Actors

4.3.1 Passive investing takes over active allocation

Table 4.4 shows that assets under management have been slowly shifting from active management (almost 90% in 2004 to 65% in 2020) to passive management (6% in 2004 to 22% in 2020). The global financial crisis (2008–2009) was the tipping point for the shift from active to passive management: beyond the returns provided by the different asset management styles, fees began to be questioned and the simultaneous arrival of low-cost standardized solutions such as ETFs and the important academic literature on rewarded risk factors (see the section 4.4.1.2 for more details) put pressure on active managers who had to demonstrate statistically significant over-performance to maintain high fee structures.

The debate between alpha and beta gained momentum, and the same academic literature coined the term *pricing anomalies*

Table 4.4: Evolution of active vs. passive investment from 2004 to 2020.

Products		2004	2007	2012	2020
Global	AUM ($ trillion)	37.3	59.4	63.9	101.7
of which	**mutual funds**	16.1	25.4	27.0	41.2
	active investments	15.1	23.3	23.6	30.8
	passive investments	1.0	2.0	3.4	10.5
of which	**mandates**	18.7	28.8	30.4	47.5
	active investments	17.6	26.5	26.6	35.3
	passive investments	1.2	2.3	3.9	12.2
of which	**alternatives**	1.2	2.3	3.9	12.2
Percent	passive	6%	7%	11%	22%
	active	88%	84%	79%	65%

as beyond the simple CAPM model (in which the only systematic rewarded risk factor is the market factor). Slowly, the idea emerged that active (but systematic and easily replicated) investment strategies could persist. Prior to 2010, the doxa was that rewarding strategies uncorrelated to the market factor would either fail to cover their costs or would correct themselves once invested by a sufficient number of participants (giving rise to *alpha decay*). More recent academic output however suggested that it is not always the case, which opened up older hedge fund strategies to the public domain, being repackaged in ready to use investment tools like ETFs. As such, the "beta" part of the linear regression (4.1) has since been supplemented by more rewarding factors $F_1, \ldots, F_K$:

$$R - R_f = \alpha + \beta\, R_m + \sum_{1 \leq k \leq K} \beta_k\, F_k + \epsilon. \qquad (4.2)$$

Risk factors have long been identified in their use in explaining the structure of covariance between tradable instruments, but not as sources of returns.[8] With price anomalies, the factors have begun to expand into the realm of investment strategies.

The business of ETFs. On paper, ETFs offer the advantage of a buy and hold product, even if it is composed of a portfolio with variable weightings. The structurer of the ETF decides the rule for updating the composition of the tracked portfolio and makes a defined commitment on the tracking error to this portfolio. In general, the tracking error is low and strict for equity-based ETFs, while it can be vague and very lazy for corporate bond ETFs (which are much less liquid.[9]) In addition, management fees (which are typically low compared to an active fund manager) and operations (such as rebalancing costs, or managing dividends or corporate events) are detrimental to the performance of the effective ETF compared to the paper portfolio.

---

[8]Typically, a Principal Component Analysis (PCA) on returns, when properly processed technically (the components can be cleaned up using standard Random Matrix Theory), provides factors that are effective in explaining the structure of the covariance matrix, but are not rewarded.

[9]While a liquid stock trades around 50,000 times a day, a liquid corporate bond trades only around 7 times a day.

Some asset managers who structure ETFs successfully optimize every layer of their product, from securities lending revenues to execution optimization. To take this a step further, a small fraction have used total return swaps to provide synthetic ETFs, delegating all the financial engineering and trading to an intermediary investment bank, but incurring the counterparty risk of that same investment bank. This has led to a debate that highlighted the pros and cons of the two different replication setups, with different alignments of interests, both from a regulatory and industry perspective. Indeed, while the US generally provides more physical ETFs, European structurers tend to favor synthetic ETFs.

As a result, two ETFs tracking the same index may perform differently: first, at entry and exit, their bid-ask spreads may be different (the wider the bid-ask spread, the more expensive the ETF),[10] second, tracking errors may be different, third, the way dividends and corporate actions are handled may also be different, etc.

The attraction of passive investing. Investing in Capital Weighted Indices is very attractive because, in an ideal world, all one has to do is adopt a buy-and-hold strategy: price changes are reflected in the relative free floats market capitalization of the components, and thus the fraction of the portfolio held naturally follows changes in the weighting of the reference index. As a result, transaction costs are paid only once, at the initiation of the position, and long-term investors can ignore them.

Nevertheless, in the real world, weights change regularly. They are reviewed once a quarter, with a potentially significant change each year.[11] Because most of the indices have a threshold for the number of companies in the index (or a threshold for the capitalization of candidate companies), each quarter can see new entrants and deletions. In addition, takeover, mergers and acquisitions occur frequently and the stocks's free floats change. As a result, weights change in ways that are no longer consistent with a buy-and-hold strategy.

---

[10]Some structurers have agreement with market makers to ensure a tight bid-ask spread.

[11]Some cap-weighted indices have systematic rules, and others have an independent scientific committee that deals with exceptions.

Structurers (or investors) who follow capitalization-weighted indices must react and rebalance their portfolios. This is bound to generate transaction costs. As a rule of thumb, if (on average) the bid-ask spread of stocks whose weighting change is about 7 basis points and 5% of the index changes each quarter, the annual performance erosion due to the portfolio rebalancing is of 1.4 basis points, which is moderate. Add to this the market impact: selling the shares lowers the price (resulting in receiving less money than expected for the shares sold) and buying raises the price (resulting in needing more money to buy the required number of shares, and probably having to sell an entire "tranche" of the portfolio to fund it). It is difficult to put a number on these friction costs because they are a function of the assets under management of the ETFs and trackers in that same index, but some academic papers have identified an annual loss of 10 basis points associated with this market impact.[12]

Moreover, there is a principal-agent problem associated with this rebalancing. The buyers of the ETFs have delegated to the structurer the proper management of the ETF's portfolio, and the main analytics used to measure the structurer's efficiency is the tracking error. As a result, the structurer cannot afford to sell some components before the official rebalancing dates and buy others a few days later. Even though it is known to provide better performance on average, it generates a certain tracking error. It is "better" for the structurer to buy and sell at the close of the official rebalancing day, which increases the impact on the market. To avoid this, he often asks the market makers (hosted by an investment bank) to have the liquidity ready for him on that day; the market makers are responsible for buying and selling slowly before the close of the official day to have the liquidity ready and mark the price at the close. They often offer a discount of a few basis points on the closing price. This practice sounds very attractive: the structurer has no tracking error and even gets a price improvement on rebalancing days. However, it has considerable downsides: market makers, who buy the desired position slowly over a few days, push the price in a detrimental way. On average, they will have bought it at two-thirds of the difference

---

[12]The transaction costs associated with non-cap-weighted indexes are likely to be greater than this because the components are on average less liquid.

between the closing price and the initial price.[13] They then sell the desired position at the closing price, making a decent margin.

This is typical of certain problems in the financial markets: the misalignment of the interests of the investor, the structurer and the market maker is detrimental to the principal (the investor), simply because in order to protect himself, he has decided to focus on the tracking error (i.e., a nonlinear statistic) and not on the long-term performance.

4.3.2 Concentration of power within a handful of asset managing companies

The adage "big is beautiful" works for most intermediation activities (simply because of the network effect and the relatively lower weight of fixed costs), so it goes beyond investment banks and brokers; the asset management industry has also understood the benefit of concentration. Table 4.5 shows that not only has the market share of the 3, 5 or 10 largest asset management firms increased steadily over the past 40 years, but also that the share of direct investment (without intermediation) has declined sharply, going from 65% (i.e., 100–35% of assets managed by intermediary institutions) in 1980 to 28% in 2016. It is possible that the level of expertise and improved efficiency of price formation (in the sense that prices reflect quicker the information available on the tradable instruments) have driven retail investors towards intermediaries, and it is also possible that the complexity of the rules has played a role in the rise of asset managers.

Table 4.5: Concentration of the asset management industry.

Year	Top 1 institution	Top 3 institution	Top 10 institutions	All institution
1980	1.6%	5.0%	7.5%	35.0%
1990	1.9%	6.2%	9.5%	47.0%
2000	2.0%	7.5%	16.0%	56.0%
2010	4.9%	9.5%	22.0%	71.5%
2016	6.3%	16.5%	26.5%	72.0%

Source: Francesco Franzoni, June 2017.

---

[13]This two-thirds coefficient comes from the fact that buying linearly with a square root market impact results in a factor of $\int_0^1 \nu^{1/2} d\nu \propto 2/3$.

Table 4.6:   Net flows of the top 10 asset managers in the US.

ASSET MANAGER	2016 net flows ($billions)	Cumulative share of total market net flows (%)	Cumulative share of net flows of players with positive net flows (%)	Positive share of total flows per firm (%)
Vangard	276	197	50	93
BlackRock	95	265	67	118
DFA	18	277	70	2
SSGA	16	289	73	99
Ch. Schwab	13	298	75	14
TIAA-CREF	11	306	77	59
Invesco	10	313	79	100
Edward Jones	8	319	80	0
R.W. Braid	8	325	82	0
DoubleLine	8	330	83	0
Total Market	140			

Source: BCG June 2017.

The steady increase in assets under management in the sector has especially benefited a handful of market players, both in terms of accumulated assets and of fresh cash flows. Table 4.6 shows how Vanguard and Blackrock collected twice the total market cash flow in 2016 with 265% positive net flows, while the rest of the industry only collected 140%. This means that aside from these two asset management firms, all the smaller ones have negative cash outflows and are therefore getting smaller every year. This concentration among market players may stem from the importance of reputation and trust. Individuals and institutions may prefer to work with players that are already recognized.

On the institutional side, the role of asset management consultants should not be overlooked either: consultants may prefer to stay away from newcomers, in order to avoid the risk of being wrong. In any case, the bottom line is clear: the giant asset managers are ever-present, and they are building on their client base to become "one-stop shops" offering a wide range of investment vehicles, going from ETFs to hedge funds. This business model may be altered by the platformization of this activity, as platformization may be accompanied by client cherry-picking (see Section 6.1.3 for more details).

The diversity of investment vehicles is crucial, because if one portfolio dominates the market, all flows will be on the same side (buying or selling), and the price will be pushed to artificial levels. A diversity of investment horizons and themes is also necessary, so that the number of portfolio managers and investment philosophies can cover all possible sources of information (which may contradictory) and achieve a balance that reflects a holistic view of tradable instruments.

The advantage of offering a wide range of investment vehicles is that it increases the probability of crossing the buys and sells within the same asset management firm. Most regulations require marking the price outside the firm (to avoid advantaging one vehicle in the transaction), but brokers and exchanges can provide crosses at market price, with low information leakage and a lower cost (free from market-impact).

With the rise of alternative data, such as satellite imagery, transportation data, or credit card receipts (see Section 6.3.3 for more details) the cost of exploiting these new source of data has multiplied. The cost of the one-time purchase of the dataset, the hiring of a team of field experts and data scientists to extract ready-made information, and the effort to build investment signals for indices structuring and systematic quantitative strategies, would be recouped if one intermediary company make the initial investment and the multiple portfolio managers and investment firms tap into them. Again, it is best for asset managers, as intermediaries, to become distribution platforms hosting a wide range of vehicles.[14]

Buying research vs. doing it in house. With the emergence of large asset managers, there is an opportunity to rethink the role of broker-produced research. Section 2.1.2 highlights the role of brokers in disseminating information to investors: their research teams provide reports to their clients with advice on the fair value of instruments. Although brokers have fewer conflicts of interest than the issuers of these instruments,[15] it is documented by academic papers that their advice has a "long bias" (i.e., they recommend more to buy that to sell). This bias may be behavioral or simply the result of a conflict of interest with the companies, since brokers need to maintain good relationships with them to have easier access to fundamental information. In any case, large asset managers can now

---

[14]It is easy to see the similarities of their position to that of Amazon or Google.
[15]This is true for stocks and corporate bonds, but not for swaps or derivatives issued by investment banks (most often linked to brokers).

consider paying the fixed costs of maintaining large in-house analyst teams; in general, one can expect that:

- A small asset manager will rely heavily on broker research to make investment decisions, specializing more in portfolio management and risk management than in research. It will also rely on investment banks and brokers for trading.
- A medium-sized asset manager will mix broker research with his own, which will be more focused on specific topics, themes, sectors or regions.
- A large asset manager can afford to produce its own research, thus avoiding the natural bias of broker analysts (or at least being aware of and trying to correct their biases).

The case of quantitative asset managers is different, since even small ones produce their own research, and try to generate their own "investment signals" or "predictors".

Section 2.1.2 also explains that for a long time, access to broker research was bundled with execution services (paying an execution fee provides access to research through "soft dollar" accounts). But recently, with MiFID 2 in Europe, which has also spread to the US, regulators have decided that this bundling could prevent fair competition among brokers on research. Some were concerned that this would diminish investor attention on smaller firms. This reasoning is again the one developed in Section 6.2.3: without bundling different services, in this case execution and research, the provider cannot use the margin of one (i.e., execution) to fund the less attractive one (research on small market capitalization). This is true if one activity generates very regular revenue (on a weekly basis), while the other is rarely required by clients (less than once a year), but has fixed and regular costs corresponding to hiring and paying analysts on small caps every month. While the business model for brokers seems to fit this description, no evidence of a negative impact on small businesses was found.

With the intrusion of data science into the financial industry and the existence of a few dominant large asset managers, business models are changing: large asset managers, building their own teams of analysts, buy and process specific datasets themselves to extract valuable insights and signals, while broker–dealers reduce their fixed costs to gradually become data distributors, using data engineers to manage platforms where research buyers (asset managers and investors) meet research producers (which may be individuals or small, specialized research teams). This viewpoint is developed in Chapter 6.

4.3.3   Crowdedness and transaction costs

Transaction costs are a major preoccupation of the asset management industry because, like any other cost, they erode fund performance, reduce the attractiveness of the fund and decrease the asset manager's revenues. Conversely, judicious management of the costs incurred by the fund creates more opportunities to improve investment performance and therefore collect more inflows.

But unlike any other costs, transaction costs are difficult to predict. Not only do they depend on the characteristics of the fund and the investment style via the size and frequency of rebalancing, but they are also a function of the assets under management, as they are not linear. For example, choosing to overweight small-cap companies in an equity portfolio may improve the gross returns of the portfolio on paper, but it also increases the cost of implementing the strategy, especially if other funds follow the same weighting scheme. Similarly, increasing the frequency of portfolio rebalancing can improve market timing and increase performance on paper, but the resulting profit may be offset by the subsequent higher turnover. Therefore, transaction costs are an important factor in investment decisions and should be considered during the investment process. Otherwise, a strategy that may appear profitable at first glance and capable of generating a significant risk premium may no longer be so after taking these costs into account.

Transaction costs depend on several parameters other than order characteristics (side and size of the order) and asset liquidity (bid-ask spread and volatility). They depend, for instance, on the aggressiveness and duration of the execution, the scheduling of trades, market conditions, fluctuations in overall market supply and demand, the information content of the trade, and the timing of the different players operating in the market. Investors' herd behavior has become even more problematic with the rise of passive investing and tracking strategies.

As shown in Figure 2.9, an investor providing liquidity to other market participant is rewarded with lower transaction costs (that can even be negative, that it is the case for meta-orders with a relative size lower than $Q_k(m)/ADV_k(d) \simeq 20\%$), and an investor consuming liquidity "with the crowd" has to pay a premium. The liquidity provider is then rewarded with a better execution price.

The nonlinear shape of market impact. Qualitatively, the market impact is the price movement due to a directional pressure of the trade flow: when an investor buys, she pushes the price up, and when she sells, she pushes the price down. For very small orders, consuming less quantity than the first limit of the order book,[16] there is no real immediate push of the price, simply a cost that is bid-ask spread of the traded instrument. For a larger order, the average price will increase with the quantity needed, as it is needed to consume more than one limit. At this stage, note that

- If the liquidity available in the order book grows linearly with the distance to the first limit, the cost of trading will grow in a square root form.
- Even if a small order consumes only a fraction of the first limit, it influences the impact of the subsequent orders that will see less liquidity available at the touch and may have to consume more than the first limit.

Because of this mechanical effect, large orders should trade in more than one child order, to wait for the liquidity to replenish before consuming more, a few minutes later. These large orders are usually named *meta-orders*. Convergent academic researches have shown that the market impact of these large orders is made of three effects:

1. The linear costs proportional to the bid-ask spread of the traded instrument.[17] This fraction corresponds to the skill of the trader or the efficiency of the trading algorithm.
2. The square root market impact, which is proportional to the level of volatility of the traded instrument, and the square root of the traded quantity renormalized by the level of the quantity usually traded on that instrument.

---

[16]The reasoning is made for trading in order books, but the conclusions taken are the same in a request for quotes environment as well.

[17]Trading and brokerage costs (which can be significant, such as stamp duties) should also be considered.

3. The permanent market impact, which is in fact the information contained in the meta-order: if the decision to buy was motivated by news with an immediate impact, the price will move during the transaction, and therefore impact transaction costs. If the decision is independent of any information (for example, if the asset manager simply received new inputs and invests them), then the permanent impact is close to zero.

This means that the impact decays from the temporary market impact (as a square root) to the permanent impact. This decay seems to take 8–15 days for stocks. The crowding of the trading flow can influence the transaction costs: if, on a given day, all market participants are buying, then the square root component of the sum of the trades of all the participants is paid by each of them. This is the meaning of Figure 2.9.

From a quantitative perspective (18)

Asset Management is probably the field that has been the least exposed to quantitative analysis to date. Of course, Modern Portfolio Theory (MPT, introduced in the 1950s) revolves around optimizing the mean-variance of a portfolio's composition, the construction of intertemporal portfolios following Robert Merton in the 1970s, and the construction of factors to analyze portfolio exposure.

The simple construction of quantitative portfolios began to have some interest after the 2008-2009 global financial crisis. Nevertheless, today there is no methodology shared by all market participants in relation to pricing, hedging of derivatives, or optimal trading. This is probably due to the fact that there is not much data available: at the timescale of most investors (one week to several months), there are no more than 250 observations per year. Relative to this timescale, economic conditions change quickly enough that it is very difficult to be sure that 20-year-old observations tell us much about expected future risks and returns.

One way to access more data is to consider that the 20,000 or so most active stocks and the 50 most active futures

---

(*Continued*)

(Continued)

contracts multiply the 250 annual observations. Nevertheless, the returns are so correlated[a] that the dimensions to describe the 20,000 stocks are probably less than 50. This means that one can only multiply these 250 annual observations by 50 if one is talking about the systemic part of price dynamics; this raises the question of how to correctly estimate these 50 important directions of equity risk.

For quantitative analysts, there are two main ways of looking at this dimensionality issue: either via Random Matrix Theory, or by using "characteristics" (i.e., risk factors constructed in a bottom-up manner, using cross-sectional views on analytics describing listed companies) as a proxy between the 20,000 stocks and the 50 intrinsic (unknown) dimensions of stock risk. On the return side, very few asset managers seek idiosyncratic returns using a quantitative approach.[b] Most active portfolio managers make bets based on qualitative analysis of their investment universe.

Nevertheless, *alternative data* opens the door to more systematic analysis and scanning of companies. These datasets are typically satellite images, credit card receipts, supply chain feeds, text (through Natural Language Processing), etc. Quantitative analysts are needed to extract meaningful information from this data.

As a result, Asset Management is likely to be an area where quantitative analysis will grow in the coming years, driven by the simultaneous impetus of alternative datasets and product standardization around a common semantics of risk/reward profiles driven by factor investing.

---

[a]Note that correlations among tradable instruments change; for instance, all instruments are more correlated under market stress conditions.

[b]Only few systematic hedge funds are doing this.

4.4   Recent Trends in Investing

Following the academic advances of the 1950s to the 1980s with the Capital Asset Pricing Model and Modern Portfolio Theory, empirical observations have been slowly accumulating, and certain asset management firms have in turn been conducting their own research, leading to the use of "factors" to explain a portfolio's exposure to the cross-sectional characteristics of the underlying of tradable instruments.

These characteristics are, for instance, capitalization, dividend yield, exposure to certain countries, and so forth. With this type of analysis, a portfolio manager or an investor is able to get a high-level overview of his portfolio and draw conclusions in terms of exposure to different economic developments.

The next step has naturally been to provide these asset managers with financial instruments to hedge unwanted exposures. Structurers, investment banks and other asset managers have started to design such products, with a single factor exposure.

In a second phase, academic work suggested that certain combinations of characteristics could not only be factors explaining risk exposures, but also "rewarded risk factors", in the sense that they generated returns uncorrelated to the market factor celebrated by the CAPM. Such rewarded factors were dubbed "market anomalies" and began to attract attention, not only from a risk perspective, but from a return perspective as well.

After the Global Financial Crisis, the logic changed: instead of designing a portfolio with strong convictions and checking *ex-post* its exposure to risk factors (and eventually adjusting that exposure), asset managers started to do the opposite: bet on a combination of rewarded risk factors to which they wanted to be exposed.

At this stage, the evolution of Modern Portfolio Theory has now permitted to design portfolios as combinations of rewarded factors; therefore, asset management can be viewed as an engineering task of combining factors under certain portfolio constraints. This section is dedicated to exposing these trends, which are generally viewed as a combination of *factor investing* and *smart beta*.

4.4.1 Factor investing: From portfolio monitoring to portfolio design

Figure 4.2 reflects Google searches for "factor investing", showing the growing interest in the matter. The search was conducted worldwide, but the charts for the United States and Europe follow the same patterns. We observe that the trend started in 2005, but stagnated

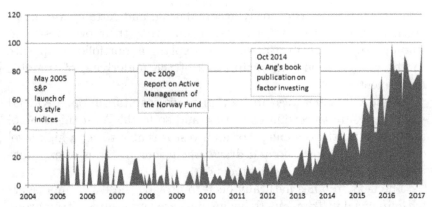

Figure 4.2: Google trend for "Factor Investing", worldwide, displays the search interest of the term relative to the highest point on the chart.

until 2010. However, the publication of the Norway Fund report on active management in 2009 is said to be the real start of investors' attraction for factor investing.

4.4.1.1   History of risk factors

The concept of factors plays a key role in the investment industry. Risk factors are identified through the analysis of market drivers and the discovery of "persistent anomalies". These anomalies, also known as "factorial premia", refer to the idea that factor portfolios (constructed from these factors) have a higher risk-adjusted performance compared to the market itself over the long run. Most academic papers explaining these anomalies consider market structure or investor behavioral bias as the origin of these anomalies.

The oldest and most well-known model of stock returns is the Capital Asset Pricing Model (CAPM). It set the foundation of the modern financial theory in the 1960s. The CAPM identifies two main drivers of returns. First, the systemic risk, which is the part of the security's volatility arising from the market exposure. It is systemic in the sense that it couldn't be diversified away, and investors get compensation for bearing this risk. Secondly, the idiosyncratic risk, an additional risk arising from stocks' characteristics, the company's foundations, and management's complexity. Based on this theory, bearing this risk is irrelevant, as it could be diluted in a basket of well-chosen stocks.

The Arbitrage Pricing Theory (APT) emerged in the late 1970s; pushing the idea of the existence of more than one factor. These other factors could change over time or vary across markets, but they are meant to explain with a good statistical significance the variability of the returns over a broad subset of stocks. This laid the foundation for a long and vigorous debate on how to identify them. Three main categories of factors distinguished themselves during this debate:

(1) First, the *macroeconomic factors* which included measures of inflation, GDP, and yield curves, etc.
(2) Then, the *statistical factor models* aiming to bring light to new drivers using statistical tools such as the principal component analysis, Bayesian techniques, and cross-sectional regressions.
(3) Finally, the *fundamental factors* which are today the most widely used ones. They capture the main stock characteristics related to valuation, quality, risk, and industry groups.

The prolific debate around factors has resulted in growing additions to the initial market factor. Most notably, the size, value and momentum factors introduced in the 1990s. These factors have since been joined by a bulk of new factors: quality, low beta, Fama–French profitability, and investment factors. Indeed, as shown in Figure 4.3, the number of factor discoveries per year have increased exponentially between 1980 and 2010. A 2015 paper reports 300 discovered equity factors and the list is still growing. Such list is refereed to as the "factor zoo", and issues raised by this inflation in factors are discussed in Section 4.4.4.

The interest in factor investing in the academic sphere has grown jointly alongside the interest from the financial industry. In 2009, a mandated group of academics published a report to the Norwegian Sovereign Wealth Fund about active management, where they explain that a substantial part of active returns comes from risk factors exposure. As a result, they recommended asset managers to systematically challenge portfolio risks with these factors and even consider using them for asset allocation. Upon this report, financial intermediaries proposed factor asset allocation strategies alternative to the traditional market-cap weighted ones. For instance, the Norwegian fund monitors the risk factor exposures of its asset allocation. The Dutch fiduciary manager PGGM applies factor tilts in its portfolio construction. The Danish pension fund ATP implements

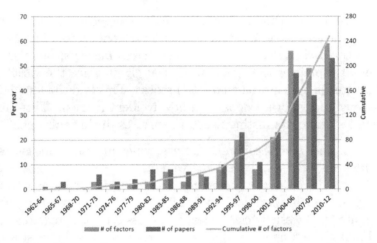

Figure 4.3: Factors discovery per year and number of paper written on factor investing.

both factor tilts and factor optimization. Large investors created a demand for a new type of index, labeled factorial, based on securities' factorial exposure. Major index providers answered to this demand, and ETF structurers and issuers provided investment vehicles, which is a kind of active management encompassed in passive investment.

4.4.1.2   Examples of asset pricing anomalies

Among the asset pricing anomalies, the financial industry distinguishes between a risk factor (rewarded risk factor) and a behavioral anomaly. The difference is subtle, but the industry agrees that a (*rewarded*) risk factor should reward an objective risk taking, usually related to the fundamentals of the company. For instance, the Size factor reflects the reality that small firms face more challenges to establish themselves as key players in the ecosystem where they evolve. As a consequence it is expected that their stocks are riskier than those of large already established companies with fewer uncertainties about their survival. However, small companies have higher growth perspectives and do not suffer from cumbersome processes and outdated technological heritage.

In contrast, a behavioral anomaly is related to market inefficiencies. It stems from investor's irrational behavior or from a mispricing (i.e., the fact that it is not possible to design the corresponding arbitrage and correcting it). In practice, it is difficult to separate the two classes.

Small size: Is the first to consider when constructing portfolios that depart from cap-weighted indices. From the definition of smart beta investment solutions, small (large) capitalization is over (under)-weighed compared to the benchmark, and since market capitalization is linearly proportional to turnover, the small-capitalization premium is usually linked to an illiquidity premium since small stocks are costlier to trade.

Quality/profitability: Captures excess returns of stocks that are characterized by low debt, stable earnings growth, and significant investment returns. Since quality is often maintained over time, the profitable companies are likely to remain profitable in the future.

Low volatility: The low-risk factor seeks to benefit from the performance of stocks with lower risk, while maintaining a high significant return superior to the more unstable volatile stocks. In other words, investors are not sufficiently rewarded for the risk they are exposing themselves to by taking highly volatile stocks.

Momentum: Invests in equities which recently well performed against equities which recently under performed. It has been coined by the saying *Buy the winners and sell the losers*.

Value: The valuation factor leads to buy the undervalued stocks and sell the overvalued ones. The Price over Earnings ratio is a closely watched indicator to build such a valuation metric.

Dividend yield: On equity markets, the high-dividend premium is related to quality and value factors, since companies capable of paying large dividends are often the more profitable ones.

4.4.1.3 Examples of factor models

Multifactor models have already been introduced in Section 4.3.1 via Equation (4.2). They use a linear model to explain returns of an index, a tradable instrument or a stock thanks to a list of factors. If the residuals do have an expectation (i.e., their theoretical mean, or average) that is significantly greater than zero, the left-hand side of the linear model is said to have some alpha. The coefficient defining the linear relationship are noted by betas and can be named "factor loadings" too. Explicitly writing time (i.e., days) in Equation (4.2) reads

$$R_i(t) = R_f + \alpha_i + \beta_i R_m(t) + \sum_{1 \leq k \leq K} \beta_{i,k} F_k(t) + \epsilon_i(t), \qquad (4.3)$$

where $R_i(t)$ is the returns of the studied time series i at the date t, R_f the risk-free rate, $R_m(t)$ market return, and the K $F_k(t)$ are the returns of the factors used in the model.

With this notation, we do not specify if Equation (4.3) is obtained thanks to a linear regression, or if the betas are given by the designer of the model. If the factors are given, a linear regression can provide estimates of the exposures (or loading) β, but collinearities can lead to a spurious regression. To save some space in the following linear relationships, α will be arbitrarily set to zero.

Factor identification or portfolio construction? Whether a factor is technical (such as a moving average on returns or traded quantities), fundamental (using financial records), or whether it is derived from alternative data (any other source), the process of qualifying it is subtle, especially in avoiding over-fitting or alpha-hacking (these aspects are developed in Section 4.4.4). The usual process starts with the construction of an indicator on a large number of tradable instruments (that is usually called the Investment Universe) such that it is a priori favorable to be long (i.e., to buy) the instruments with the largest values of this indicator, and to be short (to sell) the ones with the smallest values of the indicator.

Once this indicator is built, and because in most cases the goal is to obtain factors that are simultaneously cross-sectional and as independent as possible to the market factor, it is desirable to either center and normalize it (i.e., subtract its average and divide it by its standard deviation), or to rank its values and renormalize the obtained ranks between -1 and $+1$. This step is far from trivial, because it removes any "time series dynamics": this kind of processing neutralizes any effect of variations in time. For instance, it prevents us from knowing whether the indicator's average level of today is significantly larger, smaller or comparable to the average level 3 months ago. However, the ensuing advantage of this transformation is that the indicator approaches market neutrality: it has a low absolute correlation with the market factor, simply because the market factor is not very far away from an equal-weighted index, and reshaping the indicator to be symmetric (i.e., to span values from $-a$ to $+a$, whatever the value of a, with an average of zero) lazily orthogonalizes them.

Moreover, a last step is often to threshold these obtained symmetric values; doing so has two positive effects: to avoid taking positions on tradable instruments for which the indicator is not "very strong", and to decrease the transaction costs. Indeed, this is often achieved by keeping 20% of the most positive values and 20% of the most negative ones. Finally, obtaining weights (or loadings) for the indicator's instruments can be done by setting all positive values to $+1$ and all the negative values to -1, before ensuring that the obtained weights sum to 1.

It is important to have in mind that if the factors are meant to be used within the same multifactor model, they should be as independent from one another as possible. Not only should they not be correlated with the market factor (and it is possible to minimize this correlation during their construction), but it is also preferable that the factors be uncorrelated between themselves. This independence is desirable because it prevents to end up with a very large number of factors that are all correlated together (it would be difficult to interpret the decomposition), and moreover a linear regression performed using correlated factors would be statistically spurious.

Obtaining independent factors can be done using a risk factor model, such as employing Principal Component Analysis (PCA) to orthogonalize them, or to have a stepwise procedure to only accept the orthogonal part of a new indicator to an existing multi-factors model. It is also possible to make use of portfolio construction[18] step, starting with a list of K factors and ending up with another list of K other factors that have very nice properties in terms of orthogonality, concentration, transaction costs, etc. This process will need to add more parameters to the construction of the factor, and the fewer the parameters, the better (to prevent over-fitting). That's why academic papers use very simple, generic and arbitrary methods. If replacing the 20% threshold by another one changes dramatically the results,

---

[18]Portfolio construction can give birth to investment strategies that are named "smart beta" in this book; see Section 4.4.3.

then it suggests that the factor is not robust, hence researchers stick to simple values and explore lightly around as to check for robustness.

Moreover, orthogonalizing two factors can be done in a more naive way, which implies building their "intersection": take the 30% more and less intense values of each indicator, and only keep the four "corners" of this square; each of them will contain around 10% of the observations (if the factors are not too correlated) and the obtained two sets of corners will be more independent than the two original indicators. These intersections can however be built in a variety of forms: for instance, one can keep 50% + 50% of the first one, and 1/3 + 1/3 of the other.

Fama–French 3 factors model. The factors are: Market, Size, and Value:

$$R_i(t) = R_f + \beta_i R_m(t) + \beta_{i,\text{size}}\text{SMB}(t) + \beta_{i,\text{value}}\text{HML}(t) + \epsilon_i(t), \quad (4.4)$$

where SMB and HML, respectively, refers to *Small Minus Big* (related to "Size") and *High Minus Low* (related to "Value", i.e., "Book-to-market"). These indicators are built using the six Value-weighted portfolios formed on Size and Book-to-market value. The portfolios are formed at the end of every month of June on a universe composed of all stocks listed in NYSE, AMEX and NASDAQ, as the intersection of two portfolios formed on Size (noted by S for Small and B for Big, relative to the median market capitalization of NYSE equity only) and three portfolios formed on book to market (i.e., Book Equity/Market Equity, noted by V for Value, N for Neutral and G for Growth relative to NYSE breakpoints)

$$\text{SMB} = \frac{1}{3}\left(S\&V + B\&N + S\&G\right) - \frac{1}{3}(B\&V + B\&N + B\&G),$$

$$\text{HML} = \frac{1}{2}\left(S\&V + B\&V\right) - \frac{1}{2}(S\&G + B\&G).$$

Fama–French–Carhart 4 model. The factors are: Market, Size, Value and the monthly Momentum (12, 1):

$$R_i(t) = R_f + \beta R_m(t) + \beta_{i,\text{size}}\text{SMB}(t) + \beta_{i,\text{value}}\text{HML}(t)$$
$$+\beta_{i,\text{mom}}\text{UMD}(t) + \epsilon_i(t)$$

UMD is the Carhart implementation of the momentum factor. It stands for Up (winners) Minus Down (losers). It is also based on six value-weight portfolios formed on size and prior (2–12) returns. The portfolios, which are formed monthly, are the intersections of two portfolios formed on size (Market Equity) and three portfolios formed on prior (2–12) returns (noted by U for Up, m for medium and D for Down, relative to NYSE breakpoints):

$$\text{UMD} = \frac{1}{2}\left(S\&U + B\&U\right) - \frac{1}{2}(S\&D + B\&D).$$

Fama–French 5 factors model. Market, Size, Value, Investment and Operating profitability:

$$R_i(t) = R_f + \beta R_m(t) + \beta_{i,\text{size}}\text{SMB}(t) + \beta_{i,\text{value}}\text{HML}(t)$$
$$+\beta_{i,\text{prof}}\text{RMW}(t) + \beta_{i,\text{invest}}\text{CMA}(t) + \epsilon_i(t).$$

Robust Minus Weak (RMW) is based on six value-weighted portfolios formed on size and operating profitability (noted by R for Robust, and W for Weak). The stock profitability is computed as the annual revenues minus cost of goods sold, interest expense, and selling, general, and administrative expenses divided by book equity for the last fiscal year.

$$\text{RMW} = \frac{1}{2}\left(\text{Small Robust} + \text{Big Robust}\right) - \frac{1}{2}(\text{Small Weak} + \text{Big Weak}).$$

Conservative Minus Aggressive (CMA) is the average return on the two conservative investment portfolios minus the average return on the two aggressive investment portfolios. The portfolios are formed on size and the change in total assets from the fiscal year ending in year $t - 2$ to the fiscal year ending in $t - 1$, divided by $t - 2$ total assets.

$$\text{CMA} = \frac{1}{2}(\text{Small Conservative} + \text{Big Conservative})$$
$$-\frac{1}{2}(\text{Small Aggressive} + \text{Big Aggressive}).$$

Hou Xue and Zhang Q-factor model. Four factors: market, size, investment, and profitability (ROE)

$$R_i(t) = R_f(t) + \beta R_m(t) + \beta_{i,\text{ME}}\text{ME}_i(t) + \beta_{i,\text{I/A}}\text{IA}_i(t)$$
$$+ \beta_{i,\text{ROE}}\text{ROE}_i(t) + \epsilon_i(t),$$

where ME is market equity, I/A stands for investment to assets. It is the annual change in total assets divided by 1-year-lagged total assets. ROE: Return on Equity is the income before extraordinary items divided by one-quarter-lagged book equity.

From a quantitative perspective (19)

If building factors seems simple, identifying factors is far from easy, since it is about fighting over-fitting: Is the new factor really different from early identified ones? Should it replace a combination of existing ones? But overall: How will a factor, constructed and validated on past data, be "valid" on future data?

This question of validity requires quantitative skills. This question can be properly stated in the language of statistics. For instance, there is clearly a point on the robustness of the parameters (sometimes implicit parameters, like the investment universe, have to be checked). There is also a matter of stationarity: are the residuals stationary? While the bootstrap can be used to validate factors (especially when they are built using alternative data); it is not a magic tool and has to be used within its required assumptions (for instance, bootstrapping quantile is not a straightforward task at all).

4.4.2   ESG as a new market trend

SRI or ESG is a form of investment that systematically takes into account extra-financial criteria such as Environmental, Social, and Governance considerations in portfolio construction. While optimizing risk management, this approach aims to generate, over the long term, a return on investment and a positive social impact. This kind of investment can be found in companies (financing green products), but also states and public authorities encouraging the development of a green ecosystem.

Responsible finance, as we know it nowadays, originated in the United States in the 1920s at the initiative of religious congregations that refused to invest in securities considered to be involved in sinful activities. The more common ones are alcohol, tobacco, gambling,

pornography, and weaponry. This form of socially responsible investment disregarded all financial considerations. In the 1970s, responsible finance took a more secular and militant approach, due to major
international and geopolitical events such as Apartheid, the Vietnam
War, nuclear power, etc. The concept was appealing and growing. It
is from the 1990s onwards that socially responsible investment has
been moving closer to its current form, where moral values are no
longer thought to be taken at the expense of short-term financial performance, but a risk factor to be taken into account in the portfolio
optimization. The industry becomes more convinced of the impact
of firms' Environmental, Social, and Governance practices on their
financial results and stock market value. The approach of systematically and explicitly including ESG factors into the financial analysis
as well as in the investment process recognizes that environmental
issues, social inequality, and corporate governance can affect a company's long-term performance through several risk channels such as
the brand, the reputation risk, and the credibility of the company to
deliver on its projects. Thus, ESG is taken into account as per any
other risk factor at portfolio construction.

Datasets used in building ESG factors mainly describe characteristics of companies outside of the financial realm; therefore, alternative data is often used to this effect, especially texts that are
processed with Natural Language Processing algorithms.

4.4.2.1 Common ESG/SRI strategies

Portfolios implementing Socially Responsible Investments are usually
based on one of the following methods:

Negative/exclusionary screening. Exclusion of securities of certain sectors or companies involved in activities deemed unacceptable
or controversial. This approach however is criticized for its limited
diversification, as it implies excluding entire sectorial areas. The most
standard exclusions are related to:

Controversial activities: Exclusion of companies implicated in either
alcohol, gambling, tobacco, or manufacturing and sales of controversial weapons. The list of weapons deemed as controversial depend on which treaty we refer to. Thus, issuers base
their portfolio's construction on the cultural background of
end investors targeted by the product. Most common filtered

weapons are Anti-Personnel Landmines, Cluster Munitions, Biological Weapon, Chemical Weapon, Nuclear Weapon, Incendiary Weapon, Non-Detectable Fragment, Blinding lasers, White Phosphorous and Depleted Uranium.

Activities harmful to the environment: In the context of increased globe temperature, the depletion of natural resources, the degradation of ecosystems, the destruction of habitats, the extinction of wildlife, and pollution, it becomes increasingly important to channel private sector money away from companies undertaking harmful activities to the environment, namely involved in fossil fuel industries in upstream, supporting exploration and production, e.g., drilling and oilfield services, contract mining, offshore rigs leasing; Midstream involved in transportation services, e.g., pipelines, oil and gas storage and shipping, plants (raw natural gas gathering and processing plants, liquefaction/re-gasification plants, and generation of electricity from coal, shale oil, oil & gas, and peat).

UNGC principles: Signatories of the Global Compact leaders summit should meet certain requirements regarding human rights, labour (elimination of all forms of forced and compulsory labor, abolition of child labor), environmental responsibility, and anti-corruption considerations.

Positive/best-in-class screening. An evolution from the original exclusionary model. Rather than excluding companies for their bad behavior or implication in controversial or environmental non-friendly activities, this approach privileges the best performers within a sector or a geographical zone in terms of ESG. This includes selecting only those who meet certain thresholds or over-weighting the best performers compared to their industry peers selected in the portfolio. The following criteria serve as standard for environmental positive impact:

Environment: Pollution prevention and control (soil, accident), development of green products and services, protection of biodiversity, protection of water resources, waste management, energy mitigation and reasonable control of environmental impacts on the overall life cycle of products and services.

Social: Contribution to economic and social development of the territories of establishment and their human communities, concrete commitment in favor of the control of societal impacts of products and services, transparent and participative contribution to causes of general interest.

Governance: Efficiency and integrity, insurance of both independence and effectiveness of the Board of Directors, effectiveness and efficiency of audit and control systems, and in particular inclusion of social responsibility risks, respect of shareholders' rights and most of all of the minorities, transparency and moderation in executive remuneration.

Impact investing. Targeted investments aimed at solving social or environmental problems. Investments in particular projects designed to achieve specific measurable goals, such as building affordable housing, or renewable energy plants. The focus here is less on generating a financial return and more on using capital to create positive change in the economy.

Sustainability themed investing. The selection of assets specifically related to sustainable areas such as clean energy, sustainable forestry, female leadership, or good board governance. These strategies seek to invest in companies that are most actively working to address the chosen issues while avoiding those that are not.

4.4.2.2 The ESG eco-system

Just over half of fund flows in Europe in 2019 went into ESG products, with investors showing a strong preference for actively managed ESG funds. In total, 50.46% of inflows to European funds were invested in ESG-related funds in that same year.

Overall, fund flows totaled €574.3 billion — the second-largest figure in the industry's history, according to Refinitiv Lipper. Stripping out funds such as money markets and commodities where ESG implementation is minimal at best; then in vanilla equity, bond and multi-asset funds the percentage of ESG inflows reached 70.15% in 2020. However, ESG funds still only represented 15% of assets under management in Europe at the end of the year, with €2 trillion invested in them.

The rapid increase in ESG and socially responsible investing has given the opportunity to new market players to develop in order to build the ecosystem around it, with market regulators needing to involve themselves to deliver a sustainable financial system that works for individuals and institutional investors across the world.

Specialized rating agency: Providing extra-financial analysis of companies, giving ratings as well as identifying pure players, companies in transition and bad players. There is a need for both quantitative and qualitative data related to the various ESG criteria and fields of research. Therefore, rating agencies come into different colors and shapes depending on their mission, providing information on companies in terms of strategies, actions implemented, or results, and on their technological prowess. Going from traditional agencies, submitting forms to corporations with a series of profiling questions to assess their ESG performance, to technological agencies applying machine learning techniques — Natural language processing to extract valuable insight on the company behavior from news channels, to agencies analyzing the corporates' balance sheets to assess involvement in unethical or controversial activities.

Regulation: With the multiplication of rating agencies and ESG data providers comes the multiplications of ESG metrics, assessment methodologies and accuracy, which make it difficult to compare the ESG strategies between themselves to distinguish the pure greenwashing from the genuine methodologies. The European Commission decided to issue an EU taxonomy for sustainable finance. It is a list of economic activities with performance criteria for their contribution to six environmental objectives. The purpose of the taxonomy is to create a common language for investors, issuers, policymakers, and regulators to discuss the stakes of the environmental problems in Finance, translate the Paris Agreement and SDGs in actionable decisions and propose investment strategies. The Taxonomy proposal aims to substantially contribute to at least one of the six environmental objectives, to not significant harm any of the other five environmental objectives, and to comply with minimum safeguards. The environmental objectives are:

1. Climate change mitigation;

2. Climate change adaptation;
3. Sustainable use and protection of water and marine resources;
4. Transition to a circular economy, waste prevention and recycling;
5. Pollution prevention and control;
6. Protection of healthy ecosystems.

Auditors: Implementing regulation, issuing labels and ensuring that the labeled funds respect the minimum requirements ongoing basis. In addition, auditors intervene in green bonds certifications chain, serving as external verifier or second party opinion. Bonds must nowadays comply with a strict outline to be labelled as green described by the EU climate bonds initiative based on ICMA guidelines or the green bond initiative.

From a quantitative perspective (20)

Since ESG scores and ratings require the processing of diverse datasets, quantitative analysts have a role to play to guarantee that statistical tools have been used properly. Typically, the notion of stationarity and the curse of dimensionality (i.e., the fact that in high dimension — when the number of variable is large — the standard metrics like the variance are not able to identify meaningful trends anymore) have to be carefully checked.

Alternative data is widely used in the context of ESG, especially texts. As usual in machine learning (see Section 6.3.3), it is important to have transverse teams of field experts and data scientists to extract information from this kind of datasets.

4.4.3 From portfolio construction to smart beta

It is not always easy to define the notion of "smart beta". In this book, we took it upon ourselves to distinguish between factor investing and smart beta:

- Factor investing, defined in Section 4.4.1, is about identifying rewarded risk factors, that can be used to estimate the exposure of a portfolio or a strategy, or to design an investment vehicle, for instance style ETFs.

The factors can be technical, fundamental, or based on alternative data. They usually start with an indicator combining characteristics of companies; these characteristics are drawn from the past returns of financial instruments, the status of the balance sheet or the governance of the company, from predictions on its sales, and so on.

- Smart beta, investigated in this section, is about focusing on portfolio construction that goes beyond cap-weighted index.

4.4.3.1   Towards a normalization of the semantic of investing

If the reader put side to side the concepts of CAPM, pricing anomalies, risk factors, rewarded factors, and smart beta, she or he will have access to key elements to describe any portfolio or strategy. Over the last 50 years, investors, asset managers, investment banks, structurers, exchanges, vendors and brokers have progressively adopted the same language to describe the tools needed to build an investment strategy. This normalization of the language of investing has propagated itself to market participants, mainly since 2010. Comparatively, the tools and the language used by the investment banks to build and hedge derivatives and to monitor the balance sheet of the bank, including stochastic calculus and partial differential equations, started to be the lingua franca of banking intermediation earlier, in the 1980s.

Smart betas are an important step in this process since they put the emphasis on portfolio construction and establishes a bridge between portfolio construction and market anomalies: why does certain portfolio constructions perform better than a capital-weighted index? This is an important question, as the performance of a cap-weighted index corresponds on paper to the average performance of an investor. This theoretical property is easily explained: if all the investor's investment exactly match the free-float of the companies, then the average portfolio of the investor is a free-float weighted index. If one adds to this property a vague concept of zero-sum game, claiming that if this is an average, any portfolio performing better would require another portfolio is performing worst, then it is unrealistic that on the long run a portfolio would consistently dominate the cap-weighted portfolio: what would happen if all investors adopt it? Ultimately, it would impact the market capitalization of its components and, thus drive the cap-weighted index to this portfolio. What about the minimum variance portfolio? (see Section 4.4.3.4) It would link the capitalization of companies with their volatility and their correlations in a way that is *a priori* not economically founded.

Nevertheless, some investors are seduced by the smart beta portfolio, as this portfolio, due to its particular construction aspects, focuses on diversification and correlation between the returns of the components more than other factor-driven portfolios.

4.4.3.2 Smart beta vs. cap-weighting approach

Traditional indices have been primarily used as a reference, but thanks to their representativeness, considerable transparency, abundant liquidity, and low costs, index products have quickly endorsed the role of efficient investment tools and responded to investors' need for easy synthetic access to a whole market or industry group. However, despite all these qualities, cap-weighted investment solutions have drawbacks:

• The market capitalization weighting method is directly related to stock price movements. Therefore, stocks that have recently well-behaved, often the most volatile ones, are given greater weights in the index. As a result, some areas may become overrepresented, as was the case during the technology bubble of the late 1990s. This weighting procedure has an immediate effect on both portfolio volatility and diversification.

Similarly, if the inclusion criterion is in dollars of capitalization, it has to be indexed to an exogenous level to maintain the amount of companies stable through time. If the inclusion criterion is in number of the largest capitalization in each country, again it introduces heterogeneity from one continent to another. Of course, index providers (like MSCI, S&P, or FTSE) are trying to fix these types of issues, but it also means they are taking arbitrary decisions that all investors following their indexes will blindly, simultaneously follow. In statistics, these difficulties are called "non-stationarity issues"; moreover, this can generate crowding (see Section 4.3.3 for further details).

- Even within a given sector, valuations may vary considerably and the cap-weighting scheme does not take into account certain fundamental aspects of companies. For instance, Tesla Motors almost has the same capitalization as Renault, while it sells 70 times fewer vehicles.

  Again it may be a good idea to allocate the same weight to both Tesla Motors and Renault in a portfolio, but it is a choice that should probably be taken explicitly by the asset manager, not implicitly by importing the choices of the index vendor.

- Beyond potential crowding, the deterministic nature of some indexes rebalancing rules make them potential targets of arbitrage.[19] It is in such a case less costly to implement the investment strategy using the underlying rather than to blindly follow the index.

- Another weak point is, from a regulatory viewpoint, the fact that investors passively following an index are not taking investment decisions based on specific information on companies anymore. They behave as free riders, waiting the prices to adjust themselves to mechanically have the weight of successful companies increase in their portfolio.

  Even if information processing is a difficult task, some investors succeed because the prices are efficiently moving with information. Hence, being among the first ones to adjust the weight would mechanically increase the performance of the portfolio as other investors follow. Hence their free rider behavior forbids passive investors from taking profit from information. Somehow, their fear to miss the information pushes them to be always late.

  In terms of the efficiency of the price formation process, regulators may be concerned by an increase of passive investing: if a majority of investors are passive and adopt a free rider behavior, then a minority of investors will really contribute to form the price

---

[19]There is an abundant literature on the arbitrage of the Goldman Sachs Commodity index.

in accordance with the Grossman–Stiglitz paradigm: the market efficiency may decrease with the informativeness of the prices, and price manipulation may be easier.[20]

Hence, there is room for other mechanical portfolio constructions than capital weighted ones, and it is what smart beta are proposing to do. As often on financial markets, diversity is a virtue and having all investors adopting the same behavior is never a good sign.

4.4.3.3 Smart beta: At the crossroad of active and passive investment

Providing investors with an alternative to traditional beta while taking into account the quality and the risk of assets is not revolutionary. It has always been the purpose of active management. The strength of smart beta goes beyond redressing valuation issues: it aims at preserving the main characteristics of passive management, while actively being exposed to specific factors. The smart beta approach is based on the following pillars:

- A systematic approach based on *predefined rules*: As indices, smart beta portfolios are built by implementing a set of predefined rules. Thanks to a systematic approach, it is possible to invest in a wide universe and analyze strategies' behavior for long periods.
- *Transparency*: Investors have increasingly sophisticated profiles and wish to be able to intentionally expose themselves to specific factors instead of accepting exposure offered by an asset manager whose selection process can vary over time.
- *Long-term investment horizon*: The goal of smart beta is to hunt for persistent market anomalies measured over several economic cycles.
- *Cost effectiveness*: As smart beta strategies are based on long-term systematic investment, their implementation costs are usually lower than other types of active management.

---

[20]This concern is in line with the issue of having more trading taking place at the closing auction than during the continuous auctions: flows at the close are driven by passive strategies; it is an indicator of less active information processing.

As a result, smart beta is a crossroad between traditional indices, quantitative strategies, and active management: it is an approach that implements quantitative techniques based on simple indicators with a strong focus on transparency and cost-effectiveness. It would be ambitious to state that the current level of transparency and cost-effectiveness of all smart beta products cannot be improved, but it is clear that intermediaries providing low-cost strategies have or will have to be transparent and maintain low transaction costs.

4.4.3.4   Examples of smart beta strategies

Minimum variance. The minimum variance, also referred to as the minimum volatility strategy, is the portfolio that minimizes volatility while being fully invested. Written without long–long constraint, this problem reads:

$$\min_{w^T \mathbf{1}=1} w^T \Omega w, \tag{4.5}$$

where w is the optimal weights vector, Ω is the variance–covariance matrix. A little bit of algebra shows that the minimum-variance weights should be

$$w^{mv} = \frac{\Omega^{-1}\mathbf{1}}{\mathbf{1}^T \Omega^{-1}\mathbf{1}}, \tag{4.6}$$

where Ω^{-1} is the invert of the covariance matrix. This inversion is difficult when either the number of assets is large (but the Random Matrix Theory can help to counter this difficulty) or when some of them are highly correlated.[21]

The minimum variance strategy results in an efficient portfolio with the lowest volatility. It is constructed from low systematic and idiosyncratic risk stocks, but suffers from concentration on a few low-risk sectors or stocks with low returns. Besides, it may be exposed to small-capitalization, value, momentum, dividend yield factors, and other involuntary factors. Last but not least, it has high turnover, liquidity risk, and high transaction costs. This strategy is usually

---

[21]Note that a machine learning approach, based on backtesting and cross validation, can prevent to ever have to invert the covariance matrix.

improved first by filtering the investment universe and second by adding constraints to the optimization algorithm on maximum exposure to stocks, industry groups, capitalization levels, and liquidity categories.

Maximum diversification. There are several diversification measures in the literature, but the one we consider in this example is the following: The diversification ratio is the weighted average of stocks' volatility in the portfolio divided by total portfolio volatility. With the notation Σ_D for the diagonal matrix made of the volatility of the stocks (i.e., $\Sigma_D|_i = \sigma_i$, the associated optimization program reads:

$$\max_{w^T \mathbf{1} = 1} \frac{w^T \Sigma_D}{w^T (\Sigma_D^T \Sigma_D) w}. \tag{4.7}$$

It is straightforward to notice that maximizing this ratio drives the weights of the resulting portfolio to minimize its denominator, i.e., $w^T (\Sigma_D^T \Sigma_D) w$. Noticing that $\Sigma_D^T \Sigma_D = \Omega$ if and only if the returns are independent.

Portfolios resulting from the maximum diversification method are always less risky than market indices thanks to their higher degree of diversification. Besides, the optimization process maximizes the specific risk while keeping watch on the portfolio average volatility. Therefore, the optimal portfolio contains stocks with below-average systematic risk and above-average specific risk.

Risk parity. The goal of risk parity is to think in terms of "risk budget", it aims at attributing the same risk budget to each component of the portfolio. Therefore, it is useful to first define the marginal contribution of the ith component of the portfolio to its overall risk (under quadratic assumptions):

$$MC_i = \frac{\partial w^T \Omega w}{\partial w_i} = 2 \sum_{j=1}^{n} w_j \sigma_i \sigma_j \rho_{ij},$$

where σ is the volatility of the ith component and ρ_{ij} the correlation between components i and j. Then the requirement for risk parity reads:

$$\forall i, j \ RC_i = MC_i \times w_i = MC_j \times w_j = RC_j.$$

As we notice, marginal risk contributions are both based on volatility and correlations of each asset with the rest of the portfolio, the weights are then inversely proportional to marginal contributions, which themselves depend on the weights. The problem is complex and recursive. Unless we introduce some simplification hypothesis, we won't be able to solve it.

First case: All assets have the same volatility and the same pairwise correlation.

$$\forall i, j \ \sigma_i = \sigma_j = \sigma, \quad \rho_{i,j} = \rho,$$

$$MC_i = 2 \sum_{i=1}^{n} w_j \sigma_i \sigma_j \rho_{ij} = 2 \times \sigma^2 \times \rho \Rightarrow w_i = w_j = \frac{1}{n}.$$

The strong hypothesis of all stocks having the same volatility and all pairs having the same correlation results in an equally weighted portfolio. The only advantage it has on traditional betas is removing concentration due to market capitalization. Sectors, countries, or any overpopulated group of stocks sharing the same feature will be overrepresented.

Second case: Every pair of stocks displays the same correlation

$$\forall i, j \ \rho_{i,j} = \rho,$$

$$MC_i = 2 \sum_{i=1}^{n} w_j \sigma_i \sigma_j \rho_{ij} = 2 \times \rho \times \sigma_i \sum_{j=1}^{n} w_j \sigma_j \Rightarrow w_i \sigma_i = w_j \sigma_j.$$

Another possible proxy for risk parity is the risk-weighted scheme. Besides diluting market capitalization concentration, it adjusts for volatility but doesn't solve the concentration problem of overrepresented groups. It is possible to solve overrepresented groups by applying a weighting method in two steps: First, by forming sectorial risk-weighted baskets, and then creating the overall portfolio by risk weighting these baskets. The hypothesis of homogeneous correlation is more accurate among stocks of the same sector and between sectors themselves.

It is interesting to note that risk parity schemes have the nice intertemporal property that when the volatility of a component increases (resp., decreases), its weight in the portfolio decreases (resp., increases). If one believe that the volatility increases during market stress conditions and decreases before recovery, then risk parity provides a potentially attractive implicit market timing between the components of the portfolio.

Rebalancing of smart beta portfolios. Because smart beta portfolio are the outcome of an optimization process involving slowly varying parameters (like correlations or volatility), then one could be tempted to rebalance them very frequently to keep they in line with the slow varying target weights. This would generate excessive transaction costs, thus in practice, intermediaries providing smart beta instruments to other market participants use heuristics to time the rebalancing. The three most popular ones are as follows:

(1) *Low frequency rebalancing*: For instance quarterly rebalancing.
(2) *Rebalancing driven by threshold on portfolio weights*: Wait for the difference between the weights of the current portfolio and the target portfolio to reach a given threshold (for instance 5%) to rebalance the whole portfolio.
(3) *Rebalancing driven by a tracking error*: Wait for the tracking error (i.e., the difference between the expected risk of the current portfolio and the one of the target portfolio) to reach a given threshold (for instance 2%) to rebalance the portfolio.

From a quantitative perspective (21)

The smart beta strategies being inspired from portfolio construction, quantitative analysts can contribute to their development, either by employing tools of statistics or tools of dynamic optimization and stochastic control.

An interesting quantitative angle is to use the language of mathematics to understand the relations between all these optimization problems and to add some meaningful constraints. For instance, coming back to the Modern Portfolio Theory, it is interesting to see the commonalities between the one period portfolio problem of maximizing returns under a

(Continued)

(Continued)

volatility constraint, i.e.,

$$\max w^T \mu$$
$$u.c. \quad w^T \mathbf{1} = 1$$
$$w^T \Omega w \leq A^2.$$

That has a natural formulation of

$$\max_{w} w^T \mu - \gamma(w^T \mathbf{1} - 1) - \lambda(w^T \Omega w - A^2) \qquad (4.8)$$

using Lagrange multipliers γ and λ) and the other problems, like the minimum variance formulation (4.5) whose Lagrange multiplier formulation is $w^T \Omega w - \tilde{\gamma}(w^T \mathbf{1} - 1)$.

Nevertheless, a pitfall for experts in portfolio optimization is forgetting that most of the parameters in their optimization programs are estimates: Ω (the covariance matrix) and μ (the expected returns) are obtained via noisy statistical procedures. Even a simple program like (4.8) is in reality a deterministic counterpart for

$$\max_{w} \mathbb{E}_t(w^T R(t)) - \gamma(w^T \mathbf{1} - 1) - \lambda(\mathbb{V}_t(w^T R(t)) - A^2),$$

with the notation $\mathbb{E}$ for the expectation, $\mathbb{V}$ for the variance and $R(t)$ the stochastic vector of the returns of the components of the portfolio.

It is not sure that the variance is the desired risk measure (value at risk or maximum drawdown can be preferred or combined with it) and the temporal aspect is completely ignored in formulation (4.8) whereas a path wise optimization could be considered (add for instance transaction costs). Moreover, the relationship between the empirical covariance matrix and the future risk of a portfolio is not completely understood by now.

4.4.4 A factor zoo or a reproducibility crisis?

with the proliferation of factors of the last decade, one could ask whether the discovered factors are real, or not. Given that all these factors attempt to explain the cross-sectional distribution of expected returns of an investment universe, the needed number of factors should not exceed the number of statistically significant principal components of the returns on this universe (that is hardly beyond 20). Nevertheless, factors being constructed from characteristics of the components of the universe, they are meant to be explainable and as a consequence it is likely that more than one factor is needed to recover a single principal component. Principal components being extracted from the covariance matrix of the returns, one may argue that it may not be the adequate way to describe the cross-section; in any case, the timescale at which the covariance of the returns is computed plays a role in the direction of the identifiable principal components.

The reason behind this proliferation, as spotted by Campbell Harvey in 2017, comes directly from the process of academic publication in this field. First, journal editors competing for publication impact metrics tend to publish papers with any result beyond a reasonable statistical significance. Due to this mechanism, failed attempts at identifying factors are thus not published. Moreover, because the valuation is done on the sole time series of returns of a finite (but large) number of financial instruments, the statistical significance of the whole process, that is tracking combinations of indicators that can explain a given time series with the possibility to arbitrarily restrict the investment universe, can be questioned. The term p-hacking or alpha-hacking have been coined to describe such mechanism: performing many statistical tests on a given dataset and selecting only the results which exhibit statistical significance, instead of stating a single hypothesis and confirming it or denying it after questioning the data. In machine learning, the adequate name is simple overfitting.

Knowing the number of attempts, it is possible to provide an adjusted level of significance of the statistical test, accounting for this multiple testing bias. Cross-validation can be applied as well, but again, publishing only "conclusive" attempts introduces a bias that is very difficult to assess.

Moreover, the process of academic discovery of factors mixes itself with the business models of asset managers: almost all managers now have a "white papers" or "publications" section on their website, to convince their potential clients that the investment vehicles they provide have academic foundations. Besides, researchers often have interest on both sides: they can work as consultants or employees for an asset manager (leveraging on their academic reputation) for a few years, then return to Academia with the advantage of their expanded network. The question of alignment of interest between the private and the public sector is not exclusive to the financial sector; almost all industries are facing these potential conflicts of interest. However, the difficulty in designing counterfactual experiments in economics makes the discussion of academic discoveries more subtle.

Again, like in other domains, the availability of statistical tools coming from data sciences offers even more ways to exhibit "significant discoveries" as more tests for time series become available, the amount of false positives increases as well. Besides, researchers in finance do not always understand the technical specificities of machine learning driven tools that are designed to be used on huge datasets (think about the numbers of labels of images, pixels in images, images on social networks, etc.), whereas the number of daily returns of financial instruments is relatively low.

Another term in the debate is the one of "reproducibility crisis", because it seems difficult to reproduce academic papers (or asset managers' white papers), or when it is possible, small variations of the parameters of the procedure (like the investment universe, the size of time windows, the lags, the number of parameters in some regressions, etc.) seem to change the results significantly, showing a lack of robustness. The debate is open on this aspect, and a few elements are established certain:

- It is very difficult to review data-driven results conducted on one dataset only; there is probably a lack of capability to *share data with the reviewers on an open-source platform* to disclose the statistical procedures in full transparency.
- The more theory (or a thesis) is supporting the result, with *identified counterfactuals* (i.e., the capability to empirically falsify a theory; a key element in developing scientific theories as noted by Karl Popper), the better.[22]

---

[22] Alternative data may be a useful support to test a thesis at different time scales and geographical scales.

- The community of researchers should find a way to *share empirical failures*, especially attempts conducted during PhD thesis.[23]
- Last but not least, *conflict of interest should be disclosed*[24] in each paper; the list of current and former collaborations with market participants (especially asset managers) and the funding obtained by the researcher, her or his students and by the laboratory should be explicitly listed. It would also be desirable to list the industrial brochures, marketing material and white papers citing the paper.

4.5   For More Details

There is a lot of academic work supporting the sections of this chapter, it has been difficult to make a shortlist. Staring by generic concepts in asset management, it is of course important to cite the Grossman–Stiglitz paper (Grossman and Stiglitz, 1980) explaining how information processing has to be rewarded, and that information will never be instantaneously incorporated in prices because of that. It explains the importance of active investment that is focussed on extracting information. On the opposite, passive asset management freely follows the information that is already incorporated in the prices. Nevertheless, passive management itself is not an easy task, rebalancing is subtle: Green and Jame (2011) shows that it is better to not blindly follow index providers and Gârleanu and Pedersen (2013) provides an extension of the Modern Portfolio Theory[25] in case of transaction costs. Another pitfall of passive investment is to rebalancing alongside a crowd of other passive investors, generating more transaction costs (Stoll and Whaley (2010) details the well-known case of commodity indexes); Indeed, the effect of herding behavior on transaction costs were illustrated in Figure 4.2, based on

---

[23]If a PhD thesis in finance is usually a collection of three papers, it could be advantageously completed by the list of unfortunate attempts. This would be a good practice for a young researcher, and very informative for the community.
[24]Or mixed interest between the industry and the academia.
[25]See Markowitz (1952) for its seminal paper, and Merton (1975) for the first meaningful proposal in the context of intertemporal investment, i.e., following the paths of the portfolio.

Ancerno database, the same data used in Briere *et al.* (2020). Moreover, Section 2.6 summarizes the effect of market impact on optimal execution in a crowded environment.

Active investment is of course even more complex, and the industry struggles in putting together an understanding of good practices of alternative investment and hedge fund successes. Avramov *et al.* (2013) and references therein propose a solid start in understanding hedge fund return. As for an example of active strategy based on the careful study of FDA agreements of new drugs, see Klein and Li (2015). As well, Avellaneda and Lee (2010) is a good starting point to make sense of statistical arbitrage.

Since asset managers are intermediaries, not only inside the financial system (i.e., between market participants, for instance when fund managers use financial products designed by structurers and issued by investment banks), but also between investors with savings and individuals undertaking risky projects, the alignment of their clients' interests and the funds or the people working there is delicate and exposed to the principal agent problem. Holmstrom and Milgrom (1987) is the seminal paper introducing this problem; for a modern mathematical treatment of it, we recommend Cvitanić *et al.* (2017). In practice, metrics like high watermark are used (cf. Molenkamp, 2010) to avoid that performances with high variance are at the advantage of the agent (i.e., the manager) and at the detriment of the principal (i.e., the asset owner). Other metrics like Value at Risk (see Duffie and Pan, 1997), or Sharpe Ratio are also popular (Lo, 2002 investigates how this ratio can change due to the auto-correlation of the time series of returns). In the area of the principal–agent problem: Ambachtsheer (2011) is specifically dedicated to pension funds, and Bodie and Briere (2011) is an attempt to define the specific needs of a sovereign fund.

Regulators are actively trying to level the playing field beyond issues linked to the principal–agent problem; they issue papers explaining concerns, such as the potential drawback of synthetic ETFs (see Grillet-Aubert, 2020 and references therein for details). As synthetic products often use leverage, the price formation process is disturbed from time to time by short squeezes on underlying of leveraged instruments (see Allen *et al.*, 2021 for the Volkswagen case in 2008 and Guimaraes and Pannella, 2021 for the GameStop one in 2021). Given that the financial ecosystem adapts itself to regulations, authorities are now promoting the empirical analysis of new rules once they have been in application; these reports are always insightful, like Amzallag *et al.* (2021) on the outcome of a push towards the unbundling of execution and research on the brokerage side. In any case, regulators are always trying to cope with innovations that could on the one hand provide better tools and services, but could on the other hand prevent consumers of financial instruments from clearly understanding the associated risks. The transformations due to the emergence of data science, machine learning and associated technologies and practices are typical innovations under the scrutiny of regulators. Chapter 6 addresses these innovations; but to have quick answers to the associated stakes, the reader may have a look at Shapiro *et al.* (1998) for a reminder of classic network economy, and Haberly *et al.* (2019) for the platformization of asset managers.

Asset management is linked with portfolio construction through investment vehicles being explicitly built using optimization, and from the need to efficiently combine different vehicles. Moreover, *ex-post* analysis of exposures and performances shares tools with quantitative portfolio construction, especially through the use of covariance matrices. To go further in portfolio construction, one should start with Modern Portfolio Theory and Markowitz's seminal paper Markowitz (1952) (for early works read this historical paper: Markowitz, 1999), and quickly jump to its intertemporal version with Merton (1975) as it takes a trajectory-wise approach instead of one with strong i.i.d. assumptions. Using standard quantitative optimization on large portfolios immediately raises the issue of the correct estimation of the covariance matrix. such issue is addressed with Random Matrix Theory, which is detailed in Tao (2012). As well, see Meucci (2009) for a more generic statistical approach to portfolio construction. It is important to understand that RMT classically relies on i.i.d. assumptions too and that other approaches can be used to match the current estimate of the risk of a portfolio with its effective realization during the coming weeks, months or quarters. One of them is to combine alternative data with empirical correlations; a good framework allowing to go back and forth from the difference between the portfolio and its underlying components to the risk measures is hierarchical clustering (see De Prado, 2016, for detail and Marti *et al.*, 2021, for other frameworks). Building a portfolio with quantitative tools immediately goes beyond the co-dependencies between the returns of components of the portfolio, because a portfolio is looking for a balance between risk (that is captured by the codependency) and returns. And the expected returns can strongly drive the shape of the portfolio; for theory and examples of this dialog between risk and returns on long-only portfolios, see Lehalle and Simon (2021). Roncalli (2013) is a great start to focus on risk budgeting, and Choueifaty and Coignard (2008) for maximum diversification (that is a case where expected returns do not play any explicit role in the portfolio construction).

The rise of factor investment by the industry really took place with the publication of Ang *et al.* (2009): an evaluation report for the Norwegian government pension fund. The history of factors however began earlier with the market factor of the CAPM (see Lintner, 1965; Mossin, 1966; Sharpe, 1963; Treynor, 1961, for its origins). Later Arbitrage Pricing Theory emerged in Roll and Ross (1980), and statistical risk factors using Principal Component Analysis started to be intensively used with Stock and Watson (2002) (see references therein for further details). Section 4.4.4 detailed different kinds of factors; see Chen *et al.* (1986) for macroeconomic factors, Rosenberg and Guy (1995) and Rosenberg *et al.* (1976) or Yan and Zheng (2017) for fundamental factors, and Fama and French (1995) for one of the first very visible papers on multi-factors models. As well, ESG investing and its potential factors are detailed in Cavaco and Crifo (2014).

Even before the raise of alternative data and data science for factor identification (see Capponi and Lehalle, 2022 for the current landscape of machine learning in the financial sector, including nowcasting using alternative datasets), Harvey *et al.* (2015) and Feng *et al.* (2020) started to question the "factor zoo". The debate around the correct identification of factors is not over; de Prado (2020) is a reference introduction to good practices for machine learning users (Chen *et al.*, 2020 is a typical example of explanation of the cross-section of returns using deep learning) and Pukthuanthong *et al.* (2019) is an interesting attempt to statistically define what a "factor" could (or should) be. To review statistical tools to test the reproducibility of factors, it is a good idea to start with the bootstrap reading Efron and Tibshirani (1994) and its ancestor, the jackknife, with

Efron (1982). The reader will find an interesting empirical methodology to test the biases of a factor or portfolio in Bryzgalova *et al.* (2020). Last but not least, a good paper summarizing the "reproducibility crisis" in finance is Bailey and Lopez de Prado (2021).

References

Allen, F., Haas, M. D., Nowak, E., and Tengulov, A. (2021). Market efficiency and limits to arbitrage: Evidence from the Volkswagen short squeeze. *Journal of Financial Economics*, 142(1):166–194.

Ambachtsheer, K. P. (2011). *Pension Revolution: A Solution to the Pensions Crisis*, volume 388. John Wiley & Sons, Hoboken, New Jersey.

Amzallag, A., Guagliano, C., and Passo, V. L. (2021). MiFID II research unbundling: Assessing the impact on SMEs. Working Paper, ESMA.

Ang, A., Goetzmann, W. N., and Schaefer, S. (2009). Evaluation of active management of the Norwegian government pension fund. *Report to the Norwegian Ministry of Finance.*

Avellaneda, M. and Lee, J.-H. (2010). Statistical arbitrage in the us equities market. *Quantitative Finance*, 10(7):761–782.

Avramov, D., Barras, L., and Kosowski, R. (2013). Hedge fund return predictability under the magnifying glass. *Journal of Financial and Quantitative Analysis*, 48(4):1057–1083.

Bailey, D. H. and de Prado, M. L. (2021). How "backtest overfitting" in finance leads to false discoveries. *Significance (Royal Statistical Society)*, 18(6):22–25. https://rss.onlinelibrary.wiley.com/doi/10.1111/1740-9713.01588.

Bodie, Z. and Briere, M. (2011). Sovereign wealth and risk management. *Boston University School of Management Research Paper*, 8.

Briere, M., Lehalle, C.-A., Nefedova, T., and Raboun, A. (2020). Modeling transaction costs when trades may be crowded: A bayesian network using partially observable orders imbalance. In Jurczenko, E., (Ed.) *Machine Learning for Asset Management: New Developments and Financial Applications*, John Wiley & Sons, Hoboken, New Jersey. pp. 387–430.

Bryzgalova, S., Pelger, M., and Zhu, J. (2020). Forest through the trees: Building cross-sections of stock returns. Available at SSRN 3493458.

Capponi, A. and Lehalle, C.-A., editors (forthcoming 2022). Cambridge University Press.

Cavaco, S. and Crifo, P. (2014). Csr and financial performance: Complementarity between environmental, social and business behaviours. *Applied Economics*, 46(27):3323–3338.

Chen, L., Pelger, M., and Zhu, J. (2020). Deep learning in asset pricing. Available at SSRN 3350138.

Chen, N.-F., Roll, R., and Ross, S. A. (1986). Economic forces and the stock market. *Journal of Business*, 59(3):383–403.

Choueifaty, Y. and Coignard, Y. (2008). Toward maximum diversification. *The Journal of Portfolio Management*, 35(1):40–51.

Cvitanić, J., Possamaï, D., and Touzi, N. (2017). Moral hazard in dynamic risk management. *Management Science*, 63(10):3328–3346.

de Prado, M. L. (2016). Building diversified portfolios that outperform out of sample. *The Journal of Portfolio Management*, 42(4):59–69.

de Prado, M. M. L. (2020). *Machine Learning for Asset Managers*. Cambridge University Press.

Duffie, D. and Pan, J. (1997). An overview of value at risk. *Journal of Derivatives*, 4(3):7–49.

Efron, B. (1982). *The Jackknife, the Bootstrap and Other Resampling Plans*. SIAM.

Efron, B. and Tibshirani, R. J. (1994). *An Introduction to the Bootstrap*. CRC press.

Fama, E. F. and French, K. R. (1995). Size and book-to-market factors in earnings and returns. *The Journal of Finance*, 50(1):131–155.

Feng, G., Giglio, S., and Xiu, D. (2020). Taming the factor zoo: A test of new factors. *The Journal of Finance*, 75(3):1327–1370.

Gârleanu, N. and Pedersen, L. H. (2013). Dynamic trading with predictable returns and transaction costs. *The Journal of Finance*, 68(6):2309–2340.

Green, T. C. and Jame, R. (2011). Strategic trading by index funds and liquidity provision around s&p 500 index additions. *Journal of Financial Markets*, 14(4):605–624.

Grillet-Aubert, L. (2020). Opportunities and risks in the financial index market. *AMF Reports*.

Grossman, S. J. and Stiglitz, J. E. (1980). On the impossibility of informationally efficient markets. *The American Economic Review*, 70(3):393–408.

Guimaraes, B. and Pannella, P. (2021). Short-squeeze bubbles. Available at SSRN.

Haberly, D., MacDonald-Korth, D., Urban, M., and Wójcik, D. (2019). Asset management as a digital platform industry: A global financial network perspective. *Geoforum*, 106:167–181.

Harvey, C. R., Liu, Y., and Zhu, H. (2015). ... and the cross-section of expected returns. *The Review of Financial Studies*, 29(1):5–68.

Holmstrom, B. and Milgrom, P. (1987). Aggregation and linearity in the provision of intertemporal incentives. *Econometrica: Journal of the Econometric Society*, 55(2):303–328.

Klein, A. and Li, T. (2015). Acquiring and trading on complex information: How hedge funds use the Freedom of Information Act. *The Financial Management Association Conference.* European Financial Management Association, Amsterdam, Netherlands.

Lehalle, C.-A. and Simon, G. (2021). Portfolio selection with active strategies: how long only constraints shape convictions. *Journal of Asset Management*, 22(6):443–463.

Lintner, J. (1965). Security prices, risk, and maximal gains from diversification. *The Journal of Finance*, 20(4):587–615.

Lo, A. W. (2002). The statistics of Sharpe ratios. *Financial Analysts Journal*, 58(4):36–52.

Markowitz, H. (1952). Modern portfolio theory. *Journal of Finance*, 7(11):77–91.

Markowitz, H. M. (1999). The early history of portfolio theory: 1600–1960. *Financial Analysts Journal*, 55(4):5–16.

Marti, G., Nielsen, F., Bińkowski, M., and Donnat, P. (2021). *A Review of Two Decades of Correlations, Hierarchies, Networks and Clustering in Financial Markets.* Springer.

Merton, R. C. (1975). Optimum consumption and portfolio rules in a continuous-time model. In *Stochastic Optimization Models in Finance*, pp. 621–661. Elsevier.

Meucci, A. (2009). *Risk and Asset Allocation.* Springer Science & Business Media.

Molenkamp, J. B. (2010). Performance-based fees and moral hazard: Aligning the interests of investors and managers. *Rotman International Journal of Pension Management*, 3(1). https://icpmnetwork.com/company/roster/companyRosterDetails.html?companyId=17775&companyRosterId=48.

Mossin, J. (1966). Equilibrium in a capital asset market. *Econometrica: Journal of the Econometric Society*, 34(4):768–783.

Pukthuanthong, K., Roll, R., and Subrahmanyam, A. (2019). A protocol for factor identification. *The Review of Financial Studies*, 32(4):1573–1607.

Roll, R. and Ross, S. A. (1980). An empirical investigation of the arbitrage pricing theory. *The Journal of Finance*, 35(5):1073–1103.

Roncalli, T. (2013). *Introduction to Risk Parity and Budgeting.* CRC Press.

Rosenberg, B. and Guy, J. (1995). Prediction of beta from investment fundamentals. *Financial Analysts Journal*, 51(1):101–112.

Rosenberg, B., Marathe, V., *et al.* (1976). Common factors in security returns: Microeconomic determinants and macroeconomic correlates. Technical report, University of California at Berkeley.

Shapiro, C., Carl, S., Varian, H. R., *et al.* (1998). *Information Rules: A Strategic Guide to the Network Economy.* Harvard Business Press.

Sharpe, W. F. (1963). A simplified model for portfolio analysis. *Management Science*, 9(2):277–293.

Stock, J. H. and Watson, M. W. (2002). Forecasting using principal components from a large number of predictors. *Journal of the American Statistical Association*, 97(460):1167–1179.

Stoll, H. R. and Whaley, R. E. (2010). Commodity index investing and commodity futures prices. *Journal of Applied Finance*, 20(1):1–40.

Tao, T. (2012). *Topics in Random Matrix Theory*, volume 132. American Mathematical Society.

Treynor, J. L. (1961). Market value, time, and risk. Unpublished.

Yan, X. S. and Zheng, L. (2017). Fundamental analysis and the cross-section of stock returns: A data-mining approach. *The Review of Financial Studies*, 30(4):1382–1423.

Chapter 5

Risk Management at the Scale of an Investment Bank

5.1 Why Do We Need to Monitor Model Risk?

Previous chapters have shown that the financial ecosystem is made of intermediaries selling and buying risks, having in mind that the ultimate buyers of risk should be outside of the financial system. Remember that we call "risk" a future promise; typically the seller of a Future contract promises to deliver the underlying, and the seller of a vanilla option promises to give to its buyer the opportunity to buy (or to sell) the underlying at a given price (the strike) at expiry. Structured products are a mix of promises. A natural way to monitor the risk in the balance sheet of an intermediary is to decompose it along risk factors; this decomposition is meant to be locally linear and is hence additive. A large intermediary, having a lot of clients, has hence good chances to "net" its risk along these directions. We have seen in Chapter 3 that there is some uncertainty attached to such decompositions: are the dynamics of these risks factor really observable? have some risk factors been forgotten? are the decomposition updated frequently enough?

At the first order, it is convenient to split the risk factors into large asset classes: Interest rates, Foreign exchange (FX) rates, Equity, Credit and Commodity. More exotic risks like weather forecast, retail customer behavior or natural catastrophe damages are also exchanged, but it is a marginal part of the total risks exchanged through the financial system. The buyer or the seller of a risk can be motivated by hedging (or unwinding) its exposure to a specific mix of factors, or on the opposite take an exposure to these risks. She or he can also simply act as an intermediary between another seller or buyer. A number of financial products designed to exchange risks are standardized ready to trade on dedicated markets. Trading in such products offers both sufficient liquidity and enough transparency to allow most economic actors to use them efficiently. This is in general the case for:

- FX markets where daily exchange over all currencies amounts to $6.5 trillion USD.[1]
- Equity indices and options on dedicated listed market.
- Interest rates swap mostly cleared in CCP.

Besides, these standardized products are particularly efficient for financial risk transfers without generating too much counterparty credit risk (since they are cleared). However, investors, corporate clients and financial institutions also need tailor made products that are suited for their particular needs. These products are not readily available and need to be designed and then structured in order to propose the desired risk return profile to the client. For instance structured products can either be simple combination of standardized products or can be more complex. In the first case,the structured product is easy to hedge for the emitting investment bank: simply buy all the components and package them together. In most cases, the complexity of the structured product is such that a perfect static replication is impossible. As a consequence, the investment bank assumes a model for the dependency between known risk factors and the mix of risks it is now exposed to (i.e., because it is on the other side of the trade). A mechanism close to a Taylor expansion, described in Section 3.1.2, allows to net the exposure to these factors with exposure to other factors on its balance sheet, and to hedge (or replicate) the remaining risk on exchanges.

---

[1] 2019 Central Bank Survey.

5.1.1 What is a model?

For an intermediary, the purpose of a model is to be able to look at all possible changes in the variables of interest given other variables (i.e., risk factors, or covariates) changes. This knowledge is used to give a "fair value" to the structured product, to define a hedging strategy that minimizes the uncertainty of the final value of the portfolio made of the structured product and a mix of exposures to the covariates of the model. It allows also to estimate a margin of error that will be added to the fair price to compensate for the residual risks. Such a model is referred to as a "valuation model" but financial institutions routinely use a number of other types of models. Here are a few examples of the roles of some of these models, but certainly not an exhaustive list:

- define regulatory capital requirement for market risk: Value-at-Risk (VaR);
- define plausible stress scenarios;
- estimate the credit quality of a counterparty, i.e., its rating;
- forecast client behavior, for instance in the prepayment of mortgages;
- forecast future market prices, this is the role of analysts' predictions.

We can also propose the definition of a model given in 2011 by the US regulator in a reference document:

> The term *model* refers to a quantitative method, system, or approach that applies statistical, economic, financial, or mathematical theories, techniques, and assumptions to process input data into quantitative estimates. A model consists of three components: an information input component, which delivers assumptions and data to the model; a processing component, which transforms inputs into estimates; and a reporting component, which translates the estimates into useful business information.

5.1.2 What is model risk?

All models are simplified representation of the complex dynamic relations between all financial risk factors. In some cases, they don't perform as anticipated or the assumptions upon which they were build are no longer valid, and thus significant mispricing, and thus large losses can result from such model failures. This simply means that models come with specific risks that need to be properly addressed by their users: these are the model risk, i.e., the risk of a failure of the model, that reality could be too far away from what is modeled.

Here is a synthetic definition of model risk given by the US regulator:

> The use of model invariably presents *model risk*, which is the potential for adverse consequences from decisions based on incorrect or misused model outputs and reports. Model risk can lead to financial loss, poor business and strategic decision making, or damage to a bank's reputation.

The following sections will go through a set of examples of model failures in order to illustrate the difficulty of model risk management. Then a specific focus will be put on valuation models and some of their usual shortcomings. Finally, a few general guidelines for model risk management will be proposed.

5.2   Examples of Model Failures

5.2.1   CHF deposit rates

This first example is very simple. Table 5.1 covers the interest rates for term deposits in CHF from the Overnight rate (0/N) to 1 year maturity (12M).

Table 5.1:   Term structure of deposit rates CHF in 1987.

	CHF deposit rates			
Today	09/03/1987	# of days	Bid (%)	Offer (%)
O/N	10/03/1987		1.0000	1.1250
T/N	11/03/1987	0	1.0000	1.1250
1 W	18/03/1987	7	1.0000	1.1250
1 M	13/04/1987	33	3.0000	3.1250
2 M	11/05/1987	61	3.0000	3.1250
3 M	11/06/1987	92	3.0625	3.1875
6 M	11/09/1987	184	3.1250	3.2500
12 M	11/03/1988	366	3.2500	3.3750

Given these interest rates, what would be a reasonable bid for a deposit starting on March 11 and maturing on May 25? The naive answer is simply to proceed to a linear interpolation between the 2-month and the 3-month bids:

$$3\% + 0.0625\% \times \frac{(75 - 61)}{(92 - 61)} = 3.03\%.$$

But back in 1987, regulatory bank reserves were computed only at month end. As a result, the cost of liquidity over the end of the month was significantly higher than between two end of months. As one can observe, the cost of funds during the first month is close to 1% and as high as 3% when crossing the end of month. In practice, the funds can be lent for 2 months at 3% and another 14 days at 1%. So the correct answer is

$$\frac{3\% \times 61\,\text{days} + 14\,\text{days} \times 1\%}{75\,\text{days}} = 2.63\%.$$

Lesson to be learned from this example. Market practices and operations are very important, hence even very natural and naive assumptions can be false.

5.2.2 The Value-at-risk model

To measure capital requirement for market risk, major banks use an internal model approach based on the VaR (Figure 5.1). The VaR is defined as follows:

> Given a confidence level $\alpha \in (0, 1)$, the VaR of the portfolio X at the confidence level α is the smallest number x such that the probability that the change ΔX of the value of the portfolio X exceeds $-x$ is less than $1 - \alpha$. For Market Risk Capital Requirement, X is the portfolio of financial products in the Trading Book[a] over a period of 10 trading days (or 1 day but with a scaling factor $\sqrt{10}$) and a confidence interval of 99%:
>
> $$\mathbb{V}_\alpha(X) = \inf\{x \in \mathbb{R} : P(\Delta X + x < 0) \le 1 - \alpha\}.$$
>
> ―――――――――
> [a]The *trading book* refers to assets held by a *bank* that are available for trading and hence regularly traded.

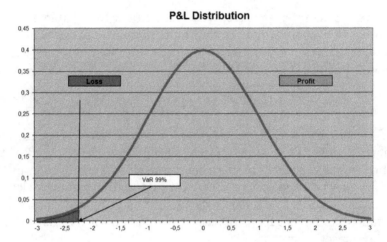

Figure 5.1: VaR model.

Using this convention, $\mathbb{V}_\alpha(X)$ is always a positive number. A *back-testing exception* is an occurrence for which $\Delta X < -\mathbb{V}_\alpha(X)$. Internal models for most banks suffered numerous exceptions during the 2008–2009 crisis (and yet again recently during the COVID crisis in March 2020).

With the 99% threshold, 29 Back-testing exceptions were registered in 2008 for a large European bank as shown in the Figure 5.2. This is definitely way too many exceptions to accept for such a model to be used in predicting the required capital to cover market risk. After the major drawdowns of the crisis, regulators and risk managers retained several lessons.

There are two main approaches to approximate the profit and loss (i.e., P&L) distribution of a portfolio. The first method is based on historical events (typically 1 year rolling window) to approximate the probability density function. The second method is based on Monte-Carlo simulations of the joint distribution function of risk factors. This requires the calibration of the variance-covariance matrix (in general on a fairly recent period). The 99% confidence level expected tail loss from the resulting total P&L distribution is taken to compute the VaR. The historical approach is often preferred because it does not require any distribution assumption which makes it simpler to implement. However, it is difficult to cover all risk factors in particular the ones that are not sufficiently liquid to generate

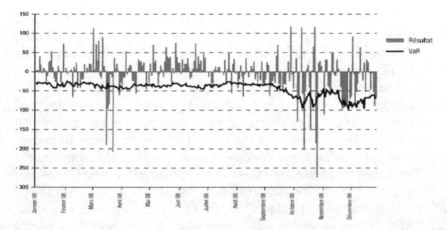

Figure 5.2: VaR failure at 2008.

appropriate daily shocks. The Monte-Carlo VaR can more easily integrate sparse information on the fairly illiquid risk factors as long as a robust estimation of the variance-covariance matrix remains possible. Generating fat tails for risk factors can be quite challenging in a Monte-Carlo set up. Finally, it has some difficulties to generate scenarios with joint probability distributions that express crisis situations for which historical correlations become irrelevant.

Lesson to be learned from this example.

1. The VaR is usually calibrated over a recent period and as the risk factors joint distribution is not stationary, it can become quickly inappropriate; in some cases, risk factors were simply missing from the VaR framework resulting in an excessive number of back-testing exceptions and hardly any jump in the VaR. *A calibration over a stressed period* somehow restricts the analytics to a given (and extreme) market context, as proposed post crisis by the Basel Committee (in the scope of the Fundamental review of the Trading Book, FRTB) will result in the capital requirement being more adapted to cover future crises even if unfortunately, the next crisis is unlikely to look like the previous ones.

2. The VaR is measured over a limited time horizon: 10 days. The market liquidity to cover some risk factors is not in line with such an assumption even more so during stressed periods. We observed during the 2008 crisis that the sudden lack of liquidity of

some structured products (credit derivatives in particular) caused far greater damage than the VaR could forecast, surely because exposures were kept on the books far longer than 10 days. The FRTB *defines different liquidity horizons* to differentiate between the various risk factors depending on their liquidity.

3. Finally, during the last crisis a large portion of the losses accumulated by banks were generated by counterparty credit risk which incurred losses because of the default of counterparties to derivative trades. The variation of the counterparty credit exposure is not taken into account in the VaR, while default is poorly modeled in most VaR frameworks (probability of default lower than the confidence interval). Hence the FRTB *includes a specific Default Risk Charge* as well as counterparty credit risk applying a kind of VaR to the credit valuation adjustment (CVA).

The experience of the crisis prompted the Basel Committee to propose a new set of rules to enhance the market risk capital framework: introduction of a Stressed VaR computed on the most stressed period over the last 10 years; introduction of a default risk charge to cover the default in trading portfolio; specific treatment of credit correlation portfolio sensitive to default correlation; introduction of liquidity horizon in the VaR measure; introduction of a CVA VaR covering counterparty credit risk.

5.2.3 Forward rate agreement disruption

A Forward Rate Agreement (FRA) is an over-the-counter (OTC) derivative contract between parties that determines the rate of interest, to be paid or received, on a loan beginning at a future date. The FRA determines the rates to be used along with the termination date and notional value. FRAs are cash settled with the payment based on the net difference between the interest rate and the reference rate in the contract. The classic hypothesis states that it is equivalent to:

- Borrowing for 6 months at the current Euribor 6M rate.
- Borrowing for 3 months at the current Euribor 3M rate and locking in future rate at which to borrow for 3 months in 3 months' time with a FRA 3/6.

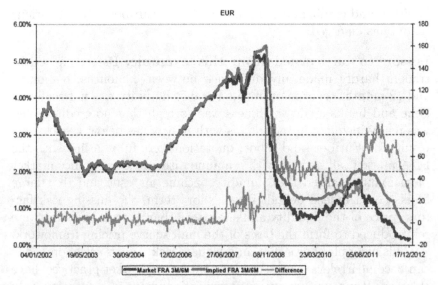

Figure 5.3: Difference between the market FRA and implied FRA in EUR rate during 2008 crisis.

It becomes straightforward to work out the theoretical value of a FRA 3/6 EUR reference rate in such mono curve framework:

$$\left(1 + \frac{n_{\mathrm{FRA}}}{360} \times \mathrm{FRA}_{3/6}\right) = \frac{1 + \frac{n_{6m}}{360} \times \mathrm{Euribor}_{6m}}{1 + \frac{n_{3m}}{360} \times \mathrm{Euribor}_{3m}}$$

Figure 5.3 plots in red the implied FRA rate computed with the formula above, the market FRA rate in blue and the difference in green on the right vertical axis. We note that the theoretical FRA rate and the one corresponding to traders' executed trades was almost the same until the sub-prime crisis where the implied FRA rate became much more expensive than the real traded one. This is because the theoretical formula given by the pricing model does not account for liquidity and credit risk embedded in the Euribor rates. Indeed, banks prefer to borrow for a 6 months term rather than borrowing for 3 months and locking the rate for the next 3 months with a FRA 3/6: as a result Euribor 6M is higher than the synthetic cost obtained with Euribor 3M and a FRA 3/6. As such, a new pricing framework based on a multi-curve set-up that properly includes the liquidity and credit information included in Euribor rates of various tenors has emerged.

Lesson to be learned from this example. Before the crisis, traders hardly made any difference between 3 months, 6 months and 12 months tenor instruments because liquidity was not really an issue and banks creditworthiness was so high that no credit spread was really included in term loans with maturities below 1 year. As a result, the Euribor (and Libor) quotation were fully in line with the FRA market, all defined with a unique discount curve. Once market participants realized that liquidity became an issue and that large banks could indeed default in the short term, the missing risk factors (price of the liquidity and short term bank credit spreads) were reintroduced to form the basis of the multi-curve pricing framework.

This example shows that an adequate risk factors selection today can become irrelevant once market context, or market practices, have changed. It means that current assumptions have to be continuously questioned to be able to detect this change of regime as soon as possible.

5.2.4 Collateralized debt obligation

A collateralized debt obligation (CDO) is a credit structured product that pools together cash flow generating assets or derivatives and repackages them into specific tranches that can be sold separately to investors with various risk appetites. A CDO is the name for the pooled assets — such as mortgages, bonds and loans or credit default swaps (CDSs) — that are essentially debt obligations that serve as collateral for the CDO. The tranches in a CDO vary substantially in their risk profiles. The safest tranches are called "senior tranches" because they are the last to be affected by the default of the collateral. As a result, the senior tranches of a CDO have a high credit rating and offer lower coupon rates than the junior tranches, which offer higher coupon to compensate for their higher default risk.

In this example, CDO tranches are characterized by: the basket of underlying, typically between 100 and 125 CDS referencing investment grade corporates, the attachment and detachment points "A" and "D" and the expiry date until which defaults are registered. For a CDO[A, D], investors receive a premium for selling protection on the reference portfolio and are exposed to the losses incurred by the portfolio over the life of the transaction. However, since any losses incurred on the underlying portfolio are distributed starting from the bottom of the capital structure, the investor is not exposed to the first A% (attachment point) of losses. Hence, the pay-off is equal to the sum of the losses on the basket of CDS minus the attachment point, capped at (detachment − attachment) point.

$$L = \min \left\{ \max \left(\sum_{i=1}^{n} (L_i - A), 0 \right); D - A \right\}.$$

The marginal distributions of the loss for the issuer of each CDS in the basket is derived directly from the CDS market assuming the recovery rate is fixed at 40% for all issuers. Pricing CDO tranches is all about correlation. Therefore, we need to specify a joint probability distribution for the basket default process. A possible approach is to represent the correlation through a copula function.[1] Using Monte-Carlo simulations or semi-analytical pricing we can calibrate the model to find the adequate correlation that reproduces market prices. However, the market trades only a few tranches of any given underlying credit like CDX.[2] Base Correlation was introduced in 2004 to build a Correlation structure (often called correlation skew) and allowed to price any customized (bespoke) single CDO tranche. The methodology is as follows: first, bootstrap expected losses for all market single CDO tranches, then compute the correlation for liquid Index single tranches in order to match the market price, and finally map from Index CDO tranches to customized single CDO tranches.

First of all, the CDO is a perfect example of risk intermediation: the investment bank hold in its balance sheet the portfolio of 100 CDS, and instead of providing a vehicle instrument that provides an exposure to this portfolio as a whole, it slices it in "stochastic tranches". The tranches are stochastic because nobody knows which CDS will be in which tranche until the underlyings face credit events: the risk is completely re-engineered in such a way that the more stable CDS are continuously allocated to the senior tranches, and

---

[1] Copulas are mathematical tools used to model the interaction between assets by computing the joint distribution.

[2] CDX: Credit Default Swap Index. It is a financial instrument equivalent to a basket of credit derivatives, usually from 100 to 125 CDS. It can be traded itself or used as the underlying basket for a CDO.

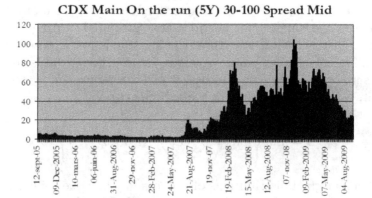

Figure 5.4: Mid Spread of the CDX Main 5Y [30; 100].

the riskier ones in the junior ones. Different investors, seeking exposure to different risk profiles, are buying the adequate tranches. This reattribution of risk in separate investment vehicles is a typical risk intermediation business.

Figure 5.4 shows the time series of the most recently issued and hence the most liquid CDO of the super senior tranche between $A = 30$ and $D = 100$ that takes as an underlying the CDX. We note that the value of the tranche spread was almost 0 (indeed less than 5 bps) before the financial crisis and went above 100 bps during the crisis. That is for the most senior tranche of the CDO composed of investment grade debt and structured to be resilient to multiple default events. Other tranches were even more impacted. Figure 5.5 gives the correlation parameter of the base correlation model allowing to reproduce market prices during the period between July 2007 and July 2011. We note that the correlation derived from the Gaussian copula reaches 100% at the beginning of the crisis and remains constant for a certain period (in fact it is capped within the model at 100% as any correlation). This means that the Gaussian copula approach was unable to reproduce market prices after March 2008 because it had already reached 100% correlation, a limit of the model thought unreachable before the crisis.

5.2.4.1   Stochastic recovery: The missing parameter?

Alternative models introducing stochastic recovery rates, allowing far higher losses to be reached, performed better during the crisis

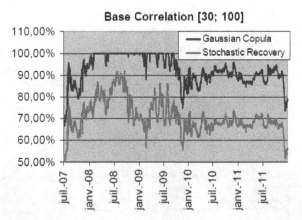

Figure 5.5: Model implied base correlation with fixed and stochastic recovery.

and quickly became the new market benchmark. Nevertheless, representing the complexity of the joint dynamic of default and recovery rate of baskets of CDS is intrinsically very difficult and even the enhanced model including a stochastic recovery rate were still very rough approximations and made it difficult to properly hedge the structured credit portfolios. Some of the products like CDO2 (CDO squared[3]), designed before the 2007 crisis were far more complex to value as they were effectively referencing hundreds of CDS.

5.2.4.2 From zero recovery rate to realistic recovery rate: Bond pricing

Pricing bonds has always been regarded as a rather easy financial problem to solve, inspired from the actuarial and economic literature. It is simply the sum of future cash flows discounted with actual interest rate, to which we add an additional credit spread for a given issuer and maturity. One straightforward approach is to add a credit-type term, a z-spread, which is equivalent to adding an additional discount on each coupon and the principal so as to find the market price of the bond.

---

[3]CDO2 or CDO squared: CDOs for which the underlying debt instruments are themselves CDOs.

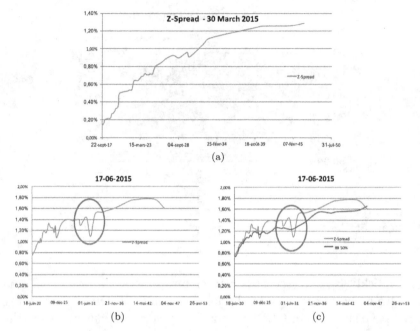

Figure 5.6: Italian Government bond curve on March 30, 2015 in panel (a) and on June 17, 2015 in panel (b) and (c): In all the three panels: z-spread and credit spread is shown in blue. The red line in panel (c) represents the model with a recovery rate.

$$B(t_0, T) = \sum_{i=1}^{N} C_i \cdot D(t_0, t_i) \, e^{-Z_B(t_i - t_0)} + D(t_0, T) e^{-Z_B(T - t_0)}, \quad (5.1)$$

where:

C_i is the fixed or floating coupon for date t_i,

Z_B is the Z_{spread} for bond B and

$D(t_0, t_i)$ is the discount factor of the risk free curve for a cash flow at date t_i.

Figure 5.6(a) and 5.6(b) show for a large spectrum of maturities the Italian Government bonds z-spreads over Euribor 6 month at March 30, 2015 and June 17, 2015, respectively. In Figure 5.6(b) we observe that something weird is happening around 2030 and 2035 maturities. It is hardly conceivable to have 0.4 % return difference for two bonds from the same issuer with just 1 year maturity difference with maturity in the 20-year bucket. In fact, using a z-spread as in the equation above is equivalent to assume a zero-recovery rate. Implicitly, we are saying that in case of default (z-spread going to infinity) the bondholders lose all the notional:

$$\lim_{Z_B \to +\infty} B(t_0, T) = 0,$$

which is in general not the case. An alternative valuation model inspired by a credit approach can be constructed. A specific default probability and a non-zero recovery rate are integrated in the valuation process in order to take into account that, in case of default, the bond has already paid some coupons and part of the notional is recovered. We see that in the case of Italian Government bonds, the credit approach valuation largely resolves the problem of the spread curve: the distortions around 2030 maturities are now more or less gone (Figure 5.6(c)). We should also note that bonds with the same maturities, but with very different coupons (1% or 6%) behave differently in case of default depending on the recovery rate. This explains the distortions observed in the z-spread model.

$$B(t_0, T) = \sum_{i=1}^{N} C_i D(t_0, t_i) \, Q(t_0, t_i) + D(t_0, T) \, Q(t_0, T)$$

$$+ \mathbf{R} \int_{t_0}^{T} D(t_0, u) \, dP(t_0, u),$$

(5.2)

where

$Q(t_0, t_i)$ is the survival probability of issuer at time t_i,
$P(t_0, u)$ is the default probability of issuer at time u and
$\mathbf{R}$ is the expected Recovery Rate as a percentage of the principal in case of default. By convention the recovery rate is applied to the principal only and does not cover lost future interest payments except accrued interest at the time of default.

Lessons to learn from this model failure.

- Keep in mind that *there will always be hidden factors* which we haven't thought of, or for which we thought the impact would be marginal and for the sake of simplicity we disregarded in the model until a new episode happens to prove us wrong.
- When a factor is missing in a model, the estimated price of assets via this model is different than what it should be. As a consequence, some intermediaries will accumulate assets that look cheap

in their (wrong) model compared to the market price and will happily hedge them with short positions in similar assets in terms of maturities that look expensive in their model.

The usual consequence of a missing risk factor is that the associated risk appears cheaper than what it should be, thus balance sheets of investment banks will fill with this risk, that is stored inside the financial system.

It is exactly the opposite of what one should expect: this risk does not circulate anymore until it reaches a natural buyer outside of the system. On the contrary it creates a false incentive to store this risk inside the financial system, and sometimes it is even worst: agents outside of the financial system become eager to buy products embedding this risk factor because they appear far less risky than what they really are.

When model risk realizes, the financial system is no more operating well; that is why regulators and risk departments of intermediaries are continuously monitoring the size of inventories. The indication of a growing inventory may be the sign that a risk factor has been forgotten, either by one intermediary, or by one type of intermediaries (structurers, market makers, etc.), or by the financial system as a whole. The "big is beautiful" paradigm may end up with participants that have such a large inventory, linked with almost all other market participant, that they become systemic: when they fail, the system fails to operate as expected. Systemic risk is the risk that the financial system does not provide the features it should provide to the real economy. In some cases, it can create a bubble of risk inside the financial system, or worst, propagate the risk to some actors of the real economy that will have been seduced by apparently rewarding investment vehicles or financial instruments.

5.3   Valuation Models for Structured Products

The particular link between Structured Products and valuation models has been highlighted in Section 5.1: valuation models are designed to value and manage the risk of structured products that cannot be statically replicated perfectly with standard products available in the various existing liquid markets. Chapter 3 reviewed the different participants in the market of structured products:

- The investor looking for a tailor-made risk/reward profile (for instance the risk/reward profile of an Autocall).
- The structurer, designing the product.
- The investment bank, offering the product and managing the corresponding risks.
- Hedge funds, taking some exotic risks off the investment bank.

The *investor* in an Autocall has a view on the equity market dynamics: stock price will rise and in any case not fall below 60% of the current price. If this anticipation proves correct then the investor will receive a boosted coupon (far higher than the coupon of a risk-free bond). He takes a risk and expects a reward.

The *structurer* designs the product to meet the needs and anticipation of the investor. Even if the structurer often hedges the risk on a back-to-back basis with an investment bank, he has a clear understanding of the complexity of valuing and hedging such products in order to have a good grasp of the final value of the product and all the potential risks involved. In the end, the structurer only keeps a counterparty credit risk facing the investment bank that is largely mitigated by collateral agreements and initial margins.

Investment banks do not take the other side of the investor's bet. They hedge as much as possible the risks arising from the structured product using products tradable in liquid markets, like futures and options. The model is the link between the structured product offered to the investor and the hedge available in the market. The model is continuously recalibrated to fit the prices of most hedging instruments available; the portfolio of hedges is also adjusted continuously during the life of the structured product. In practice, most investors have a static view on the market, while the investment banks will always have a dynamic view. Rebalancing the portfolio can be costly and investment banks are usually more efficient at rebalancing cheaply their global portfolio when they trade across a large spectrum of clients with various anticipations and interests. If the prices of the hedging products are not moving as described in the model, the link between the value of the structured product and the value of the hedge portfolio is disrupted, generating P&L leakages that is a typical model risk.

Hedge funds sometimes offer macro hedges to the investment banks when they accumulate specific risks that cannot be hedged in a liquid market (correlation, out of the money volatility, etc.). A good example is the accumulation by European investment banks of quanto correlation between EURJPY and Nikkei that will be described thereafter. Because they offer structured products linked to the performance of the Nikkei in EUR (most of the time as a component of a basket), they simply accumulate exposure to this risk factor and there is no tradable product to hedge this risk. If the implicit level of correlation at which these products trade becomes too distant from historical values (always possible since all the banks have the same exposure), it might be a fair bet for hedge funds to offer offsetting products to investment banks at such extreme price.

5.3.1 Risk neutral pricing

The first risk to hedge is typically the directional or underlying risk. In our Autocall example, if the market goes up as anticipated by the investor then the bank will have to pay a large coupon, far larger than the risk-free rate that the investment bank may have collected holding the cash of the investor. In order to hedge this risk, the investment bank will simply buy a certain amount of the underlying (equity index for example) that will compensate the loss on the coupon paid. The framework of the Black and Scholes model to price equity options gives a precise intuition of the hedge. The underlying price dynamic is usually modeled as a geometric Brownian motion, where the first term, μ is the expected return and σ is the volatility.

$$\frac{dS_t}{S_t} = \mu dt + \sigma dW_t.$$

Under the hypothesis of Black and Scholes (complete markets, constant volatility, no transaction costs), one can construct a portfolio eliminating the risk coming from the underlying S_t and then using the absence of arbitrage opportunity, which establishes that the return of such a portfolio is equal to the risk-free rate r (the dividends and repo rates are neglected for simplicity).

The premium of a European Call option $C(T, S_t)$ at date t is the solution of the following Partial Differential Equation:

$$\left(\frac{\partial C}{\partial t} + \frac{\partial C}{\partial S} rS + \frac{1}{2} \frac{\partial^2 C}{\partial S^2} \sigma^2 S^2 \right) = rC,$$

with the terminal condition for a call $C(T, S_T) = \max(S_T - K, 0)$. The dynamics of the self-financing strategy duplicating the value of the option at maturity is defined by the delta (δ_t) specifying for each time t, the quantity of the underlying security to hold and the initial investment required. Note that under the Black–Scholes assumptions, the expected return μ of the underlying price does not contribute to the option valuation. In fact, the only expected return intervening in the option value is the risk-free rate r. As a result, the Black and Scholes formula that links the option price to the underlying price and a set of other parameters (σ, r, T) in the "real world" could also be applied in a virtual world where the risk premium is equal to zero and the only expected reward is the risk-free rate. This universe exists only because dynamic self-financing portfolios exist and replicate the payoff of the options. In this world, agents are neutral to the risk because they can hedge it perfectly.

5.3.2 Itô–Taylor expansion

When building more complex models, more sources of risks are introduced and a similar approach is applied in order to hedge these risk factors. The generalization of this hedge approach is very similar to the Taylor expansion of a deterministic function. Locally, the partial derivatives of the value of the instrument are used to design a hedge portfolio. In order to correctly value these derivatives, a good representation of the joint dynamic of all risk factors is required. For example, assuming that there is no correlation between changes in equity prices and volatility will produce one set of partial derivatives; assuming the correlation is different from zero will give another set of partial derivatives. The value of the product and the replication portfolio won't be the same under such different hypothesis! As an example, let us consider a Stochastic Local Volatility model in the context of FX options:

$$\begin{cases} \dfrac{dS_t}{S_t} = \mu dt + V(t, S_t)\sigma_t dW_t^1 \\ d\sigma_t = \alpha_t \sigma_t dW_t^2 \\ \langle dW_t^1, dW_t^2 \rangle = \rho\, dt. \end{cases}$$

Assuming that there is a complete market for European Options, one can always define $V(t, S_t)$ in order to fit all market options for any given value of volatility, α, and the correlation between the changes of spot and volatility, ρ. Then, using these options to hedge the volatility risk, one can create a portfolio comprising the underlying FX and European options in order to hedge the value of any structured product against moves of the spot and volatility surface. However, depending of the value chosen for α and ρ, the value and the hedge portfolio can change significantly leaving model risk arising from the non-tradable risk factors in the model.

5.3.3 Redefining model risk

Even if, by nature, the model risk is unexpected, one can try to define a range of alternative scenarios to quantify the amplitude of the possible drawbacks when the model risk occurs. Hence without pretending to be exhaustive there are nevertheless at least three ways to look at model risk in the context of valuation models:

(1) A range of values achievable under various acceptable models.
(2) The risk that the model price will be significantly different from the market price, when such price is revealed.
(3) The risk that the "current market model" jumps to another model.

5.3.4 One way market and concentration of risk

A typical situation encountered in financial markets is one-way markets. It does not mean that there are more buyers than sellers or vice versa as the name could suggest. For every transaction, there is always a buyer and a seller, but one has a static view (the investor) and the other has a dynamic view (the investment bank). The difference is that

• The investor looks at his own anticipation of the future, i.e., its own probability distribution, to make its expectations on future price moves. When an asset manager enters in a position, she has a positive expectation of the outcome, i.e., she expects that the value of the derivative product will rise in order to receive a large payoff at maturity or alternatively to sell it with a profit.

- On the other side of the trade, the investment bank should not make a bet on the price of the underlying of a derivative product going up or down. It should rather enter in a hedging (or replication) strategy to cheaply create an optimal replication portfolio.

Because of these two perspectives, situations where both the buyer and the seller end-up winners can happen.

For instance, in a Black and Scholes set-up, when the investor purchases a call option, she will make a profit if the spot price moves up; the investment bank will be able to hedge the call option and make a profit even if the spot price goes up, as long as the realized volatility is lower than the volatility that was used to price the option at inception: *a smooth rising trend will result in both the investor and the investment bank turning a profit on such a trade.* This is typically an example that is not a zero-sum game.

Since investors tend to buy the same products again and again, investment banks can usually easily hedge the underlying risk and most of the volatility risks arising from such concentrated exposure as long as there is no change of market context. But more exotic exposure such as quanto correlation, dividend or far out-of-the-money volatility exposure can be challenging to hedge, especially after large movements in the underlying.

5.3.4.1 A perfect calibration! Now what?

In the framework of the Stochastic Local Volatility model of Section 5.3.2, it is possible to calibrate market prices of European options for a large range of values of ρ and α. All these models are equivalent with respect to the calibration of market instruments. However, depending on the product that are evaluated with this range of models the outcome can be:

- quite close for option types not too sensitive to these additional parameters such as Asian or simple digital,
- significantly different for option types like double-no-touch or forward start which are far more sensitive.

To be ready to face model risk, it is usually recommended to use a range of values for the unobservable model parameters. Thanks to this, observing different P&L associated with different values of the unobservable parameters allows to cover some uncertainty.

Table 5.2: Price range for various option types.

EUR/USD 2007	B&S	Dvega	LV	Max	Min	(Max–Min)/ (Max+Min)*2
Double-No-Touch	71.89	69.02	67.23	69.96	67.16	4.1%
One Touch	84.22	81.47	80.75	81.94	80.74	1.5%
Digital European	89.73	88.36	88.6	88.6	88.49	0.1%
Fwd Call	0.69	0.89	0.88	0.91	0.78	15%
Down & Out Call	0.58	0.73	0.73	0.74	0.7	5.5%
Down & Out Hurdle Call	0.58	0.76	0.74	0.76	0.72	5.5%
Range	13.45	7.53	8.72	8.74	7.99	9%
Lookback	6.2	3.6	4.0	4.0	3.7	8.9%

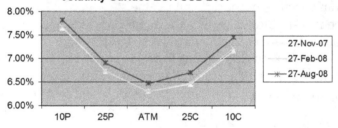

Figure 5.7: Volatility surface for EURUSD FX spot.

It is also recommended by the regulator to compute additional capital buffers. These two complementary approaches are efficient to cover the model risk arising from this diversity of calibration and the uncertainty of model parameters that must be estimated rather than calibrated. Table 5.2 and Figure 5.7 show the price differences using Stochastic Local volatility model calibrated on the same smile surface and compare them to the simpler B&S and DVega models. The parameter α is chosen in $[0; 150\%]$ and ρ in $[-50\%; 50\%]$.

In Table 5.2, model risk is define as the difference between the maximum and the minimum price reachable with various α and ρ parameters, divided by the average of the maximum and the minimum.

5.3.5 Model parameters estimation

Since estimating model parameters is based on statistical tools, these estimates suffer from the same weaknesses as statistics do:

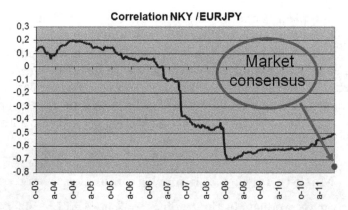

Figure 5.8: Historical estimation of correlation Nikkei and EURJPY.

- First, they are estimated based on historical data, and what was true in the past will not necessarily be true in the future.
- Second, every statistical estimation assumes stationarity of the parameter which makes the model vulnerable during crisis periods.

The following example describes the Quanto Equity Call option, which is an equity option with the pay-off function:

$$\max\{\text{Nikkei Performance} - K\%, 0\} \text{ paid in EUR (instead of JPY)}.$$

European investors are interested in the performance of global indices with baskets including EuroStoxx50, S&P 500 and Nikkei 225 but the resulting basket performance is paid in Euro for the convenience of the investors. Two new risk factors come into play: first the correlation between Nikkei, EUR/JPY exchange rate and then the volatility of the EUR/JPY. While the foreign exchange volatility is easy to derive and hedge from the mature market of EUR/JPY options, no product sensitive to the correlation between Nikkei and EUR/JPY is quoted on any market. The fact that there is no intermediation on this variable makes the job of intermediaries very difficult. Figure 5.8 shows the historical estimations of EUR/JPY and Nikkei correlation. The average historical correlation is at -50%, the worst-case scenario is at -70%. Surprisingly, when investment banks first tried to hedge this risk by asking other institutions for quanto European option prices, they received prices corresponding to a quanto correlation of -74%: even worse than the worst-case historical estimation.

This is typical of one-way markets: all investment banks accumulate the same long correlation exposure and do not want to buy any more even at rock bottom prices. This is where hedge funds might step in as they do not have any exposure with investors and it can be a reasonable bet (not an hedge anymore) to buy the correlation from investment banks at the market level. We note from this estimation process that the correlation is far from stationary and this underlines a weak hypothesis in the model design.

5.3.6 Mark-to-market and mark-to-model

All derivative products in the trading book need to be valued daily. Hence, on a daily basis most structured products are mark-to-model in the absence of a market price. However, as soon as a product becomes tradable, the bank must switch to a mark-to-market valuation whatever the difference between the model price and market price. Even if the derivative desk believes that a robust replication strategy to lock the model price can be put in place until maturity, since market makers, arbitragers and other participants will use market prices, the bank has to stick to the mark-to-market approach. Besides, because of risk limits (VaR, Stop loss) and counterparty default risk there will frequently be situations where the bank will have to unwind its position before maturity and this will always occur at the market price, creating a loss if the market price is lower than the model price. The following episode of convertible Bonds[4] in 2004 is a good illustration. Convertible bond prices can be obtained by complex models with multiple risk factors: equity prices, volatility, Credit spread of the issuer and interest rates. However, model prices and market prices can diverge. Starting mid 2002, the volatility starts to drop steadily (see Figure 5.9) affecting the value of all convertible bonds (bond plus call). The model value falls below market value as fund managers (specialized in convertible bonds) buy from market makers to prevent prices from dropping too fast and to defend the net asset values of the fund they manage. Luckily convertible

---

[4]Convertible bond is a type of debt security that can be converted into a predetermined amount of the underlying company's equity at certain times during the bond's life, usually at the discretion of the bondholder. It is very similar to a bond combined with an American Call option.

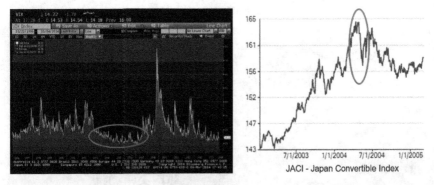

Figure 5.9: VIX short-term volatility of S&P 500.

bonds are difficult to sell short, so the discrepancy was able to last for quite some time. At some point, it became cumbersome to artificially maintain market prices and everyone revised their position at once. At that moment, market prices dropped sharply to converge towards the model prices which better reflected the large drop of volatility.

5.3.7 Missing risk factor

A good example was presented in Section 5.2.4 with the pricing of a CDO with a Gaussian Copula and a fixed recovery rate, which became unable to fit market prices anymore. This situation is not uncommon in particular because market dynamics can change significantly and risk factors that were once almost constant and could thus be genuinely neglected in the model can suddenly become volatile, producing significant price impacts. The cross currency basis spread between EUR and USD is a good illustration of such a situation. A cross currency swap is equivalent to the exchange of a long term floating rate loan in USD with a floating rate loan in EUR for an equivalent amount. It is expected that major international banks have sufficient access to liquidity in various currencies for the spread paid to exchange a EUR loan with a USD loan to be close to zero. Indeed, Figures 5.10 and 5.11 show that for the first 10 years of existence of the EUR, the spread was close to zero and hardly moved. With this in mind, it makes it easy to not take this risk factor in the valuation model. From 2008 onwards, it becomes clear that the market dynamics of this spread is unrecognizable!

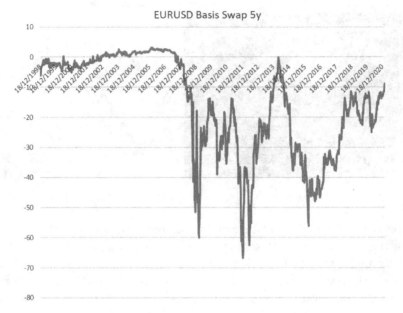

Figure 5.10: EUR/USD cross currency swap 5 years spread.

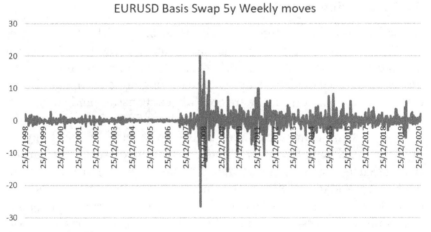

Figure 5.11: EUR/USD cross currency swap 5 years spread weekly changes.

A key development with the 2008 crisis was that suddenly banks and European banks in particular were perceived as riskier counterparties than previously thought. Hence, US asset managers became reluctant to lend USD to European banks. As a consequence, those banks had no alternative but to use the cross currency swap market to cover their medium term USD funding requirement. This created an excess demand that translated into a complete change of the market dynamic of this spread with significantly negative spreads and a dramatically different volatility. In this new context, including this risk factor in the valuation became mandatory.

5.3.8 Change of model consensus

Constant maturity swap (CMS)[5] prices can be replicated with a static basket of swaptions with different strikes. Initially, the model used at-the-money (ATM) volatility for all swaptions present in the replication basket. Everyone knew it was an approximation but since all used the same approximation there was no price discrepancies between market participants. In 2000, the most advanced investment banks managed to introduce the volatility smile properly in the replication portfolio. It turned out that the price with smile was significantly higher than the price without smile because of the shape of the smile curve. At some point, the consensus jumped from an "ATM" replication to a "Smiled" replication, creating huge losses for the desks that were not able to change their models at the right time.

5.3.9 Change of paradigm

Collateralized derivatives pricing. Most derivative products are typically cleared in CCPs. The remaining bilateral transactions between two banks are covered by ISDA netting agreements completed by a Credit Support Annex (CSA). The CSA defines how the collateral is posted daily between the two banks to cover the mark-to-market value of all trades covered by the agreement. The cash collateral generates interest calculated at OIS[6] which is different from the rate used to discount uncollateralized cash flows, the Euribor. The difference between the two rates used to be small and constant,

---

[5]Constant maturity swap (CMS): is a variation of the regular interest rate swap in which the floating portion of the swap is reset periodically against the fixed rate of a long-dated IRS (typically 10 year).

[6]OIS: Overnight Index Swaps. A swap where the overnight interest rate is exchanged with a fixed rate.

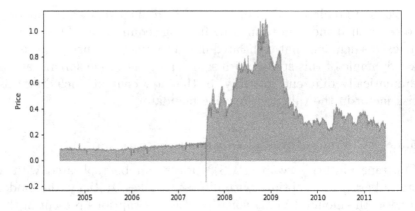

Figure 5.12: Euribor 3M swap 1Y – OIS swap 1Y. Period: 2005–2011.

and was generally neglected. Figure 5.12 shows that the difference between OIS and EURIBOR became significant and volatile during the liquidity crisis of 2008–2009. Taking this difference between the two interest rates into account significantly changes the value of long-term collateralized derivatives. The following equation describes the additional term in the valuation of derivative products representing the cost/benefit arising from collateral posting:

$$V(t) = \mathbb{E}[e^{-\int_t^T r_{\text{BOR}}(u)du} V_T]$$

$$+ \mathbb{E}\left[\int_t^T e^{-\int_t^u r_{\text{BOR}}(v)dv} \left(r_{\text{BOR}}(u) - r_{\text{OIS}}(u)\right) C(u)du\right],$$

where $C(u)$ is the amount of collateral posted at date u.

This change of model generated significant impacts within most bank's interest rates derivatives portfolios because they host the longest dated trades (up to 50 years in some currencies).

Multi curve pricing. Pricing of interest rate products used to be based on a single curve for all products (remember the FRA example). As liquidity spread between 3-month tenor and 6-month tenor appeared during the 2008 crisis (see Figure 5.13), this framework needed a complete review. In this new paradigm, the first curve is the discount curve that will be used to discount all the future cash flows. Since market quotes correspond to collateralized derivatives transactions, the discount curve is bootstrapped using OIS swap rates.

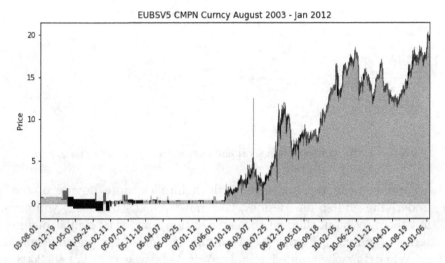

Figure 5.13: Euribor 3M Swap 5Y plus spread vs. Euribor 6M.

Then a 3-month forecast curve is derived from quotes of 3-month tenor FRA (1/4, 2/5, 3/6,...), IRS fix vs. 3-Month Euribor and the discount curve; for each additional tenor (1 month, 6 month, 12 month), a new forecast curve is built along the same principle as the 3-month forecast curve: the 6-month forecast curve uses FRA (1/7, 2/8, 3/9) and IRS fix vs. 6-Month Euribor.

5.3.10 Gamma feedback

Hedging large derivative portfolios may impact market prices of hedging instruments. When most participants are exposed to the same risks, which is typical of one way markets, this impact is magnified. In some cases, the market impact can even impact the underlying if the concentration is very significant. In this latter case, the price impact will change the hedging requirement of all participants and that will put even more pressure on the price of the underlying (negative gamma). This generates a feedback that can be devastating.

Hedging a short call option on a single stock implies a negative gamma exposure for the investment bank: when the stock price rises, the bank must buy more underlying stock to hedge the position. If the number of shares to buy is large, that will definitely have a market impact and raise the price of the underlying. This will also generate

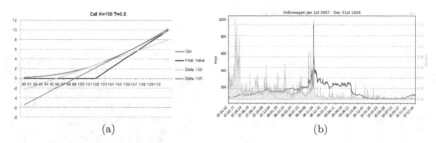

Figure 5.14: Hedging of a short call option: theory (a) and practice (b).

additional hedging requirement which implies more buying of the underlying and so on. Besides, you may even discover that you are not the only bank short of the same option (or a very similar one in terms of gamma). Figure 5.14 is an illustration of the phenomenon.

When Porsche wanted to take over Volkswagen (VW) in 2008, it bought call options from a number of investment banks in order to spread the huge size they were looking to buy between market participants. Banks all had negative gamma positions that required to purchase stocks as the stock price went up! Figure 5.14(b) illustrates the continuous progression of the price of VW in 2008 when the general market, represented by the DAX index, declines. The spike at the end of 2008 is a different phenomenon linked to short sellers unable to borrow the stock anymore and forced to cover their short exposure by buying back in the market at whatever price. This type of situation is difficult to prevent, because it is difficult to spot and does not appear in historical data until it is too late. The Front Office will argue with the Risk department that there is nothing to worry about. When the same structured instruments are sold to many clients, strict limits are required to limit unhedgeable exposures that inevitably accrue with the size of the exposure. As a result, at some point the trading desks will have to find a hedge otherwise the bank will simply stop to offer the product. In such a situation, a bank with strict limits is likely to be one of the first to hedge. But hedging a small position is often feasible at a reasonable cost: when everyone else rushes to hedge, the price impact will be too big and the cost of hedging will rapidly become prohibitive.

A very similar situation occurred in 2021 with GameStop. This time the buyers were a group of individual investors acting in concert to buy call options: first, all option sellers need to buy stocks to hedge which moves the price higher; at some point, short-seller come into play needing to buy back their short positions and are victim of a spike. Then the situation goes slowly back to normal after having generated huge transfers of wealth.

5.3.11 Model risk management framework

In order to limit the impact of model risk, a proper framework needs to be implemented within the bank. The first pillar is the model design. The team in charge of developing the model needs to clearly state the purpose of the model, the input data used in the calibration, the mathematical motivation, the implementation in a system and the user validation. Finally, a comprehensive documentation must precisely describe all these features for future review and updates.

The second pillar is setting up a model validation process. Three key features drive the model validation team's effectiveness: independence from the model design team, competence and influence, which is the authority to require enhancements from the design team. The robustness of the model should be tested by monitoring the sensitivity of the model output to small changes of the inputs. Model outputs should be regularly benchmarked against outputs of alternative models or market consensus. Finally, the model output must also be backtested against the actual outcomes. The outcome of the validation process should be an evaluation of the conceptual soundness and accuracy of the model, as well as the design of risk mitigants in the form of a restricted validity domain, accounting reserves and capital buffers.

The third pillar is a strong governance. Policies and procedures should describe the roles and responsibilities of all stakeholders: model designer, model validation, senior management, internal audit. They describe the various processes associated with model risk management: periodic reviews, validation committee, model inventory.

The last pillar is a well-designed communication covering the reporting of model performance, uncertainties and evolution to all stakeholders, including the top management. Models are not just a quant issue, they impact the whole bank!

Main components of risk management. Models are imperfect representation of a complex reality but remain very useful in practice.

Being aware of model limits is key in using them appropriately. Some shortcomings frequently affect valuation models: stationarity of model parameters, one-way markets, missing risk factors, risk concentration impacting illiquid hedges or even creating gamma feedback loop on the underlying, changes in the market dynamics. In order to limit the model risks, the most important attitude is to limit the volume of risk that are not hedgeable even if it means a loss of business. Banks should also setup a proper model risk management framework covering:

Model design: Purpose, input data, mathematical motivation, implementation, user validation, documentation.

Model validation and periodic review: Independence, Competence, Authority, Mathematical, soundness, Relevance of Input Data, Pertinence of model hypothesis, Implementation, Calibration, Robustness and stability, Model Parameter estimation, Validity Domain, Model Reserves, Documentation.

Governance: Policies and Procedures, Annual Reviews, Model Inventory, Model Validation Committee, Internal Audit.

Communication of model performance, Model uncertainties and Model evolution.

From a quantitative perspective (22)

Risk management is naturally a playground for quantitative analysts. It is nevertheless not only a matter of models and data, but quantitative risk managers are meant to give sense to the mix of equations and analytics they have access to.

It has been underlined that one important component of the intermediation of risks is the *risk replication* (or *payoff hedging*) process, that leverage on two assumptions: the chosen risk factors are meaningfully capturing future risks, and the counterparties (i.e., other intermediaries or natural buyers and sellers outside of the financial system) are really allowing to net the risks they buy or sell. Risk managers are there to assess how much these assumptions reflects reality: are some terms missing in the considered Taylor expansions? is the risk

---

(*Continued*)

(Continued)

really cancelled when buyers or sellers accepted to transact as counterparties of the hedging process? If not, one may be in a "one way market context", in which all market participants are massively buying the same risk and the hedging is netting out some risk exposure virtually only: the liquidity is slowly drained, giving birth to increasing transaction costs up to the point no more meaningful counterparty will be there and the risk will realize itself in a bad way.

5.4 For More Details

They are not as many books on risk management for intermediation that one could expect. A reference is Crouhy *et al.* (2005), that reviews most of the topics and gives practical examples. Two important papers set the cornerstones to now basic concepts on model risk: Cont (2006) focusing on the possible models, and Rebonato (2002) focusing on possible prices. It is interesting to have a look at Schoutens *et al.* (2003) to read some views about the limits of a "perfect calibration" with respect to pricing exotic options.

To go further in a technical manner, one can start by reading about early questions on the robustness of the Black and Scholes model with Karoui *et al.* (1998) (this notion of robustness can have sophisticated mathematical extensions, see Biagini *et al.* (2017)), and think about adding new risk factors as a filtration enlargement[7] (i.e., adding a risk factor demands to enlarge the natural filtration) and hence reading Aksamit *et al.* (2017) is a good idea. Albanese *et al.* (2021) shows that the counterparty risk itself can be injected in the mathematical formulations of hedging strategies. More practically, Kealhofer (2003) details the concepts around debt valuation and recovery rate and Piterbarg (2010) to read more and the consequences of the difference between two interest rates (i.e., OIS and EURIBOR).

---

[7]In probabilistic terms: the filtration is the sequence of sets, indexed by the time t, containing all the information at each time t.

Regulators and policymakers are of course concerned by the model risk, essentially because it can generate systemic risk. To investigate the notion of systemic risk, read Zigrand (2014) and then have a look at Federal Reserve (2011) or Rowe (2014) to adopt a regulator perspective.

Last but not least, a good context to think about model failures is the very long term risk. Typically the longevity risk is of this kind: read Barrieu *et al.* (2012) and think about the impossibility to anticipate the meaningful risk factors over more than 50 years.

References

Aksamit, A., Jeanblanc, M., *et al.* (2017). *Enlargement of Filtration with Finance in View*. Springer, Cham, Switzerland.

Albanese, C., Crépey, S., Hoskinson, R., and Saadeddine, B. (2021). Xva analysis from the balance sheet. *Quantitative Finance*, 21(1):99–123.

Barrieu, P., Bensusan, H., El Karoui, N., Hillairet, C., Loisel, S., Ravanelli, C., and Salhi, Y. (2012). Understanding, modelling and managing longevity risk: key issues and main challenges. *Scandinavian Actuarial Journal*, 2012(3):203–231.

Biagini, S., Bouchard, B., Kardaras, C., and Nutz, M. (2017). Robust fundamental theorem for continuous processes. *Mathematical Finance*, 27(4):963–987.

Cont, R. (2006). Model uncertainty and its impact on the pricing of derivative instruments. *Mathematical Finance*, 16(3):519–547.

Crouhy, M., Galai, D., and Mark, R. (2006). *The Essentials of Risk Management*. McGraw Hill, New York.

Federal Reserve (2011). Supervisory guidance on model risk management. *Board of Governors of the Federal Reserve System, Office of the Comptroller of the Currency, SR Letter*, pp. 11–17.

Karoui, N. E., Jeanblanc-Picquè, M., and Shreve, S. E. (1998). Robustness of the black and scholes formula. *Mathematical Finance*, 8(2):93–126.

Kealhofer, S. (2003). Quantifying credit risk ii: Debt valuation. *Financial Analysts Journal*, 59(3):78–92.

Piterbarg, V. (2010). Funding beyond discounting: Collateral agreements and derivatives pricing. *Risk*, 23(2):97.

Rebonato, R. (2002). Theory and practice of model risk management. *Modern Risk Management: A History'*, (pp. 223–248) RiskWaters Group, London.

Rowe, D. (2014). Prudent valuation versus confidence accounting. *Risk*, p. 46.

Schoutens, W., Simons, E., and Tistaert, J. (2003). A perfect calibration! now what? *The Best of Wilmott*, p. 281.

Zigrand, J.-P. (2014). Systems and systemic risk in finance and economics. Technical report, London School of Economics and Political Science.

Chapter 6

Could AI and FinTechs Disintermediate Historical Participants?

The financial industry has been disrupted by three major innovations: First, Big data has played a key role in the development of the industry, then machine learning and nowadays artificial intelligence (AI) are both changing the way we are doing business. These innovations were rapidly adopted by the financial sector as it is the first ranked sector in terms of technology consumption. Compared to other sectors, the amount of data handled is far bigger than the rest of the industries. In the heavy industry, for instance, the data are essentially generated from sensors deployed on the field. These sensors were constructed with a clear view of their purpose and used to asses a certain physical metric that gives insight on the state of production. What really matters is not the amount of data we can store but the quality of each metric that we dispose of, which is solely determined by the sensor's quality. In contrast, the financial industry is a worldwide interconnected network where the smallest information in a tiny country could storm the entire system and put it in dire straits. Therefore, we need to keep track of a lot of information related to the real economy, to asset classes, financial products and interdependencies, as to stay alert to potential hidden risks. Needless to mention the growing need for continuous now-casting and short term forecasting of real economy for investment purposes which increased the complexity of managing non-structured data composed of numerical information, text (from web and news) and images (from satellites).

All these implications make the financial industry the number one field of application for new technologies. In this chapter,[1] we will focus on the impact of these new technologies on the financial system and how they changed its landscape. We will discuss the impact of FinTechs on improving customer relationships by personalizing the service to enhance their experience. We will also look further into the role of technology to better connect the financial system to the real economy.

6.1 Impact of "Cheap Intelligence" on the Financial System

In the 1990s, investment banks were among the owners of some of the largest computing power and storage capacity on the planet. One might expect them to be at the forefront of innovations produced by data science and Artificial Intelligence (AI), but they are not. If it is private companies that have taken the pole positions on the podiums for image recognition or Natural Language Processing from the major universities, it is the GAFAM and not the financial institutions. Market participants are trying to catch up as best as they can, one of the indicators is for instance the growing number of research initiatives they have been funding at the Institut Louis Bachelier or Turing Institute for the past two years.

This section describes the major areas of application to be expected from AI technologies in the sector of financial markets. Beyond expected technical changes, this section targets to foresee the evolution in practices and positioning of business models due to the application of these technologies. To start with, a superficial reasoning, simply inspired by the area successes of the GAFAM and their consequences would expect a "disintermediation" of the financial sector, since this is what happened in the other areas where AI has been used with success. This disintermediation, often summarized as "uberization", is clearly one natural consequence of the deployment

---

[1] The first section of this chapter is an augmented version of *La finance de marché à l'ère de l'intelligence bon marché* published (in French) in *La Revue d'Economie Financière*, 2019/3 (135), pp. 67–84.

of data sciences in a sector. There is nevertheless a specificity of the financial sector: it has been explained in the previous chapter that it is essentially a network of intermediaries. How can disintermediation impact a sector that is primarily made of intermediation? To answer to this question we will rely on the literature on the organizational impact of modularity to understand the expected effect of AI technologies on market participants. This section also explains what these technologies are, and particularly the fact that they are made up not only of a very large amount of computer code but also on "reference data" necessary for their operation (i.e., to "learn"). It will insist on the fact that the presentation of the main areas of application of AI on financial markets is not enough to understand the transformations that can be expected in this sector. Indeed, AI does not come alone: it also brings with it many of the software industry's recent practices, which revolve around the notion of modularity. These practices have led to the platformization of players, already underway among the most innovative of them, such as Blackrock with Aladin and Goldman Sachs with Marquee.

This section is organized as follows: the first subsection recalls what artificial intelligence is, and establishes a link between the development of Formal Mathematics initiated at the very end of the 19th century and the recent successes of AI. It emphasizes the role of data in the implementation of this technology. The second subsection traces different areas of application of AI in market finance: customers and products, risk management, and nowcasting; the next section focuses on the organizational transformations linked to the implementation of AI, drawing on recent developments in the brokerage industry, which is the simplest form of financial intermediation. The fourth subsection details the consequences of the most important of these transformations: the platformization of actors. The last section concludes on the regulatory aspects as well as on what may emerge as new sources of uncertainty.

6.1.1   From learning machines to cheap intelligence

Although scientists have been working in "Artificial Intelligence" since the beginning of the 20th century, the objects of their research have evolved considerably, and the term now covers a wide range of techniques. The first approaches continued the famous "Hilbert program" launched in 1900 around this simple question: *was it possible to develop simple grammatical rules that could guarantee that "any grammatically well-formed sentence would be accurate"?* This ended with a disappointment for mathematicians since the answer, being negative, showed that the field of mathematics is too vast to be reduced to a grammar (as Kurt Gödel showed in particular), but it was also the launch of theoretical computer science: this "grammar" would be a programming language, and the "well-formed sentences" would be computer programs.

It is in this direction that Alan Turing defines artificial intelligence thanks to his famous "test": a machine only deserves the title of AI if it manages to pretend to be human during a conversation. If this happened for the first time in 2014, it was not through the laws of logic, as Turing could have imagined, but through the use of statistics and probabilities. At the root of this shift of paradigm, the Second World War prompted engineers to develop self-guided missiles, robust to "random" disturbances. The mathematics of uncertainty subsequently made it possible to explain the performance of Rosenblatt's perceptron, the first neural network to learn from data without an explicit model, by "statistical learning". Similarly, while Deep Blue, the IBM robot that defeated Kasparov in 1996, was an heir to Turing, trying every possible combination faster and deeper than a human could; AlphaGo, DeepMind's AI, defeated Lee Sedol in the game of Go in 2016 without knowing the rules but having learned to play it from a huge database of games (not to mention the billions of games it played against itself on Google servers).

From the industrial applications point of view, these two approaches are complementary: IT and logic inherited from Turing have produced the Robotic Process Automation (RPA) that flourishes in the back-office of banks, while deep neural networks, heirs to Wiener's work, make large-scale risk calculations for investment banks and insurance companies.

The recent craze is turning to neural networks , no doubt because of their apparent analogy with our brains, but also because they seem to be able to make predictions without understanding the underlying phenomenon. They are the fruit of several decades of trial and error, which began in the 1960s and were crowned with success about ten years ago by the progress of electronics, and consequently of computer science. These technological advances combined with advances in theoretical statistical learning have given rise to a range of functionalities that are qualitatively different from those provided by conventional statistics, known as "artificial intelligence".

Luciano Floridi used to say that what we call AI is actually *the ability to solve complex tasks without being intelligent.* The complexity of the tasks that these new machines can solve is nevertheless relative; it is limited to three types of use. First of all, neural networks can reproduce the perception functions of most animals: identifying what they see, hear or read. Today, it makes it possible to build personal assistants, translators, conversational agents, or monitoring systems using software components (i.e., packages) that are freely available on the Internet. Second, they can make statistics "along very large databases". For example, from the dataset of the sequence of movies viewed by all Internet users, they will suggest the next movie that a new user will like. It is a question of finding very quickly the movie that Internet users usually watch after those that the user has just watched. This feature allows to make recommendations, or to recognize a scene from photographs or any other form of data. Finally, they can solve combinatorial problems approximately; this is how AlphaGo works, just like the risk calculation engines of banks or insurance companies. They can quickly discard unrealistic answers and isolate a few likely scenarios on which they focus their computational skills.

Despite the term artificial intelligence, we are still quite far from the capacities of the human brain, which not only learns without having to be confronted with such large datasets but above all requires less energy. It should be pointed out that the learning phase of these new machines requires a lot of very well labeled data. Collecting and classifying this data is tedious work often done by humans. The micro-tasking platforms like Amazon Mechanical Turk allow the auctioning of data cleansing that is then tagged and stored and finally used to calibrate artificial intelligence. Artificial intelligence could thus not exist without these tasks performed at low cost by humans, so we are entering more into an era of "cheap intelligence" rather than of AI.

6.1.2   AI in the heart of the financial industry: Personalizing the customer experience, improving risk management and bringing prices closer to economic reality

To review the expected applications of AI technologies in the financial sectors, it is convenient to split them in three areas that have just been listed: perception, statistics along large databases, and approximate resolution of combinatorial problems. It is also good to split them in three domains of application:

(1) It is first of all in the context of *customizing the customer experience* that AI can be used. This is not surprising as it is common to many other sectors, although it has some particularities when it comes to financial market activity. The best example of this is robo-advisory decision support, which first developed in B2B, between product structurers and institutional investors, before reaching individuals. Within an institutional framework, product distributors began around fifteen years ago to provide their clients with internet portals that make it possible to analyze the composition of their portfolios, identify potential "weaknesses" (in terms of exposure to predefined risk factors), and propose investment solutions to cover these risks or to set up a desired exposure to a risk factor deemed to be remunerative. In practice, the institutional client provides the detailed composition of all or part of its portfolio, selects a collection of risk factors (such as the "international companies" or "high-dividend companies" factor), provides information on its exposure objectives (e.g., no exposure to the international share of corporate returns, twenty percent exposure to high-dividend companies), and the software proposes a complementary portfolio which is in line with the objectives by exploiting historical data, including correlations between the various possible assets. AI can improve these portfolio decision support tools, on the one hand by making better use of data (i.e., "making statistics along factor performance histories"), and on the other hand by solving the combinatorial problem of constructing the complementary portfolio (i.e., "approximate combinatorial problem solving").

The protection of consumers of financial products will also be able to benefit from innovations stemming from AI. Typically, the questionnaire used to assess the risk appetite of an individual wishing to acquire an investment product is nowadays very generic and very dry. It results in a score that is compared to a level of risk declared on the standardized sheet describing the product. Drawing on the attention-grabbing and Natural Language Processing technologies implemented by social networks, this questionnaire can be replaced by a dialogue with a chatbot, which will have access to the risk metrics of the products in which it is planned to invest. Financial education applications, perhaps coupled with this interactive questionnaire, could also be developed.

(2) Risk intermediation is the second theme impacted by AI. Investment banks, driven by changes in regulations following the 2008–2009 Global Financial Crisis, have moved from a "risk inventory" activity to a "flow driven" activity, that can be formulated as a shift from a *balance sheet intermediation* business to a *market intermediation* one. The previous chapters of this book explained the mechanisms behind the intermediation of risks, but for the current development simply say that the level of risk is set implicitly by regulators through minimum capital requirements. The capital required is different for each type of risk (banking or market risk), and also depends on the nature of the financial products carrying it (cash or cleared products, listed or OTC products, etc.). When an intermediary considers that the capital cost associated with issuing or owning a type of financial product is too high, it no longer stores the associated risk. Instead, it will try to quickly resell (respectively buy back) the products of this type that it buys (resp. sells) via a risk replication or risk hedging mechanism that have been explained in the previous chapters.

Artificial intelligence can be useful in this context. First of all to facilitate flow management: AI-based recommendation systems will help the investment bank or broker's operators to find potential buyers or sellers. This will enable it to better manage the flow of its buys and sells to maintain very low exposure to risks that it no longer wishes to keep in its inventory.

AI also makes it possible to estimate more quickly and accurately the risks associated with holding financial products.[2] These are extremely cumbersome calculations, having to take into account all the possible combinations of risk realizations that made banks and insurance companies the owners of the largest computers on the planet in the 1990s and 2000s.

(3) The latest application of AI to financial markets is associated with the emergence of what is now known as *alternative data*. These are non-financial data, but they reflect economic reality, and are hence linked to the valuation of financial products. Satellite images, which have become more accurate and cheaper in the last ten years, are a good example: they can be used to assess the quality of crops, measure the brightness of cities (and therefore their activity), count vehicles in car parks, etc. Transcripts of speeches by company executives at their general meetings, communications to financial analysts, or mandatory corporate disclosure documents are also available, often free of charge. The texts of patents filed by companies, job offers, or traffic on their web pages, are also part of these "new data" that allows the evaluation or revaluation of many economic variables.

These are very large volumes of data, which cannot be analyzed, even approximately, by humans. Recent advances in AI, which can be used to understand images or to grasp the meaning of a text, make it possible to use this information to construct new indices of the health of the economy at all scales: macroeconomic or microeconomic, or even simply indices of supply or demand in certain sectors or sub-sectors. These real-time or near real-time estimators of economic variables are not predictions; they attempt to estimate the current state of the economy in small increments. This area has been called "nowcasting" by analogy with "forecasting". Asset managers, bank strategists or traders are now able to build dashboards using these indices. Thanks to nowcasting, their decisions, which play a major role in shaping prices and allocating capital, are more faithful to the

---

[2]We are talking here about estimating the sensitivities faster and on more risk factors.

state of the economy, reducing the risk of a "virtual", endogenous, price formation which would only result from an endogenous financial activity.

While customization of the customer experience, more effective risk management and better connection to the real economy through alternative data are the three main directions in which innovation can be expected, this is a process that started a few years ago and is still in its infancy. There is still research to be done and methodologies to be put in place. Changes in governance will sometimes be necessary, including in the area of regulation and compliance.

6.1.3 AI leads to fragmentation of the sell-side

The list of natural innovations introduced by AI in the areas of customer experience, risk management and the use of non-financial data does not answer the question of the effect of these innovations on the functioning of financial markets. The effect of AI on other sectors seems clear: whether it is in the publishing, television or film industry, transport or catering, the ability to assemble different services on the fly to create a personalized offer for each consumer results in a new form of disintermediation. Platforms generate customized menus from assemblies of services from different vendors. Amazon offers its customers the opportunity to bring together consumer goods from very different suppliers at very distant locations in one order; Uber Eats makes custom menus that no restaurant has ever thought of putting together because they don't know the consumption history beyond their doorstep. Whereas media companies used to offer a single package of articles frozen in a paper newspaper, whereas television channels used to offer only one linear program schedule tailored to the "average customer", recent technologies are moving away from focusing on one representative agent to addressing both customers and suppliers on an individual basis. For the management of a company in one of these sectors, it is no longer possible to manage its margins horizontally, accepting a drop in profitability on some products compensated by more comfortable margins elsewhere because the search engines of the platforms that select the best bidder, micro-service by micro-service, are machines for provoking adverse selection.

The financial market industry has already seen this scenario unfold in the brokerage world since the mid-2000s: the introduction of competition between trading platforms in 2007 under the European Directive on Markets in Financial Instruments (MiFID) triggered such a paradigm shift. Explicitly focused on ending the monopolies of national markets (Euronext, London Stock Exchange, Deutsche Boerse, etc.), this European directive (that had a counterpart in the US: Reg NMS) formalized the responsibility of brokers in the routing of buy and sell orders in the form of a "best execution" duty: they must obtain the best price for their clients' orders. Thought in a "pre-AI" world, this requirement was intended to establish healthy competition between platforms: the intermediary (i.e., the broker) would match each client's order with the best offer, in line with Monge's optimal transport problem so well described by Cédric Villani. This is not at all what has happened: the emergence of AI-related techniques has led to order fragmentation; Smart Order Routers acted as "liquidity search engine", disintermediating trading platforms and thus transformed the business of market making. In a few years, traditional investment banks lost their dominance on making equity markets at the profit of a new type of market participants, using statistical learning, the high frequency market makers. Within a few years, brokers lost control over high touch execution to algorithms produced by a few players, and their margins fell. The brokerage ecosystem is today polarised around a large number of trading platforms providing a wide range of services (multilateral order book, bilateral quotation system, Dark Pools, systematic internalization, reverse fee model or not, etc.) from which the algorithms of a few major players will draw to assemble, in real-time and in a personalized manner, the liquidity requested by each user. The second version of MiFID, which entered into force in January 2018, opened the door to a revolution of the same magnitude for the provision of financial analysis by preventing brokers from bundling this service to the fees charged for execution. This pairing allowed them to pool the margins earned in execution brokerage and in financial analysis. MiFID 2 enables the emergence of financial analysis platforms using AI-powered search engines and data driven research that could aggregate services from multiple brokers to create customized offers to clients. This development should replace monolithic and not very agile players with a collection of suppliers who keep a very close eye on their costs, and whose products will be re-assembled on demand by a few gigantic distribution platforms.

Brokerage and trading is the simplest form of intermediation and has been, therefore, the first to be transformed by AI technologies. All other investment services will be transformed in the same way, provided that regulations continue to move towards less monopoly and more symmetry of information. The role of regulation is far from negligible and does not only go in one direction: standards introduce fixed costs that are barriers to entry for financial start-ups (i.e., FinTechs). The subsequent slow down on innovation gives the historical players time to appropriate the know-how of these younger companies, for example by entering into their capital, such as the NASDAQ which bought Quandl (a recent alternative data provider) in December 2018. However, as the competition takes place on the international stage, harmonization is necessary so as not to give an advantage to young shoots born under more lenient regulatory auspices. In the area of markets and trading, for example, Europe has not been able to foster the emergence of a local giant such as Intercontinental Exchange (ICE), which was born in 2000 in the United States and succeeded in buying out the NYSE-Euronext group, each component of which is more than two hundred years old, and which continues to threaten many European players.

Fostering innovations from AI. In order to understand and support AI innovations, it is therefore not enough to list the most likely application areas; it is crucial to understand the process that will give rise to these applications, and how they are expected to propagate in the market enterprise ecosystem. An abstract framework allows to read this process: Artificial Intelligence should be seen as a "general-purpose technology" in the same way that the steam engine and electricity have been. Therefore its use in a specific sector or for a particular activity is not always self-evident and does not always come at zero cost. It is necessary to invest to discover "secondary innovations" adapted to each use. The Interdisciplinary Institutes of Artificial Intelligence (3IA), created in France following the Villani report, are structures designed to stimulate secondary innovations by promoting contacts and projects around a cluster of experts in AI and data sciences: each industry can host innovative projects, led by experts in the field of application. If the financial sector has been excluded from the 3IAs, it is up to financial institutions to create similar structures. The Banque de France, investment banks and insurance companies have often set up "Labs" along the same lines: a small group of experts in AI and data science hosts business teams around well-defined projects and over short periods of time, in order to develop innovative solutions.

6.1.4   The link between AI and technology is not anecdotal: The players are "platforming themselves"

It should not be overlooked that AI technologies are above all coupled with advances in computing: according to Moore's Law, the capacity to record, store and process data is multiplied by 1,000 every 10 years. This growth has influenced the software industry and its practices, and particularly the expansion of open-source softwares, which is no stranger to the pace of innovation in data science in general and AI in particular. Beyond the AI libraries distributed for free by data processing giants (such as TensorFlow for Google and PyTorch for Facebook), the world of software development has organized itself to digest the millions of lines of code produced annually in open source. The software industry became modularized and then organized around "platforms". The industry of financial markets, which is essentially a software industry, is taking advantage of these new practices by developing internal platforms that unite all the components used by the different departments of each market participant:

- The first virtue of these internal platforms is to disseminate expertise by ensuring that functionalities are developed only once in a company and then improved through feedback from all teams using it.
- Their second virtue is to allow teams to consume software services provided by subcontractors or partners and to produce themselves services that will be consumed by external customers.

It seems that the transformation brought about by the modularization of market participants' functions is likely to lead to the vertical disintegration of firms. The few winners will be first and foremost the operators of the platforms; the most innovative players have already moved in this direction. Blackrock's Aladdin platform operates

$14 trillion, twice as much as Blackrock's assets under management, and Marquee is at the heart of Goldman Sachs' strategy, which seeks to unify its investment bankers' tailored offering with an increasingly technological environment where AI would become an essential element of decision support.

Whether or not they become the GAFAM of the financial industry, all players have an interest in playing the game of platformization by fragmenting the services they provide and bundling them within software modules. The tools provided by artificial intelligence will re-assemble this constellation of micro-service, from different suppliers, to build on-the-fly a personalized offer for each customer. Until now, this customization was done by humans who, without having the ability to draw from a very large library of choices, sought to offer their customers an assembly of adapted products and tried to suggest in-house improvements to the functionalities of these products. The emergence of AI obviously raises employability issues that is beyond the scope of this book. What has been witnessed in the past is this sequence: first, robotization does not destroy jobs, it even creates some; but then, the expertise capitalized in the machines leads to a relocation of production centers.

Nevertheless, some specificities of AI, and in particular of the AI assembly line, should be highlighted at this stage of the analysis; setting up an AI requires at least three components:

(1) first, the availability of computer code, which is often an open-source library produced by a university or one of the major data science companies;
(2) second, a collection of datasets that will be presented to the software so that it "learns" the relationships present in what it contains;
(3) third, ad hoc computer code that assembles the libraries, presents the data to them, and specifies the criterion (often named *loss function* by the machine learning community) which defines the learning task. This criterion may, for example, be a customer classification rate of success, or the difference between the risk predicted by the AI and the risk that was observed a few weeks later, or the difference between the activity of industrial centers nowcasted by the AI from satellite images and the industrial production of these centers as assessed by the balance sheets of the companies located there.

The libraries used are coded and corrected collectively; they are stored on one of the platforms hosting open-source software, such as SourceForge or GitHub. Error tracking and correction, as well as the integration of new features, are in the hands of a small team of researchers and developers who ensure the consistency of the library and its alignment with certain principles set out at its creation. The quality of the data collection that will be used during the learning process is crucial: the AI will do nothing more than draw on this data to capture the relationships between the different variables that will be presented to it later in production. The role of data is therefore as important as that of defining the loss function (i.e., the criteria for successful learning). The cleaning, storage, and labeling of this data have a great influence on the outcome of the learning, and there is no question today of putting it in the hands of machines. Human operators are in charge of this process. This sequence of tasks have created new professions: "data scientists", "data engineers" or "data analysts", whose importance should not be overlooked. Ironically, AI, which can perform complex tasks without being intelligent, will replace the back offices of financial firms but will rely on other back offices for data preparation and tagging: jobs are transferred from the companies or departments that provide financial services to the back offices that prepare the data to be presented to neural networks during the learning phases, prior to deployment. These new functions are not always grouped together within the same company, as they often use micro-tasking services, which outsource labeling or data cleaning tasks via an auction system. Finally, Indian engineers, Chinese students or American housewives connected to these micro-tasking platforms form a large network of decentralized back offices.

6.1.5 The sources of uncertainty related to AI remain to be mastered

The secondary innovations produced by the confrontation of Artificial Intelligence with the specificities of the financial industry will, therefore, be deployed in three directions: towards customers and products personalization, towards risk management, and towards the real economy and nowcasting, via alternative data. But they will not come without consequences on the organization of this industry. First of all, AI is not an isolated technology: it cannot be detached from the open-source components provided by the giants of data science (the GAFAM, NATU or BATX). As a result, it goes hand in hand with a very high degree of modularization of financial services and a platformization of the companies that produce them. It is very likely that a few giant platforms will eventually become the preferred intermediaries between a constellation of unitary functionalities and the assembly, on-the-fly, of services customized to the characteristics of each consumer of financial services. AIs will be involved at both ends of the chain: in the manufacture of unit functionalities, and in the identification of the particularities of each consumer, mainly in terms of risk profile. Some major players have already competed to become the owners of these industry nexuses. All industries are groping around to find the adequate method to encourage the production of secondary innovations to AI. Bringing together in a single place, an "AI Lab", AI and data science professionals with business experts focused for a few months on a well-identified project seems to be one of the emerging solutions. The financial market participants are looking for a path to innovation that does not increase systemic risk. One of the first aspects to be taken into account is linked to the modularization of functionalities and platformization: on the one hand, it is more complicated to guarantee cyber-security in a world where services are distributed, on the other hand, a strong dependence of AIs on a small number of IT resources (either software libraries or delocalized hosting services) gives rise to a new type of systemic risk that could be caused by a malfunction of one of these resources since it would affect a large part of the actors in the financial system in a transversal way.

Finally, market supervisors explicitly or implicitly require that firms providing financial services be able to explain the economic sense of their activity. The famous triptych *count to understand, understand to act* is a good illustration of the current weaknesses of AI techniques:

- On the one hand, the quality of the data used during the learning phase is often outsourced and rarely well documented.
- On the other hand, these techniques do not provide a "model" in the usual sense, and therefore do not allow the relationships between variables to be understood, but only implicitly exploited in production.

- Finally, the action will often be produced by a platform that combines several modules or atomic functionalities; identifying the responsibility over the end-to-end production chain in such a context is particularly complex.

Nevertheless, these concerns are not totally new issues for the financial industry:

- the nature of the data used to quantify risks is sometimes already questioned, for example in the ambiguous case of contributed data;
- the economic meaning of the models used is not always clear, as they often consist of an overlay of technical calculations;
- and the link between the different models and the action that is ultimately taken is therefore difficult to establish.

As was the case for high-frequency trading, the intrusion of technology into a space that is rather dominated by humans allows us to take a step back from the nature of financial services, to clarify the issues at stake and to better regulate.

6.1.6   Focus on Aladdin and Marquee: Two generations of platforms

Blackrock's Aladdin and Goldman Sachs' Marquee are often cited as references to illustrate the "platformization" of the financial industry. However, they are very different. The first came from the world of asset management and was mainly built around the outsourcing of IT services, while the second, more recent, comes from an investment bank, and should enable Goldman Sachs to continuously improve the services provided to its clients. The commonality between Aladdin and Blackrock is a logic of pooling fixed costs with competitors or clients while Marquee remains focused on exclusively improving Goldman Sachs' services while being open to interoperability. This subsection provides a short description of each of them.

Aladdin: Outsourcing an infrastructure. Aladdin's story is one of transforming a "cost center" into a source of revenue over 20 years: "Technology Services" revenues, mainly due to Aladdin (an acronym for "Asset, Liability, Debt, and Derivative Investment Network"), represented 5% of Blackrock's total revenues in 2018.

The development of an internal platform for generating risk monitoring reports for Blackrock investment funds began in 1987. It was in 1994 that the first external users were able to take advantage of this tool. To reassure on possible "information leaks" between the platform users and its parent company, an independent company, Blackrock Solutions, was created in 2000. It groups together most of the technological solutions BlackRock used: portfolio management, operations (including middle and back offices), trading, and the development of analysis and monitoring tools. These different modules are based on a financial datasets. According to Blackrock's website, a force of 1,000 developers maintains and develops this platform and its modules.

Aladdin is marketed as a service: a customer's need is analyzed and only the necessary modules, customized as required, are deployed. However, this is not a human resources service offering: only the technology is outsourced to Aladdin, the user must have the human resources to operate it. This is, therefore, the standard model for outsourcing a software platform: the savings are made on the recurring costs of the IT teams, as well as on the fixed costs of interfacing or developing new functionalities. Blackrock Solutions reports that its clients save 10–30% of the costs associated with maintaining the systems that Aladdin replaces; Blackrock Asset Management does not derive a particular competitive advantage from having originated this platform. Of course, to have build Aladin is a sign of maturity and a proof of the ability to develop a vision of the asset management business; these are good marketing arguments, but it is not a key part of Blackrock's strategy as an asset management company.

In addition, while Aladdin incorporates components that provide access to traditional asset management company subcontractors, such as financial data providers or broker/dealers and custodians, it is not possible (as of 2021) to replace any of its other components with one that would be developed by the user. For example, it is not possible to substitute another home-made risk model for the one proposed by Blackrock Solutions. Nevertheless, Aladdin's success shows the financial industry's appetite for external technology solutions that include business logics.

Marquee: A collection of modular and interoperable services. Marquee is a more recent project, which Goldman Sachs started in 2013 in the spirit of an internal technological revolution. The figurehead was Martin Chavez (Chief Information Officer from 2014 to 2017, then co-head of trading activities until 2019). While Aladdin is an undeniable success of the old model of infrastructure outsourcing, the Goldman Sachs platform is not yet a success but is positioned on an innovative model based on components that each user can access via an API. In a interview with The Block Crypto (August 13, 2019), Martin Chavez defines this new paradigm very well:

> [Market participants used to think in term of buyers and seller of financial services, or provider and users of] market infrastructure – all of those dichotomies are going away and so it's going to be much much harder to know, is this a client? Is this a competitor? Is this a counterparty? And we all really need to start thinking more about the ways in which we're overlapping with other participants in the financial ecosystem as opposed to, is it a competitor? Are you with us or against us? That thing needs to go away. The whole financial ecosystem is re-inventing and re-architecting itself around API boundaries and the new question that matters hugely is where are you going to be the best producer? One of the very few best producers of some service that's encapsulated by an API and in every other place you probably need to be an astute consumer of an API service produced by somebody else. Anybody who's not doing that is going to be missing the biggest and most important technological change in all the other tools you mentioned are important implementation tools. That's the big picture.

In contrast to an outsourcing project, Marquee remains primarily focused on the services provided by Goldman Sachs. Its aims to offer personalized access to each functionality provided by this investment bank and to allow to access them in many different ways. There are modules for financial analysis, portfolio risk analysis, creation of financial metrics, financial product construction, and data access. In addition, the platform offers other modules to Goldman Sachs employees. While the traditional data offering aims to provide generic access to commercial databases, Marquee offers access to Goldman Sachs' private data. Indeed, investment banks produce financial information, which is made available via this platform. Similarly, the creation of financial products is usually reserved for the internal departments of investment banks: in a early stage Goldman Sachs developed a module allowing its own departments to easily create index-based derivatives, connected to the calculating agents and traditional distributors of financial data (usual suppliers to the banks, but who are in the role of clients for this functionality), and then this module was integrated into Marquee, and thus made available to its clients. Within Marquee, the organization of porosity between clients, suppliers and investment banking business lines is made possible by software modularity. But it is AI that gives it value: not only does AI open the door to the customization of its components around the uses of each customer, but it also allows the platform owner to be at the center of information exchanges between its customers, suppliers and its own teams. This is the interaction graph that makes the commercial success of social networks, but which is transposed here to the ecosystem of market participants, and whose "likes" are replaced by financial transactions.

6.2 From New Technologies to FinTechs

6.2.1 A brief history of practices in new technologies

The "FinTech" name is the contraction of Financial Technologies, it encompasses companies that are building solutions for the financial industry using technologies born with the rise of electronics. In this context, is covers innovations coming from data sciences and blockchains.

6.2.1.1 A detour by distributed ledger technologies

It is very easy to find an history of Distributed Ledger Technologies (probably because it is very recent), and the development of DLT is not saying a lot about the best way to use it. In very short: DLT gained traction with the seminal paper advertising the Bitcoin blockchain. It allows to maintain a collection of consistent ledgers, allowing to support alternative currencies without the central will of a large institution (like traditional currencies, attached to a country and a Central Bank, are). It also provides a way to resolve a trade "locking" both sides of the trade until it is sure that the transaction can be done (i.e., checking that the buyer has the cash and removing the cash from his bank account and checking that the seller have the share and moving this share from her account to the account of the buyer).

It is easy to guess that this ability to resolve transaction has the capability to change the way market participants organize themselves in three layers with back, middle and front offices: the main reason of the old organization is to be able to focus each layer on some unitary reconciliation tasks. With a blockchain, there is (in theory) no reason to check for failures that will not happen anymore: if the shares, the contracts, the cash accounts are on blockchains and moreover if the referential of instruments are also on such ledgers: first the time series of their changes will be stored in a consistent way forever, and second only valid transactions, that can be done along the whole, end-to-end chain of accounts and symbols will be done; hence no more failure, no more need for checks, monitoring and reconciliations. One has to know that "fails" occur frequently on financial markets: an asset manager discovered after the close of the market that it sold twice the same share, or that it does not have the cash to buy one, or that it bought the incorrect financial instrument (this is often due to a mistake in the symbology, i.e., not-unique identifiers, of the instruments). The process of clearing and settlement has been built to monitor and correct these failures.

Provided that all the elements of the transaction chain are stored in a blockchain, only transactions that can occur will occur. One immediately sees two difficulties:

(1) It may be slow and it "locks" the system until the integrity of the end-to-end process is checked. This is probably not a long-term concern, since they are technological ways to shorten the time to check this integrity. The energy consumption issues with most existing blockchains is linked to the same issue since this high energy consumption comes from redundancy, that is also preventing to solve quickly transactions.

(2) In a world without need of any ex-post reconciliation, 100% of the steps are on a blockchain. This demands the cash account to be on one blockchain, and hence requires the existence of a *stable coin* that is an equivalent of a Dollar or a Euro on the blockchain. This need explains why Central Banks are working on stable-coins and links this issue with the existence of crypto-currencies.

Last but not least, the existence of distributed ledger is poten-tially a threat for traditional accounting (or, if we listen some of its advocates, it is the next revolution in accounting) because the way accounting is built around a balance sheet recording assets and liabilities, providing the capability to check and double check consistencies, rely on the fact that one never really knows of his counterparties have written the exact same liabilities (reflecting what he recorded as assets) or the exact counterparts of his assets (recorded as liabilities by someone else). Since your assets are someone else liabilities (or have been someone else's assets) and the reverse, a blockchain could prevent to write and record numbers that are already known by someone else: the DLT promises to maintain in real-time only one consistent record, at a worldwide scale.

6.2.1.2   Artificial intelligence has a very long history

The conjunction of an increase in the capabilities to record, store and process data with improvement of machine learning gave recently birth to a new technology that has been coined under the name of "Artificial Intelligence". The main components of this kind of AI are not new, and that is useful to understand where they come from to discuss how they can interact with the features provided by financial markets.

It is obvious that the desire to create artificial intelligence goes back a long time in the history of humanity; just site the myths around Golems to underline the prominence of this desire, and Mary Shelley's Frankenstein in the middle of the 19th century for modern discussions about the "ethics of AI". Let us detail a little more the history of AI.

From a mathematical viewpoint, AI started to take form with Hilbert's program: its goal was to formalize human reasoning in a grammar. Within such a grammar, there would be no need to think to known whether a sentence is correct or not, it would be enough to simply check whether or not it is grammatically correct. This ambitious program gave birth to a lot of mathematical results, the most famous being Gödel's incompleteness theorem; it shows that most human reasoning, at least when they are sophisticated enough, cannot be reduced to such a grammar. This result split the community of mathematics in two: some pursued their work in the limited set of sentences that can be expressed with this grammar, and other continued to work with the standard tools of mathematics, accepting that in their theories some assertions will be undecidable (it is impossible to prove that they are true, nor to prove that they are false, but the fact that they are true of false does not change the consistency of other assertions). The former (and smaller) group of mathematicians continued to focus on logics and Formal Mathematics; it gave birth to computer science, because Hilbert's grammar is ultimately equivalent to a programming language and an assertion is a software program written in this language. This resulted in the creation of the first programming languages (Lisp in the 1950s and Prolog in 1970s), and then later on decision trees which we see the trace of in modern machine learning algorithms (random forests are collections of decision trees generated randomly).

On the other hand, mathematicians who instead continued their work outside of these Constructive Mathematics soon started to work on the formalization of probability theory, Andrey Kolmogorov being of paramount importance in this field. Uncertainty broke into the world of Mathematics. Automation, and especially robust automation of processes pushed by the needs of the Second World War gave birth to the study of the control of stochastic processes. Norbert Wiener made the connection between such an automation and artificial life, and coined the term Cybernetics in his 1948 famous book. It was not completely new since James Maxwell, a contemporary of Mary Shelley, well-known for his work on electromagnetic radiation, published seminal works on the automation of devices to automate the speed of steam engines.

These progresses soon gave birth to the first artificial neural network, the perceptron, created by Frank Rosenblatt in the 1950s. At this time two trends of research were progressing side by side with no real relations: on the one hand the formal logic, trying to mimic the capability of humans to draw conclusions from symbolic reasoning, mainly supported by Lisp and Prolog; and on the other hand the probabilistic or statistical approach, "learning" with trial and errors for simpler tasks. This period is known as the first era of AI.

A breakthrough has been caused by two results

(1) Vladimir Vapnik and Alexey Chervonenkis went beyond the standard approach of statisticians; they decided to extend the traditional asymptotic results that were up to this date limited to situations for which the observed data are truly generated by

the model one tried to fit (for instance estimating the slope and intercept of a linear regression assumed that the data have been generated by a — noisy — linear relationship). In 1970 they proposed a mathematical framework to assess the situations where one do not know how the data have been generated, and tries to estimate the parameters of an arbitrary model. It is clearly the case for neural networks: the observed phenomenon is not generated by a neural network.

(2) George Cybenko proved in 1989 that neural network are universal approximators: provided they have enough "units" (or neurons) they can emulate any relationship between input and output variables.

These results pushed mathematicians and statisticians to use artificial neural network, and later Support Vector Machines (that controlled the complex results of Vapnik and Chervonenkis), to fit large datasets with some interesting results, including Yann Lecun's now famous LeNet that could recognize handwritten zip codes of letters. This second era of AI slowed down because a lack of data and computing power.

The veracity of Moore's law, stating that computational capabilities are doubling every year, worked in favor of the development of the next wave of results (Figure 6.1). Such a development implies that after 10 years, the computational capacities are multiplied by $2^{10} = 1,024$. This somehow implies that every decade, the multiplication of the capabilities by 1,000 changes what can be done or not, allowing to accomplish what nobody could have imagined before. Table 6.1 gives an idea of the major innovation for each decade. As we went from processors to computers, to structured databases, to distributed storage networks and distributed computing, and maybe the next huge step would be quantum computers. As far as information processing is concerned, there has also been some great achievements. We went from the scientific calculus used for simulations, to inference what we called at the beginning artificial intelligence, then to multi-varied analysis, statistical learning, data mining and finally to deep-learning.

The current era is the third for AI and has been dominated by the capability of deep neural networks to emulate three main functions (as it has been detailed in Section 6.1.1)

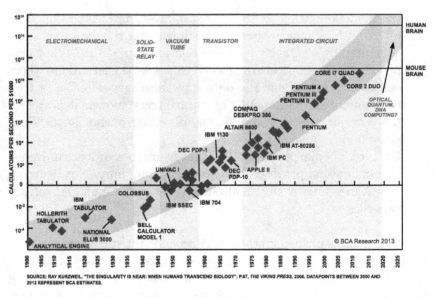

Figure 6.1: Moore curve.

Table 6.1: List of main processes in technology, computing and processing every decade.

Decade	Technology improvement	Computing	Processing
1960	Processor	Mainframe	Scientific computing
1970	Computer	Personal computer	Inference (AI)
1980	Databases	Relational database	Multivariate analysis
1990	Networks	Internet	Statistical learning
2000	Distributed storage	Web 2.0	Data mining
2010	Full distributed processing	Connected devices	Deep learning

(1) reproduce the perception functions of most animals;
(2) make statistics "along very large databases";
(3) solve combinatorial problems approximately.

This toolbox is a general purpose technology that can give birth to secondary innovations provided data scientists and experts of a given field are working together with a well-defined goal during a dedicated number of months.

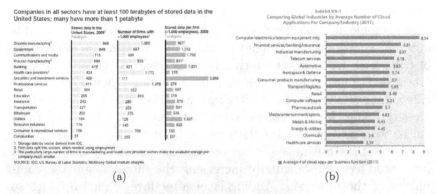

(a)   (b)

Figure 6.2: Computing power and storage per industry.
Source: (a) tcs.com and (b) blogs.saphana.com.

6.2.2   Is the financial industry ready to onboard these technologies?

The history of a failure. Figure 6.2 shows that the financial sector was one of the first in terms of computing power and storage 10 years ago. Because of that, one could expect that when Universities started to be challenged by private companies in the field of AI, market participants were among these new private challengers. But it is not the case. Obviously the financial (and insurance) sector missed the opportunity to lead this revolution. Why, having the largest capabilities in the world, and recruiting the most talented scientists, this industry could not be part of the advances in AI? This is for sure a failure in terms of innovation and research and development. It is worthwhile to take time to analyse such a defect to understand its roots and changes practices to allow the financial sector to catch up with the capability to innovate.

First of all: what is the use of all this computing power if it is not to innovate and push the limit of scientific computing? Most of this power has been used to estimate sensitivities and to store clients' historical records. It seems that in the field of risk computation, i.e., sensitivity estimations, market participants progressed step by step, with no vision, ultimately driven by regulators' demands. IT projects are usually driven by refactoring of existing libraries in the context of "technical debt reduction" than by "blue sky ideas". More than this, it seems that they have been obsessed by the construction of silos, replicating resources and teams working on the same topics (like symbologies, market data, Monte-Carlo simulations, etc.) without real coordination. Instead of thinking in terms of integration of transverse features on which all teams could contribute to, they "rewarded" performing teams with more human resources to duplicate what other teams, most often internal IT service suppliers, where already doing. Middle offices, stuck between back offices and front offices were meant to ease the process by duplicating tasks at the interface of the business and the operations; instead of this it added new interfaces, exponentially increasing the number and the complexity of the processes. Adding layer after layer ended up with so much inertia that most market participants "exfiltrated" the most agile and transverse human resources (who were eager to bear the cost of taking care of overlapping silos) to "commando" or "guerilla" teams, working side to side with the front but reporting to the slow and massive IT department. This IT department, having no R&D resources, focuses on managing the combinatorial number of middle term projects; it became very close to an external resource, working without any concern about the operational efficiency of what it was working on, since each time some of their human resources started to understand some business cases, they were "rewarded" by a reallocation close or inside the front offices.

The crucial element that added to this very fragile organization is that the best position of data sciences is at the interface of technology and the front office. Market participants put so much efforts in building a wall between these two functions, removing as much innovation capability from the technology side, that it has been impossible to simply consider that projects could be initiated at the interface of IT and the front offices. Moreover, data has never been considered as an asset, but as a temporary tool; each team building its own way to consume and rarely index them. This has been enough to completely miss the data science and AI revolution.

If only one lesson can be kept from this failure is that when you invest so much in a domain (here in computing power and data), you should consider to maintain a team of R&D attached to this domain. Of course the lesson could be extended to good practices in project management, governance and responsibility management, but it would go far beyond the scope of this book.

What are the main features of the financial intermediation.
To review the potential added value of new technologies to the financial system, it is good to start by a list established by Robert Merton in 1995. According to him, a financial system provides:

(1) A payments system for the exchange of goods and services.
(2) A mechanism for the pooling of funds to undertake large-scale indivisible enterprise.
(3) A way to transfer economic resources through time and across geographic regions and industries.
(4) A way to manage uncertainty and control risk.
(5) Price information that helps coordinate decentralized decision-making in various sectors of the economy.
(6) A way to deal with the asymmetric-information and incentive problems when one party to a financial transaction has information that the other party does not.

It is straightforward to associate technology-driven innovations to each of these domains: the payment systems are changed by mobile-to-mobile payment system, narrow banks and crypto-currencies; the pooling of funds by the economy of tokens, ICOs and crowdfunding; asset allocation by robo-advisors; uncertainty management and risk control by deep hedging, fast pricing and Automatic Adjoint Differentiation in general; price information diffusion by optimal trading, high frequency trading, liquidity fragmentation and smart order routing; information asymmetry by last look trading mechanisms and electronic brokers.

Listing like this all potential innovations will end up with a long list *à la Prévert*. To structure it, it can be useful to split such a list along three directions that have already be detailed in Section 6.1.2:

1. *Innovations toward customers*: Using AI to take into account the specificity of each client to customize its products and to use recommendation systems.
2. *Innovation for a better intermediation of risk*: Using new technologies to improve risk management, estimation of sensitivities, hedging and stress testing.

3. *Innovations to improve the connection with the real economy*: Use alternative data and machine learning to build analytics and indicators of the health of the economy for algorithmic or decision support purposes.

6.2.3   Understanding financial disintermediation thanks to two analogies

In this section, we will highlight the way new technology, based on the capability to record, store and process data via reproducing perception functions, statistics along large databases, and approximate solving combinatorial problem, lead to disintermediation.

The main argument for comparison of the use of new technologies in other industries with their use in the financial industry has already been presented earlier in this chapter: before these technologies, customers had to buy newspapers to have access to News. Even when they had an interest in only one theme (science, theater, or economy for instance); they had to buy the whole newspaper and hence pay for the production of the News in other domains. Thanks to this position of monopoly in delivery of News, owners of newspaper could have an horizontal strategy in term of margins: they could use the attraction of readers on some domains to pay journalists to produce information on other domains. Compare one domain that generates a small attraction every day (like humain interest stories) to another domain that generate large interest only very few days a year (like sciences, when a discovery of paramount importance takes place); it is able to share the margins and produce both, somehow investing in sciences thanks to the every day small attraction of human interest stories.

Once it is possible to store the news, follow the interest of every reader and process them with AI technologies (in this case essentially a *search engine* and a recommendation engine), and cherry pick only what interests each reader, the monopoly of the delivery of News is broken: thanks to these technologies each reader has his or her own "virtual News headlines". It is no more possible to cross fertilize the production of News in different domains. It is what happened with the emergence of Google News and then other web giants followed this path.

We have seen the same in TV with Youtube, music with Deezer and Spotify, transportation with Uber, shops with Amazon or restaurants with Deliveroo. Previous "old" companies, who could previously capture their customers and balance their margins between different products, had to compete on their "best" products only, because they are otherwise adversely selected by search engines.

The financial system is a connected network of intermediaries, trying to generate stickiness of their clients by selling them a unique suite of services, rather than the best service on one specific domain. This is a natural business model because as we have seen in the previous chapters, financial intermediation is cheaper when you have more (and diverse) clients; it allows you to net your exposure to risk factors. Focusing on a few products would expose the intermediary to a one way market; at least it should make business on a suite of products that are complementary in terms of risk exposure.

AI technologies nevertheless produce disintermediation: we have seen in Section 6.1.3 how the brokerage business has been affected by these technologies, reassembling liquidity on fragmented markets like Google News reassembled information around each clients' needs. The next two subsections are detailing two other analogies, to help to understand and foresee what could be their future effects on financial intermediaries.

6.2.3.1 Analogy 1: Amazon disintermediates retail stores like electronic execution services disintermediate brokers

Figure 6.3 is a schematic way to show the analogy between the retail sector and the trading in the financial industry. First, we observe several similarities between retail and finance services. Looking for an item in a specific market or seeking liquidity in market venues is essentially the same thing. In both cases, there are some middlemen which connect the demand to the offer. On financial markets, these middlemen are called brokers or market makers. They provide liquidity to investors via marketplaces that are often called multilateral trading facilities (*multilateral* because buyers and sellers meet there). Similarly, middlemen in the retail sectors are the owners of stores. They help producers to sell their goods and customers to buy them. The equivalent of liquidity is simply the availability in the inventory of the store.

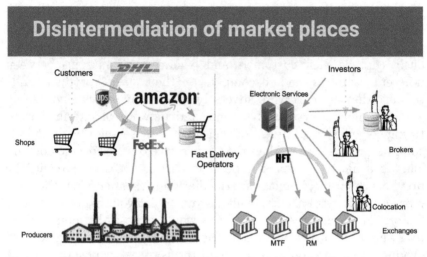

Figure 6.3: Analogy between the development of Amazon and the development of electronic execution services.

Both industries were disrupted by automation and electrification of service. On one side, Amazon-like companies developed a new business model on the Internet. Connected to all stores and producers, they provide the customer with a multitude of products coming from the various producers, different brands and franchises and different geographical zones via delivery services. On the other side, brokers started to develop Alternative Electronic Services (AES). Both are providing an equivalent of search engine: the equivalent to the "search" area of the web side of online stores like amazon is a web interface where a trader, an asset manager or an investor can enter characteristics of the shares she or he wants to buy or sell. She then clicks on a button to see the amount of liquidity available to buy or sell, and the price increase to consumer more than the "first limits" of this aggregated orderbook. Once she is ok with a balance of price and quantity, she clicks again and sends the order that is split to as many trading facilities as needed, and it comes back with a traded quantity at an average price that can be aggregated back to form the overall average price for the whole asked quantity.

The search engine of online stores is replaced by the Smart Order Router (SOR) of the electronic execution service. The delivery services like DHL or FedEx are replaced by high frequency traders or market makers who are taking liquidity from one place to bring it to another place in exchange for a small fraction of the bid-ask spread.

While marketplaces like Amazon are also providing recommendation engines to bring to clients attractive products, brokers are providing portfolio analysis tools providing analytics on the exposures of the clients' portfolio to different risk factors, associating them to the possibility to buy tradable instruments like ETFs, Futures or Swaps providing some hedge to these exposure. Moreover, market makers and dealers are building tools to recommend which client to call to unwind their inventory when they want to balance their risk: who has good chances to be eager to buy the risk that is over-abundant in my balance sheet?

Amazon and AES began to gain notoriety in their field of operation, they profit from economies of scale and become more visible to clients. Traditional store (respectively traditional broker) close their shops to open a new one within Amazon (closed their low touch execution desks to subscribed to AES services from the few large AES providers) in order to reach many more customers and leverage their tech investment. Instead of acting as a single shop, Amazon chose to become a mall composed of several shops including its own. Every manufacturer can thus build its shop on Amazon and sell through its network taking profit from its search engine and recommendation engine. This logic of hosting is extended further. Amazon started to give its former "competitors" the possibility to use its logistic network. Moreover, it provides new services of cloud computing, storage, and CPU. The same is also true for Electronic services: the few brokers having invested in electronic services provide "white-labeled" AES to other brokers that resell the same services to their clients without necessarily declaring that the services are provided by a third party. They also gave the possibility to plug a direct market feed and direct market access to other brokers and clients.

6.2.3.2   Analogy 2: Distribution of mobile applications vs. structured products

The second analogy concerns the life cycle of mobile applications and the life cycle of structured products. Section 3.3.3 describes in detail the life cycle of structured products, here we simply compare it to the life cycle of applications for mobile phone.

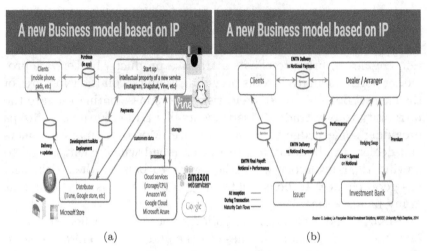

(a)   (b)

Figure 6.4: Comparing the distribution of mobile apps (a) to the distribution of structured products (b).

The goal of this analogy is to emphasis the breakdown of the value chain for mobile Apps and for structured products (Figure 6.4). Again we went from the standard distribution model of softwares to a chain of a collection of participants, each being specialized on a specific element. The same is happening in finance, and structured products migrated from a model within one big integrated bank to a collection of specialized participants. The reader can refer to the quote of Martin Chavez of Section 6.1.6 that goes in the same direction.

The life cycle of mobile Apps is the following:

(1) You have a small start-up with the IP of a product.
(2) It relies on a web giant like Amazon Web Services or Microsoft Azure to host its infrastructure, paying usage fees rather than owning its own cloud of servers.
(3) It uses a distributor of Apps that has access to retail clients, typically iTunes Applestore for iOS or PlayStore for android OS. This distributor has a reputation: typically some are checking the integrity of the Apps more than others; the client chooses one because of its menu and because of its reputation, i.e., its rating.
(4) The user pays the distributor and then can do "in App purchase" that are more rewarding for the start-up.

Compared to the previous business models, where the producer of the software had to own the creative team with good ideas, the infrastructure to produce the software, and to take care of the distribution and of the marketing and advertising, this new way is made of specialized components. Each participant of the value chain focuses on what it does well, and the fixed costs are a strong driver of the split: the infrastructure, with hardware costs, is in the hands of few major players, same for the distribution because building a reputation on a platform is a long-term effort, while the creators of the ideas are small independent units.

If one thinks about how structured products are distributed, it is now possible (but it is not always the case today), to have the same kind of life cycle:

(1) A small team has the idea of the structuration of the product, mainly the formula for the coupon. This small team believes there is a business case, because market participants and investors would demand the kind of risk-reward profile and exposure their coupon is providing.

(2) This team relies on an investment bank to provide a swap on the returns of the coupon; this is of course subtle because there is a transfer of IP there: the team has to explain to its provider (i.e., the hedging desk of an investment bank) the formula of the coupon. It exposes itself to the risk of copycat by this big bank; clearly a blockchain could allow to store the IP in a smart contract, somehow stamping to its creators.

(3) The equivalent of the distributor is the bank accepting to put its signature on the underlying of the structured product (issuing the bond), it has to have a good rating to be attractive to clients.

(4) Then there is an exchange of flows during the life of the products via the coupons, that shortcuts the issuing bank, between the structurer and the client.

Like all analogies, comparisons are odious. These two examples are mainly a way to illustrate how technologies change business models and the way to operate: their main feature is to split the value chain. For such a split to operate, one needs two elements:

(1) A platform, bearing the fixed costs for a lot of providers of features incarnated by software components.

(2) Componentification: each provider of services splits them in units of value with standardized interface (to provide interoperability with the platform).

Market participants are going in this direction; who will be the owners of the few dominating platforms? who will identify the features it is competitive on and focus on their production?

6.3 Focus on the Three Main Expected Areas of Innovations

6.3.1 Improving the relationship with clients

This area of improvement by new technologies is not specific to financial markets, the reader will find plenty of resources detailing how they can "personalize the customer experience".

(1) *Standardization vs. customization*: At first glimpse, standardization and customization are contradictory concepts. We need to standardize the processes in order to automatize our daily tasks but at the same time, we want to customize the product for each customer. Nevertheless, before customizing, we need to break down the process into tiny standardized components that are then re-assembled and parametrized in a different way for each customer. This provides customization. Of course, it is required to know well clients to build personalized products based on standardized blocks. This knowledge is achieved thanks to data collection and analysis.

This book is not dedicated to retail finance, but it is worthwhile to mention *financial inclusion*. Thanks to these new technologies, it may be possible to give an access to financial and insurance product into countries that had not access to them. Previously it required physical sales points, shops or agencies to offer access to financial and insurance products; nowadays, a smart phone is enough, and it can be done at low cost, especially once standardization occurred.

(2) *Future organization of financial intermediaries*: This chapter already reviewed ways financial intermediaries will have to rely on common or interoperable platforms. The specialization of each

intermediary on its strong points will for sure influence the business models and the end-to-end life cycle of products and liquidity. The role of regulators will be of paramount importance because the higher the barrier to entry for challengers, the more time old participants will have to adapt or buy the new comers. It could kill innovation. Up to now regulators wanted to be *neutral to technology*, i.e., they do not focus on how a service is provided, but on customer protection and well functioning of the financial system whatever the tools that are used. That is a very good practice since, as it has been already underlined in this book, the automation often allows us to better understand a feature, and hence to better regulate it. Nevertheless it is important to take into account the transformation of the business models. For instance: if really positive innovations demand to intermediaries to split their business, the costs related to compliance (that are currently pooled over different services offering services of different quality) could prevent this positive move.

(3) *Innovation of the financial infrastructure towards clients*: Section 6.2.1.1 develops the stakes of Distributed Ledger Technologies in the contact of financial markets. Platformization will influence infrastructure, blockchains should reduce frictional costs and the need of too many reconciliation steps. The middle offices should be reduced, and the importance of back offices for data curation should rise. Data privacy, as ethics of algorithms (mainly via a good understanding of the biases of the data), should be central topics.

From a quantitative perspective (23)

There is a need for quantitative analysts to understand and model the behaviour of clients, and capture the most important risk factors that are able to describe their needs. Data scientists and traditional "financial quantitative analysts" have to work together to build models and recommendation engines needed to put in place these new practices.

Robo-advisors are a good example of such a need for collaboration: the data scientist will design a system to record

---

(Continued)

(Continued)

the risk aversion of the client, via explicit question and using its past investments; thanks to this database, she will model the wishes of the client, that are not the same for each period of his life. On the other hand, the financial analysts will extract information from past investments in terms of risk-reward profile, build a risk model and select low cost tradable instruments to build a portfolio. The portfolio construction should go beyond the standard "modern" portfolio theory (created in the 1950s), since it has to be intertemporal, at least following the model proposed during the 1970s by Robert Merton. During the life of the portfolio, the clients' wishes can evolve, the risk-reward of instruments can change too, thus interactions should be planned, ideally conducted by a chatbot or another interactive conversational agent, to adjust the portfolio. One can dream that interactive session of financial education would be triggered by such changes, or simply to help the user to improve his financial proficiency.

6.3.2 Better risk intermediation

From a pure technical perspective, smart contracts and blockchains can help to intermediate risk in a smoother way. Section 6.2.1.1 already explained how Distributed Ledger Technologies can be used in financial markets. It also underlined some of its limitations (like the need of a stable coin to fully take profit of a DLT). Moreover, using a blockchain to resolve trades would require pre-financing of all transactions, whereas today financing can be found at $D+1$, and sometimes $D+2$ (like for Future contract: the investor deposits an initial margin, and then takes new positions at day D; at end of D it will receive a margin call if needed, that it will pay the day after). This would require "over financing".

From trading and balance sheet perspectives, risk intermediation is based on risk replication (to enable to price and hedge future payoffs) and estimation of tail losses (in the scope of capital requirements and stress tests). Machine learning can help in performing such tasks in two ways:

(1) Generating more realistic time series that can be used for Monte-Carlo simulations, stress-tests or extreme quantile estimation.
(2) Leveraging on Automatic Adjoint Differentiation (AAD), that is a technology widely used in machine learning toolboxes, to estimate sensitivities.

These tools can be used by all market participants, and especially regulators, to estimate the quantiles of value of future payoffs quicker, and with more realistic assumption (especially on the autocorrelation of financial time series that is often underestimated today). One can especially dream about generating more realistic long term time series, for instance in the scope of long-term risk, longevity and sustainable development. Nevertheless one should not minimize the fact that sometimes machine learning tools are used like black boxes; in such a case they will reproduce the biases that are in the data they are fed with. Typically if a Generative Adversarial Network is traded to generate time series with data that never saw a crisis, it will probably never generate "difficult" market contexts.

From a quantitative perspective (24)

Machine learning techniques have to be well known to be disassembled and reassembled for specific usage in risk management or risk replication. In fact statistical learning and stochastic control have a lot in common: from a theoretical perspective, a neural network is controlling the trajectories of its weights during the learning phase to minimize its loss function. Stochastic approximation is the common field allowing to understand how the parameters of a learning algorithm converge during the learning, but also how numerical scheme used in stochastic control (forward scheme like Monte-Carlo approaches, or backward schemes like Euler approaches) are converging to the desired solution.

Since the most natural formulation of risk replication is done via stochastic control (the replicating portfolio being the control), they are a lot of commonalities between machine learning and hedging. The same way the replicating portfolio

(Continued)

(Continued)

follows the partial derivatives of the payoff with respect to risk factors, the weights of a learning algorithm follows the partial derivative of the loss function with respect to its weights.

The emergence of partial differential equations in hedging (via Hamilton–Jacobi–Bellman dynamics) emerges under Brownian (or Levy) assumptions, whereas in machine learning only the historical measure (i.e., described by the provided dataset) is used. Learning algorithms are hence influenced by the bias of the data they learn with, and stochastic control is influenced by its regularity[a] assumptions on the uncertainty surrounding the economic condition.

---

[a]"Regularity" on a Levy manifold, i.e., supported by a Brownian with jumps.

6.3.3   Toward a better connection to real economy

With the availability of new sources of data, like satellite or drone images, credit cards tickets, supply chain or transportation data, web site traffic, it is possible to build indicators of the health of economic entities like brands, companies, cities, regions, countries, etc. Moreover, these indicators can be localized in time (few months) or space (along a coast). This has several implications:

- It is possible to have more instance of economic phenomena; for instance "micro-crises" at the level of small regions (like the 2015–2016 oil crisis in Texas). One can observe how the economic difficulties propagates at the finest level. This opens the door to draw conclusions from more examples in economics.
- Asset managers and investors can have access to more information to shape their investment thesis, that will be more connected to the reality of these indicators.
- This new discipline, coined with the term "nowcasting", provides a faster access to information, that should propagate faster in prices. As a consequence, prices will be more informative, but investors not using these alternative data will be less rewarded for their investments (the price will already have changed when

they will understand a new economic context). That is a natural consequence of the Grossman–Stiglitz paradox: if one does not make the effort to extract new information, it will not earn money from its investments.

- All market participants should take care of these information, at least to focus their attention on the most intense economic events.

A very important feature of alternative data it that they are not well structured in the sense that they are not daily numbers associated to tradable instruments; they are updated at different frequencies (for instance satellite images do not have the same accuracy every day, and some zones can be fully masked by clouds) and they can contain information on a subset of economic entities (for instance brands) that are not always easy to connect to tradable instruments. Data scientists are key in exploiting these unstructured data; they should work with field experts on their side, to make sense of data (what kind of companies' sales are affected by credit card tickets? how to characterize the crop under a pixel of a satellite image? what kind of wheel a car manufacturer is using for each of his cars? etc.).

From a quantitative perspective (25)

Alternative data are in the situation explained in Section 6.1.3: no data scientist alone nor field expert alone will be able to exploit them the best way. Interdisciplinary teams, focused on well-defined projects, should be formed to address each kind (or conjunction) of data. This team should mix data engineers, data curators, machine learning scientists and field experts during a few months to give sense to the data.

6.4   For More Details

There is not a lot of academic publications addressing the impact of new technologies on financial markets, since it is only the start of it, but some studies on the impact of technological advances on other sectors could allow some analogies. Nevertheless some institutes, like the Alan Turing Institute and the Louis Bachelier Institute are pushing researchers to investigate in these directions.

First of all the concept of creative destruction and general purpose technology can be found in Aghion *et al.* (2018), Acemoglu and Restrepo (2020) and David (1990). Besides, the software nature (as opposite to the hardware-based industries) of the financial sector gives a very specific role to modularization, platformization and software components, they are studies in Baldwin and Clark (2003), Baldwin *et al.* (2009) or Plantin *et al.* (2018). The importance of networks and information asymmetry in financial markets plead in favor of reading Shapiro *et al.* (1998) that had a great influence on the strategy of the web giants like Facebook or Google On its side, the disintermediation itself has not been intensively studied by academics; two good entry points, focusing on network effects more than on the intermediation of risks, are Crouhy *et al.* (2021) and Feyen *et al.* (2021). The reader can refer to Rencher (2019) to understand its influence on the commercial aviation industry.

Since the functions of back-offices of banks will probably migrate to generic back-offices of data curation, it may be informative to have a look at academic papers studying the existing platforms of this kind, like Berg *et al.* (2018) or Ross *et al.* (2010).

Last but not least Mittelstadt *et al.* (2016) and Mökander *et al.* (2021) are addressing the subtle question of "ethics of algorithms", to which Kearns and Roth (2019) give a nice introduction.

6.5 Conclusion

The financial ecosystem is made of intermediaries: the buy-side (including asset managers, investing the savings of individuals or institution), the sell-side (including agency brokers, providing access to tradable instrument and information related to their valuation), structurers (that are designing and signing products involving promises on future evaluation of — potentially complex — formulas), investment banks (that are buying are selling financial instruments, including structured products, made of — potentially non linear — exposures to risk factors; they are balancing their balance sheet as much as possible), market operators and vendors (providing technology, data and operations to other participants), market makers and proprietary shops (that are making the markets, taking liquidity risk to provide liquidity on different instruments), and regulators.

This network of intermediaries are involved into operations of buying and selling risks, mixed or not. The hope is that the circulation of these risks ultimately finds natural buyers and sellers of these risks outside of the financial system; when it is the case, the system as a whole operates like an anonymous intermediary between actors in the real world. Corporates wanting to be protected against an exposure to price changes, institutions or risky projects looking for capital, individuals wanting to protect their savings from the erosion by time, are the end user of the financial system. It allows them to buy and sell protections against risks that are incarnated by financial instruments, which prices are reflecting the imbalance between offer and demand and expectations of all market participants about their future values.

New technologies, driven by technological progresses like data sciences and distributed ledgers, have a lot to offer to this ecosystem. Nevertheless, they come with different practices (platformization and breakdown in components, or features) and require (or provoke) changes in the way to operate. Most probably few large platform operators will emerge, and most other participants will focus on well identified sets of features.

In terms of generation of secondary innovations, it is needed to host in small teams data scientists or specialists in distributed ledgers with field experts. These teams should be focused on well identified, prototype-driven projects, during 6–18 months. The simultaneous support of the front office and the IT teams is mandatory, demanding more collaboration than ever between technologists and front officers. Last but not least, one of the big lessons to learn from the failure of market participants to lead the revolutions of AI and distributed ledgers is that when you spend so much money in equipment and human expertise in a field, you should host a research and development lab dedicated to this field. It has not been the case: most of the researchers hired by market participants have been focused to the front office and not to technology, while these companies were massively spending money in technology, considered as a back-office, secondary activity.

- Personalization will reach a new level within the sector of retail financial services products.
- Online social norms and platforms will be widely used: users will be able to take control of aspects of the financial supply chain, from decision support to financial intermediation.

- The Fintechs take advantage of the emerging networks and platform-based services to lower their costs, improve compliance and focus on markets where they own competitive advantage.
- New data sources and analytic sophistication will continue to advance, develop and play an essential role in the era of transition.

The remaining open question for traditional financial services firms is about when and how could they be proactive in managing the change and further profit from it?

References

Acemoglu, D. and Restrepo, P. (2020). Robots and jobs: Evidence from us labor markets. *Journal of Political Economy*, 128(6):2188–2244.

Aghion, P., Jones, B. F., and Jones, C. I. (2018). *Artificial Intelligence and Economic Growth*. In Agrawal, A., Gans, J. and Goldfarb, A. (Eds.), University of Chicago Press, Chicago, pp. 237–290.

Baldwin, C. and Clark, K. (2003). *Managing in An Age of Modularity. Managing in the Modular Age: Architectures, Networks, and Organizations*. Blackwell, Malden, MA, USA.

Baldwin, C. Y., Woodard, C. J., *et al.* (2009). The architecture of platforms: A unified view. *Platforms, Markets and Innovation*, 32:19–44.

Berg, J., Furrer, M., Harmon, E., Rani, U., and Silberman, M. S. (2018). Digital labour platforms and the future of work. *Towards Decent Work in the Online World*. Rapport de l'OIT.

Crouhy, M., Galai, D., and Wiener, Z. (2021). The impact of fintechs on financial intermediation: A functional approach. *The Journal of FinTech*, 1(01):2031001.

David, P. A. (1990). The dynamo and the computer: An historical perspective on the modern productivity paradox. *The American Economic Review*, 80(2):355–361.

Feyen, E., Frost, J., Gambacorta, L., Natarajan, H., Saal, M., *et al.* (2021). Fintech and the digital transformation of financial services: Implications for market structure and public policy. *BIS Papers*.

Kearns, M. and Roth, A. (2019). *The Ethical Algorithm: The Science of Socially Aware Algorithm Design*. Oxford University Press, New York.

Mittelstadt, B. D., Allo, P., Taddeo, M., Wachter, S., and Floridi, L. (2016). The ethics of algorithms: Mapping the debate. *Big Data & Society*, 3(2):2053951716679679.

Mökander, J., Morley, J., Taddeo, M., and Floridi, L. (2021). Ethics-based auditing of automated decision-making systems: Nature, scope, and limitations. *Science and Engineering Ethics*, 27(4):1–30.

Plantin, J.-C., Lagoze, C., Edwards, P. N., and Sandvig, C. (2018). Infrastructure studies meet platform studies in the age of google and facebook. *New Media & Society*, 20(1):293–310.

Rencher, R. J. (2019). Progressive disintermediation of the commercial aviation industry ecosystem. Technical report, SAE Technical Paper.

Ross, J., Irani, L., Silberman, M. S., Zaldivar, A., and Tomlinson, B. (2010). Who are the crowdworkers? shifting demographics in mechanical turk. In *CHI'10 Extended Abstracts on Human Factors in Computing Systems*, pp. 2863–2872. ACM.

Shapiro, C., Carl, S., Varian, H. R., *et al.* (1998). *Information Rules: A Strategic Guide to the Network Economy*. Harvard Business Press.

Index